Instant MOM

NIA VARDALOS

HarperOne
An Imprint of HarperCollinsPublishers

HarperOne

HarperCollins books may be purchased for educational, business, or sales promotional use. For information please e-mail the Special Markets Department at SPsales@harpercollins.com.

HarperCollins website: http://www.harpercollins.com

HarperCollins®, 📖®, and HarperOne™ are trademarks of HarperCollins Publishers.

FIRST HARPERCOLLINS PAPERBACK EDITION PUBLISHED IN 2014

Designed by Janet M. Evans

Library of Congress Cataloging-in-Publication Data

    Instant mom / Nia Vardalos. — First edition.
      pages cm
    ISBN 978-0-06-223184-0
    1. Vardalos, Nia. 2. Vardalos, Nia—Family relationships. 3. Motion picture actors and actresses—United States—Biography. I. Vardalos, Nia. II. Title.
PN2287.V345A3   2013
791.4302'8092—dc23   2012045930

14 15 16 17 18 RRD(H) 10 9 8 7 6 5 4 3 2 1

For my daughter:

I thought I knew love and then I met you.

CONTENTS

THIS IS THE BEFORE-I-START-TYPING PROLOGUE

I'm nervous.

To be honest, I'm sweating like I've just accidentally bought pot cookies in a tiny foreign municipality with faint ties to the UN.

So I get up and walk around my office.

I'm really perspiring. But like many of us, I don't exude that sexy JLo gyrating in a music video golden-hued glow. No. When I'm anxious, I have a gray, sallow pallor and a shiny upper lip of sweat beads glistening through a stubborn mustache that won't respond to the gabillion dollars I've spent on laser treatments.

Great. Now my forehead is oily. By tomorrow I will grow a new zit there, and my husband will start the day speaking directly to it.

I pause now and open a window. Breathing deeply, I think about going downstairs to the kitchen. Again.

I can't stop stalling. Stalling is a euphemism for snacking.

In the kitchen, I grab celery sticks and mineral water. Okay, fine, that's a complete fabrication and what the romantic-comedy movie version of me would do. In reality I gobble down a Yoo-hoo and a Ho Ho.

Back in my office, I sit down again and stare at this page.

Writing a book is unfamiliar territory for me.

When *My Big Fat Greek Wedding* came out, I politely demurred to the kind requests to write a career memoir. My two reasons were simple: I'd feel like a blowhard dispensing industry advice. And as some film critics would agree, I don't know much.

I don't want to write some career memoir with a quaint title in ironic font, like *I'm Not Pretty But I'm Photogenic*. Hmmm, how about *You're Never Too Fat for a New Purse*? I do love purses. Most ladies know we can upgrade a dull outfit or gloomy mood by just switching out a purse. Could I simply write about my accessories mania . . . ?

I'm stalling again. Since typing the first paragraph, I have gotten up three times for snacks. Not good. Maybe I can walk off these extra calories by pacing. I'm trying that now. I'm walking through the house. My dogs are following as if we're all in the love montage of a Disney movie.

I worry if I'm doing the right thing in telling this story.

When the adoption of our daughter was finalized, I too-tight hugged our superb social workers and asked one question: "For all those years, why didn't I know about the kids in foster care waiting for parents?" Their reply was carefully put: "Well . . . we've been waiting a long time for someone like you."

Oh.

They needed a spokesperson. They needed an advocate. They needed a blabbermouth like me.

But I like my privacy.

However, like many movie reviewers and studio heads, I often wondered why the success of my first movie happened to me. Well, maybe this is the reason. Maybe I'm supposed to be using my big mouth to talk about adoption.

Sometimes if something scares me, I lean right into it. I'm not a brave person—I'm more of a fearless idiot.

So I became the spokesperson for National Adoption Day. I live in Los Angeles, and flew many times to New York to do press. But because I was firm with show producers that I wouldn't reveal anything about my fertility struggle or regarding my daughter, they would allot me only a few minutes of airtime after twenty minutes of a booted-off dancing contestant dissing the judges, or a reality celebrity talking about her sex tape.

I get it. Facts and figures about adoption are not sexy. Celebrities doing it with each other is good TV. We like those segments. It's comforting to stand around in our faded housecoats, spooning in our tasteless cereal and squinting at morning TV through last night's flaked mascara while declaring everyone a slut. And we all buy those magazines and peer at pictures of celebrities without makeup. Come on, you have a subscription and so do I. We validate and support that salacious aspect of the media we complain about for being so focused on negativity and tacky subjects.

So when it comes to adoption—if there's an irresponsible foster parent or a kid whose home placement didn't work out, the media jumps on that story because fear sells newspapers. Anxiety makes us tune in. And we do.

I couldn't play the drama game; I couldn't give those talk-show producers my personal backstory, the tragic theater they needed for a must-see segment. I only wanted to tell the nice stories. I needed to talk about how in the world of adoption, I have met astonishingly good people who strive to make a difference. I've met great kids living in kind foster homes, who eventually age out of the system without a family to call their own. I have met people whose hearts ache to be parents, who don't know the ways to adopt. Studies have shown worldwide there are as many prospective parents as adoptable children. But some people think they don't have the financial means to adopt. Numerous people can't find credible information on how to adopt. Countless prospective parents are waiting to be "matched." I was once in that position.

I now know the many ways to become a parent. Sure, some methods are expensive and time-consuming, some can lead to heartbreak. Some work for many. Some don't. And some are amazingly simple and accessible to everyone. One way worked for me.

I don't want to come across as a proponent for motherhood for all women. Of course it's not for everyone. Needless to say, it's completely possible to live a wholly splendid life without children. I won't send my gender careening back into the Dark Ages with any suggestions that we're unfulfilled without motherhood. This applies to men too. Of course parenthood isn't for everyone. It's a choice. While there is pressure on all of us to get married and have babies, it would be absurd to suggest it's the right fit for everyone. So this book isn't saying that at all.

In the same way, when I was having difficulty becoming a mother, I was assured by good friends and my supportive family that I could be happy without parenthood. Observing my completely fulfilled professional friends and family who did not have children, I tried to accept this was what was intended for me.

But I wanted a family and had to walk over hot coals to find my daughter.

Being a mother . . . actually being my daughter's mother has changed me. My daughter filled a raggedy hole in my heart. She is the love of my life.

When (brace yourself for a humblebrag) I received an award in Washington, in my speech, I vowed to continue to spread the word about adoption. Inwardly, I knew the reality: it's been tricky to get the word out. But the occasions I was given more airtime, like on *The View* and *The Talk*, yielded incredibly positive results. The director of a child-placement agency told me they got so many hits, their site crashed. She said, "Keep talking, the kids are flying out the door."

But how do I keep talking? As I said, it's not like the morning talk-show circuit is itching to have me dryly list facts and figures about adoption. I'm not getting starring roles in hipster movies that will yield more talk-show bookings. I don't want to get airtime by making a sex tape with someone in celebrity rehab. I mean, not right now. So I wondered how I could disseminate adoption information.

Both (here comes some name-dropping) Katie Couric and Joy Behar urged me to write an adoption book about my real experience. I said I'd "think it over," which is my polite way of shrieking, "No waaaaaaaaaaaay."

Then this happened: a friend asked me to counsel her friend who was going through infertility. I hesitated. The mutual friend's entreating expression affected me, reminding me I was once in that position, reaching out for help. So I met with the woman. In a private, quiet setting, we began to talk, she told me her story . . . then she asked what had happened to me. And . . . I told her my story. I chronicled the events that led me to adoption. I told her the truth and understood why I hadn't wanted to tell the real story before. It's because I am an inherently optimistic person and I wanted to move on from that bleak time, not revisit it.

I am absurdly happy now because I am a mom. But I could see this woman was still so angry about her fertility experience. I told her the futility she was feeling would pass. We were quiet for a bit, both wishing she could accelerate forward to that better time. She then asked me to tell her how to adopt. I outlined what had taken me years to learn about the world's adoption systems—which routes were expensive, which were time-consuming, which foreign sites were shams, which weren't. I told her how to do it.

Months later, the woman called me again. She had adopted a baby boy from Ohio, and the joy in her voice made me ecstatic. I walked around all day beaming like I'd just found a Twizzler in a coat pocket. Next I counseled a couple—and they adopted a four-year-old boy from another country. Then I set up a gay friend with a Foster Family Agency—he is in the process of adopting a teenage girl.

I am not telling you this for more humblebragging. I am telling you because I was experiencing a strange feeling—I felt useful. Like a good recipe you've just got to share, like a shoe sale you've got to email your girlfriends about, I enjoyed explaining the process of adoption.

I've never revealed the truth behind my daughter's adoption. The stories I have told publicly have glossed over the facts so I could quickly segue into circulating information. Although I do make fun of my family for fun and profit, plus often use relatives as the basis of many of the characters in my screenplays, I twist specifics so they're not recognizable. Now I'm disquieted to write with veracity about what really happened. It's not that it's shocking and tell-all-y so if you're looking for gossip, sit back. I'm merely nervous because I've never written just the truth.

I'm a middle-child Canadian, which basically means I'm annoyingly nice and I like everyone to be happy. To describe the events that led me to my daughter means I will have to reveal information that is not exactly pleasant, not exactly funny. I'm not comfortable with the fact that trying to become a mother was a difficult ten-year process that sucked the fun out of me. I hate talking about infertility. Ever. I really hate it.

I fret I will have to fend off invasive questions for the rest of my life. I hope this can be the one and only time I have to delve into it. Really. Let's be friends, come over for dinner. My only BFF requests are (1) please don't ask me about infertility, and (2) please don't place your purse that was just on a bathroom floor/subway seat/grocery cart on my kitchen counter.

Also, the simple fact is my daughter deserves her anonymity. My family and in-laws are private citizens so it's best I don't detail their feelings in this matter. The same goes for the social workers and adoption attorney we worked with: I would love to print their names, but their work is best done with confidentiality. My husband, Ian Gomez, an actor too, is always working in films and on TV shows from *Felicity* to *The Drew Carey Show* to *Cougar Town*. But we are very private people. We rarely talk about our personal lives in the press unless we're making fun of each other. We don't let magazines shoot pictorials in our home, won't allow media pictures of our daughter, and up until this point, have never released her name. But now with school and sports teams, it's impossible to keep this a secret anymore.

I've become conscious of two things. First, each time I told my story it got easier to leave behind the feelings of shame because Mother Nature and I had clashed in an epic cage match. Second, I've realized there's a difference between secrecy and discretion.

My goal is to provide a "how to adopt" book and still retain my daughter's privacy.

So here I am. About to start writing.

Oh wait. Two more snacks later, I just have to do one more thing. I wait for my daughter to come home from school. I ask for her permission to write a book about her. She cocks her head, smiles, and says okay. Then she wryly offers a few pointers on which stories should be in the book.

Even though I promise my daughter I will alter certain facts to preserve her privacy and dignity, I worry when she's a teenager she will find this embarrassing. But since being horrified by your parents is an almost inevitable part of teenhood, I figure I might as well write the book while she's too little to wrestle the computer from me.

I now assure myself that if I refer to projects I was working on for context and timing, it won't make this book that autobiography I don't want to write. Also, I tell myself to reveal the truth, even though to people in comedy, talking about our real emotions feels like a TV after-school special. Finally, I pledge to limit those cute kid quips that make people's teeth ache.

I close my office door. I put the snacks down. I am going to start writing now.

So here is the true story of how I finally became a mom.

Instantly.

Birth

It's late 2008 and I'm lying on the couch at my home, holding my three-year-old daughter as she cries.

We're both gasping for breath.

Just a minute ago, I was standing in the kitchen as she walked by, sucking on a hard candy. She was happily jumping on the couch, when she suddenly grabbed her neck and looked at me. The candy had lodged in her throat. She tried to swallow it. She couldn't breathe. She was white.

Being a parent requires courage and, unfortunately, I'm a bit of a sucky 'fraidy-cat. I sleep with a light on. I get out of an elevator if I'm alone when a man gets in. I never walk down back alleys.

But in that moment, like anyone would, I ran toward my daughter. I knew exactly what to do, because to adopt, you have to take a first aid course. I knew not to put a finger in her throat and push that candy even farther in. I knew not to touch any part of her neck. I knew not to panic. I just grabbed my daughter, turned her upside down, and jumped—and finally that candy fell out.

She breathed. She cried. She was okay.

Now, as I am lying on this couch, holding her against my body, we both breathe in. And out. I try to relax so she'll feel soothed, comforted, and safe. I try to think of what else I should do now. I don't know. I wonder if the feeling of being an adult, being a grown-up will ever come naturally to me.

I love being in charge. I am completely comfortable whether I'm throwing a giant dinner party or directing a microbudget independent film. I don't get stressed and I don't yell. I like to calmly problem-solve and enjoy getting things done. However, as a grown-up in sophisticated situations, I am not completely at ease. In scenarios that require decorum and restraint, I usually want to make a fart joke and run. But, as a mom, I try to *act* like an adult, especially at this moment.

Tight against each other, my daughter and I eventually calm down, now listening to our hearts beating. We are very still. I realize this is what it might have felt like if I'd grown her inside me. She would have heard my heart beating; I would have felt her move.

Instead, I met my daughter just recently. I've only been her mom for a few months. The adoption isn't even finalized. Anyone who ever wondered how much they could love a child who did not spring from their own loins, know this: it is the same. The feeling of love is so profound, it's incredible and surprising. I love my daughter so much I want to carry her around in my mouth.

As I'm holding her now, I am in an emotional place I'm not used to. I feel content.

This is new. It's not at all how I felt for a very long time. For years, I felt exactly the opposite.

A Fistfight with Mother Nature

It's 8:00 A.M. in early 2003 and I am driving through a rare and raging rainstorm in Los Angeles.

My hands are shaking.

I don't want to have a horrible accident on the freeway that an infamous ex-football player once made famous. It's a cliché, so of course utterly true, that L.A. people don't drive well. I'm not talking about me. I'm from Winnipeg—I took my driving test the day after a snowstorm—I'm tough. However, nothing prepared me for early morning Los Angeles morons driving and reading a script they forgot to tell the intern to cover, plus sexting a mistress whilst sipping a gluten-free soy-free GMO-free not-at-all-free power shake.

Therefore, a rainstorm is a particularly foolish time for me to be on the freeway. Hard rain pounds my windshield. Wind whines against the car windows. My palms ache from how hard I am gripping the steering wheel and my eyes blur from trying to focus. I am trembling. But it's not the storm that's making me anxious. I've just been nominated for an Academy Award.

The shock of this is making my teeth clang. It's been close to a year since *My Big Fat Greek Wedding* opened, and it's still playing in theaters. So many nominations, from a Golden Globe for acting and best comedy film to a People's Choice Award, are hard to comprehend and absorb. And now this has happened. The impossible. I had written a script in an attempt to get an acting job, and this morning I'd been nominated for an Oscar for Best Original Screenplay.

But I didn't celebrate with champagne. A gaggle of friends didn't rush over to jump up and down with my husband and me, then devour a lavish brunch. Sure, I'd been woken up before dawn when the phone rang with the amazing news from my best friend, Kathy Greenwood. That led to an exciting round of call waiting from family and friends, lots of noise, excitement . . . then my husband and I looked at each other and somberly accepted the reality of what I had to do that day. He went to work, and I got in the car.

Now I am alone, driving to the fertility clinic for my early morning lab work in yet another attempt to be a mother. I am on IVF #3. For many years I have been hiding a dumb secret: not being able to carry a baby to term has made me deeply unhappy.

While I am grateful for the success of the movie, it just doesn't matter. Sure, I'm thrilled, but all I can think about this morning is how long I have been trying to carry a child to term. Over the past five years at least, I'd often been pregnant. There is no feeling of disappointment I have ever known like a miscarriage. So I am now in awful, painful, and time-consuming fertility treatments and even working with a wonderful and selfless surrogate. I don't know if this will work, but I do know I will keep trying.

Because I am obtusely obstinate.

I am the type of person to whom the word "no" is a shortened version of "try a different way." I just never accept the word "no." The fact that I'm a working actress and writer is simply because I am incredibly stubborn. Over the last years, many, many people told me "no," as in "Get lost, Fatty." They would look me right in the eye and say "no," but I just heard, "Go around me. Fatty."

It's ironic, bordering on tragic, that I share common traits with psychopaths and serial killers, in that we're focused and truly believe we're right. I have no idea how I got this way.

I am the second daughter born to two fantastic and funny parents. I was raised in Winnipeg, an excellent Canadian city of pleasant and cultured people. I have two wonderful sisters and a delightful brother. We're very close and yet all quite different. I was always a bookworm and loved performing, so I decided to be an actress even though my parents wanted me to be a dental hygienist. Or better yet marry a dentist. Yes, a Greek one.

I did community theater and many musicals in Winnipeg. Then I auditioned for professional classical theater schools across Canada and got into all of them because I was so beautiful and talented!

Actually, no. No, I wasn't. I got rejected by every single school. I was an overweight and overconfident hairy girl with a very loud voice. Nobody knew what to do with me. But I was a boisterously exuberant person living a good life in Winnipeg. I took university classes, did more community musicals, dramatic theater, some large professional productions, and made a good living working as a florist. This is a skill I still have and I will do your wedding if you ask politely. If you're gay, I will definitely do your wedding because of your absolute right to be. . . . I digress. One day this issue will be as dated as the vote for women and most of my hairstyles. Back to the backstory.

I wanted to be a professional actor so I kept auditioning for the theater schools. Then a friend put in a good word for me with a classical theater school in Toronto and I finally got in. I opened that acceptance letter and stared at it. This was what I had been waiting for. Validation. This theater school was going to train me to become a classical actress.

I moved from Manitoba to Ontario and decided to really pursue acting; yes, much to my family's dismay. If you have an image of a brave girl turning away from her people's traditional ways, then I'm not being clear. It's not like there was some sweet Greek guy offering me a comfortable life if I stayed in Winnipeg with him. No one asked me to stay. All the cute Greek boys I grew up with were like brothers to me. Most of them loved my older, perfect sister, who was actually quite worthy of their attention. I was dating one non-Greek guy who slept with my then-closest friend. So it's not like I had guys weeping, begging me to stay and marry them.

I was extremely close to my family. With Greeks, your cousins are like siblings, your aunts and uncles are more parents. The entire family is comical—everyone can tell a good story and, in a completely good-natured way, we all incessantly make fun of each other. My mom and I are extremely close. She is warm and witty and the type of person you just want to make laugh because she really cracks up hard. I do not know why I wanted to leave all that love and support in favor of an industry of judgment and denigration. But I did. I really, really wanted to go to that classical theater school and become a classical actress.

Within two weeks at that classical theater school, I knew I would never be a classical actress. I enjoyed performing Shakespeare but how many roles were there for a robust and curly-haired loudmouth? I loved my classmates, but I didn't really fit in with the classical program. This would be about the umpteenth time in my life when I would realize I was trying to jam my square peggedness into yet another round hole. The first time was in junior high school when I heard the whole class was coming to see our production of *Free To Be*. I was sure this would finally make me popular, yet instead during my performance the boys screamed, "Vardalos, shave your side-burns." Then in high school, it was when the straight-haired, straight-leg-jeaned girls ran from me when I suggested we have a sleepover *Evita* sing-along. Then during university, there was the time at my weekend job I suggested to my florist co-worker that we attach a tape recorder on a timer under a casket floral arrangement that, ten minutes into the funeral service, would emit a from-inside-the-casket knocking sound.

Even though I don't seek it or enjoy the feeling, I've gotten used to people staring at me like I'm an idiot.

Big surprise: like most people in comedy I have never been pop-ular and cool. "What?" you clutch your chest and screech. "You mean people who go into comedy are actually insecure and seeking approval?" We all know the answer is uh-huh. But c'mon, isn't every-one insecure in some way?

So here I was at the stellar theater school I had yearned to get into, and it was not a good fit. I didn't know what to do with this information. I did see one thing very clearly though—while some of my teachers were urging me to be true to myself and find out what kind of actor I wanted to be, one teacher was an absolute dink. He treated me with disdain, quite openly making fun of my ethnic physicality and weight. He actually told me he would cut me from the program if I didn't lose weight. Now, I was a big girl, but it's not like I was circus-fat. I looked around me—many of the male students were overweight and funny. But I was being chided. Just me. The men were being encouraged to be irreverent. I wasn't. This teacher made me feel as if I was all kinds of wrong for being a funny, fat girl. As if there's any other kind. I don't know if you carry your fat on the outside or if you're waving your freak flag from within—funny people are funny because we don't feel like we fit in. The less you soared in high school, the more likely you are to have success in Hollywood. Because observing and loving/hating pretty people from the sidelines is what makes us funny. Our kind knows if we're funny, we'll get some attention. And bonus: we'll stop getting picked on. My industry is filled with successful people who were once most likely to have been locked in a high school locker.

Feeling dejected and rejected at theater school, on a whim, I attended an evening performance at a comedy theater called The Second City. It was the first time I'd seen sketch comedy and improvisation. In the third act, the actors took suggestions for scenes from the audience and performed the ideas on the spot. It was so spontaneous and fun—and it felt familiar. It felt like when my cousins and I would lie around after a giant meal and just have fun in the living room, imitating our parents and each other. It was made up on the spot, just like the improvised act at Second City.

I was mesmerized and hooked.

As I said, not everyone on the staff at theater school loathed me. In fact, several of the teachers, acknowledging I didn't fit in, felt I'd be happier working in musical theater and encouraged me to leave the program and start working. So with most of my teachers' support, I auditioned for Second City. After years of performing everything from musical theater to Shakespeare, that comedy stage was my goal. I could truly envision it: I could really see myself in that cast. I walked into that audition with a ton of brash confidence. I walked out with a red-hot shame-face and not just a trickle of butt-crack flop sweat. When it came to improvisation, I had no idea what I was doing. I was not good. At all. But that didn't stop me. Nope. I just auditioned again and again, never getting into the cast. I now know this to be true about Hollywood: the really talented people are not necessarily the ones working in the industry. It's the people with the highest tolerance for swimming in a sea storm of viscous excrement who make it.

I auditioned and got jobs in musical theater summer stock companies, performing in every musical from *Anything Goes* to *Oklahoma*. In between these jobs I would waitress at a comedy club. To this day I overtip because I was such a lousy waitress—I would often win the Bartenders' Dork of the Night contest by accidentally spilling trays of beer on myself. The bartenders would openly hope I would get hired in another musical so I would take more time off.

But my eye was on getting into that Second City cast. I learned there were improvisation classes at Second City and that employees could take the classes for free. So I got a job in the box office and took those classes. I loved the improv lessons during the day. But if anyone knew what I was up to in the box office at night, I would have been fired. After the audience was in, I would guiltlessly take the phones off the hook and go into the theater to watch the performance. I loved watching the show. The first two acts were short sketches—this was material that had started as suggestions from earlier audiences and been improvised until they became scenes. The sketches that went well in the improvised act were placed into those first two acts, replacing older material that had been developed via improvisation months before. The first two acts of the show were constantly changing as new material went in approximately every six months. The third act was always improvised by the actors in their search for new material.

Well, for the three weeks I worked in the box office, I watched those first two acts of scenes diligently, mouthing every word. After the show, I'd run back and close up the box office before a manager could notice that I hadn't been in there all night.

One night before the show, an actress got sick. She had an inner ear infection and was rushed to the hospital. As the audience was filing into the theater, the stage manager ran into the box office to find the understudy's phone number. I watched with my eyes a-popping. As the phone rang, I was whispering a mantra, "Don't answer. Do not answer that phone." Maybe because I'm a witch, it rang and rang. Finally the stage manager left a voice mail and rushed backstage to figure out what to do.

Something made me stand up. As I've said, it's not bravery—it's more along the lines of senseless and resolute fortitude. I blithely went backstage, walked right up to the stage manager, and said, "I am a member of Actors' Equity and I know your show."

After a long moment in which I did not blink once, while wondering if she could call the union at this hour and find out I was still gathering enough points in professional productions to join but actually was not a member, she said, "Get out."

I said, "Okay," turned, and ran hard into the chest of a cast member, Mark, who asked, "What's going on?" The stage manager explained the actress was sick, adding, "I can't find an understudy and the box office girl thinks she knows the show." Mark laughed, lit a smoke, and looked me over. I should mention I was 220 pounds of bravado flaunting a never-in-fashion home perm. Oh, and I wore harem pants a lot. And, a gold-braided headband stretched across my zitty forehead. It was the '80s. I'm not saying I was chic for the era. No, no, I just didn't know what fashion was. I wore what I thought a thespian would wear. My harem pants were comfortable and stitched within them was an awesome gold thread that matched my superhero headband. As I said, I had a lot of confidence. I liked my look and I rocked it hard.

Mark asked, "Do you know Nun?" "Nun" was the opening scene. It was normally performed by two people: Mark and the actress who was sick. I said I knew it. Mark fired the first lines at me, and I responded with the rest of the scene. Mark grinned mischievously at the stage manager and said, "Put her on." I think it was more of a dare.

I waited while the stage manager called to get permission from the producers. The rest of the cast showed up and, after a moment of shock upon learning I wanted to do their show, acted like I wasn't there. In retrospect I think no one really believed that anyone would put me onstage without a rehearsal. I guess they were waiting for the producers to call back and fire me from my box office job, then Security would escort me from the building. The cast started to talk about replacing the actress's scenes with improvisational game scenes. But she was in a lot of scenes, and that many game scenes would have seemed strange to a paying audience. I was adamant I could do their show, calmly and urbanely smiling while my stomach boiled a nervous acid soup that made my tongue taste of urn ashes.

The stage manager hung up the phone, pulled me aside, and said, "You're on." The look in her eye let me know she actually was rooting for me but if I messed up, I would not only never work in this theater ever, but probably not work anywhere ever again. With the thought of starting a puppet theater in Winnipeg flashing through my skull, the introductory music started . . . and I just walked out onstage.

I did the show. All the scenes. It was a huge blur. I remember nothing except the cast being really nice as I performed scene after scene, and they even bought me drinks afterward. I recall profusely thanking everyone. Then, at two A.M., I walked back to my one-room apartment, sat on the couch, and burst into frantic, mucousy, blubbery tears. I had no idea how I had pulled that off.

The next day, I reported for my box office shift. The producers were waiting. They hired me and my gold headband.

I worked hard, very hard, to learn how to write material through improvisation. This was a place where irreverence was rewarded. It was expected that we would be impertinent and create scenes that challenged authority. My immature need to poke fun at social mores meant I finally fit in. For the first time, I felt in control; I knew this world and belonged in it. Plus, there weren't any physical constraints—I could do any character I felt like playing. Although the producers didn't ask me to, I worked diligently on losing some weight so I could be more versatile onstage. Years later, I learned it was thyroid disease that made my weight yo-yo. But at that time, through sheer willpower and a little unhealthy starvation, I lost ninety pounds. I made great, fantastic friends in that cast whom I truly loved working with, including my best friend to this day, the aforementioned just-this-morning caller, Kathy Greenwood. Because I'm so close with my sisters, female cousins, and girlfriends, I've always sought and collected female relationships. I love playing with the boys, but there is a bond between certain women that is unbreakable. You can spot a woman-friend in that first eye flick. We know who we are and we find each other. Woman-friends are the ones who will quietly tell you, "Yes, you do look fat in those pants." They will stay up late writing material with you and never make out with your boyfriend.

Joyce Sloane and her daughter, Cheryl (both woman-friends), two of the producers of Second City Chicago, having heard the going-on-from-the-box-office story, came up to Canada to scout me. Or as Joyce put it, to go "have a look at that girl with the balls." After the show, Joyce invited me to work at the Second City in Chicago and she and Cheryl did all the paperwork to get my immigrant working papers, green card, and eventual dual citizenship.

I arrived at the Chicago theater and sat on the lobby bench and looked around. There is a lot of history in that theater, and I had always wanted to be a part of it. The strange thing is, as I said, I may have sorcery in my blood because I always knew I was headed there. Akin to most Greeks, I have cousins in Chicago, so I spent many summers in the city. We'd drive past the theater and I'd think, *I'm going to work there one day.* I had no idea how I'd conjure it all up, but I knew it would happen.

That day, as I sat in the lobby surrounded by pictures of famous alums, I took a moment to absorb it. And I heard something. A small laugh. I looked around. . . . I was alone. People had told me this theater was haunted. There was no one there, but I heard the sound again. Was that a laugh? Yeah, a laugh.

At that moment, Joyce Sloane walked out of her office to summon me. She had a thorough and intense way of looking at a person, in a way that said she really saw you. I didn't know then that she would become my mentor, driving me to create characters and write scenes to make her proud. Joyce believed that good material doesn't rely on swearing and cheap sexual references. We had a special bond that . . . okay, okay, I learned many years later that *every* cast member felt the same way about her when we spoke at her memorial service and each declared we were her favorite. Anyway, in the lobby as she was about to officially hire me, I stood up to greet Joyce. She looked under the bench I'd been sitting on and yelled while laughing, "Chris, get out of there." I looked down. That laugh I'd heard? That was Chris Farley hiding under that bench, looking up my skirt.

Even with the support of my loving Chicago relatives, the first year in Chicago was not easy. The last Canadian hired—Mike Meyers— had recently been chosen for *SNL* over American cast members. Then I showed up. It was tense. But I get it. If this had happened in Canada—if an American had been brought into our cast and then been chosen for a juicy job over the rest of us—we'd be peeved too. (We wouldn't be openly rude; it'd be more like we'd wave a cheery good morning from across the street as you discover we've egged your car.) Anyway, most Chicago cast members didn't have a problem with me and I formed great friendships with people who are still my übertight group to this day. We were all in our twenties, brashly and protrusively opinionated. That's why we were hired; we had a lot to say.

At that time, I'd started dating my soon-to-be husband, an American, a not-Greek person—Ian Gomez. At first, I tried to not like him because the fact that our first names have the same three letters was so cute it made my esophagus burn with regurgitated bile. Anyway, we dated for a few years and after our wedding, Joyce and Cheryl urged us to move to Los Angeles to try to work in the film and TV industry. They assured us the Second City theater would always be there for us, and if it didn't work out in Los Angeles, we could come back to Chicago and be creatively rewarded by teaching or directing shows. At this point, Ian and I had made our living solely doing theater for about five years. It was foolish to leave a steady gig, but we had to try L.A. I had also been featured dancing around in a Lean Cuisine commercial (now that's a former fat girl's ultimate triumph) that had gone national, so we had over ten thousand dollars saved, which made us cocky and a tad smug. We packed our car and drove west, so hopeful, half expecting to be greeted with a network pilot as soon as we arrived in Los Angeles.

We got a cheap apartment on a grimy street that always smelled like dog poo, in an area Ian goaded me that the Hillside Strangler had once brought to national attention. Ian started getting acting work right away. But I couldn't get a part. Could not. I couldn't even get regular auditions.

Suddenly three years had whizzed by. It was the mid-1990s, I was in my early thirties and had only done a handful of lines on-screen. Ian was working as a guest star and semiregular on shows such as *Murphy Brown* and *The Drew Carey Show*. I was getting voice-over work, but not regularly. We often ran out of money. I took other jobs—answering phones or floral designing—and every few months we'd go through our stuff and have yard sales to get cash for rent. It's not as if we suffered working long hours in a coal mine. We were young and dumb and living in Los Angeles where the sun always shines but no one calls you back. It was an adventure to keep financially afloat.

At the time a lot of stand-up comics were getting lucrative network development deals. I thought about doing stand-up and even tried it once, but the rhythm is a skill I didn't have, nor the patience to learn. Plus it takes years of performing in clubs on the road from

Moose Jaw, Saskatchewan, to Beaver Lick, Kentucky, to hone a tight ten-minute act on dating or in-flight snacks. Stand-up is a tough life and you have to love the art to live it. I admire the art but know I can't do it.

Around this time, I saw Jeff Garlin, a close friend from Second City, in his solo show *I Want Someone To Eat Cheese With*. Jeff is a joyful storyteller—going off on tangents ranging from bikinis to pudding while keeping the audience engaged, entertained, and invested. I also saw *God Said, Ha!*—Julia Sweeney is remarkably adept at letting an audience release their anguish and laugh with her. Watching their shows, I was in awe of their ability to be erudite and eloquent while remaining relatable.

I ached to be onstage, in a film, on TV, anything. I was grateful to now be making a good living doing voice-overs on commercials for Bud Light, Kraft, and Home Depot. But that's not what I'd come to Los Angeles to do.

Like most actors trying to get a job, I'd given my on-camera agent a series of expensive headshots. But I had only gotten about four auditions a year. To put it in perspective, Ian and our friends were auditioning four times a week. So I asked for a meeting with my on-camera agent. I planned to suggest I meet with casting directors, so they could put a face to the headshot they'd been receiving but not booking for appointments.

I sat across from my agent and she bluntly told me she'd been sending the latest round of one hundred headshots "out like crazy for a year," but no one wanted to see me because, in her opinion, I didn't "look like anyone else in the city." I was surprised by that. I was 130 pounds, a size six, and my hair was long and curly. I thought I looked about average. Or at least normal. I mean, I was married but I did get hit on, so I didn't think I was delusional in thinking I was not a model for a building gargoyle. But I noticed my agent regarding me as if I was indeed a creature attached to the corner of her desk. This was Los Angeles, after all—the land of size zero actresses with imaginatively enhanced breasts, tiny noses, and butter-colored hair. Looking me over, my agent brusquely announced she now realized the problem. She said I was "not pretty enough to be a leading lady and not fat enough to be a character actress."

That hung in the air for a sec. I paused just in case she wanted to correct anything. Nope.

She then asked, "What are you? Latina?" I said, "No, I'm Greek," and she said, "Well, that's the problem. We're going to change the spelling of the last part of your last name from 'os' to 'ez' and send you out as a Hispanic."

I felt the blood leave my face. Change my name and sit in a casting waiting room with real Hispanic actresses, many of whom I knew? I said I didn't think I should do that.

She said, "Well, there are no Greek parts, so I can't get you work."

And she dropped me.

Dolefully agentless, I shuffled into her storage room to pick up my remaining two or ten headshots. There were over ninety of them there.

It looked like she hadn't been sending them out at all. She was either too lazy or didn't know how to market me, so chose instead to belittle me and my physicality. I yawn when people say it's a man's world and women have it so tough. We don't need the male species to oppress our ascent; we do a fine job of it ourselves.

I drove home doing that crazy snicker-snort when you don't realize people are watching from the next car. I was furious, amused, bemused, empowered, and somehow relieved. I decided to not put myself into anyone's hands again. I had given this woman several years of my life and she had wasted them and declared me not castable because I was Greek? I decided to turn my problem into the solution: if there weren't Greek roles, I would write some. I had just spent many years at Second City writing my own material. I could write myself a role.

I sat at the kitchen table and listed every family story I'd been telling at parties for years. When I was watching Ian meet my family, I saw them through unsullied eyes. I saw all the joy, all the quirks, all the devotion. When Ian was getting baptized so we could get married in the Greek church, I was truly touched by how gallant it was. And a minute later, the mercenary side of me thought, *Hmm, this could be a movie.* So after I made a list of stories about my family, I decided to shove them all into a script premise about my enormous wedding.

I had never written a movie. But I had seen a movie script. So I borrowed a friend's computer—he had the screenwriting formatting program called Final Draft and showed me how to work it. I wrote the screenplay in three weeks and called it *My Big Fat Greek Wedding*.

Yes, my real wedding is the basis for my screenplay. Although I made most of it up, I now prefer not to reveal which parts are real and which aren't because of the look of deflation I have seen in peoples' eyes when they find out the movie isn't a documentary. So please accept just this: Yes, Ian got baptized Greek Orthodox. Yes, my dad used Windex on everything, including my teenage zitty forehead. Yes, my aunt Voula had a lump on her neck she claims was her twin. Yes, really. Then the script is fact mixed with fiction topped off with my affection for my huge family who loves me to the point of suffocation.

Okay! Now I had a screenplay chock-full of Greek parts I could play. I was so naive, I thought if I could get that script to a studio, I could play a bridesmaid. I re-wrote the script for months, then eagerly gave it to my new managers. And I waited. They didn't mention it. For a month, I didn't bring it up because lately I felt tension when I walked into their office. It wasn't going well. They'd gotten me a few auditions for TV shows and while I made it close, I had not booked a job. Plus, the managers hadn't been able to convince an agent to represent me for very long. I knew I was a disappointment to them. Because they told me. Often.

Three months later, I nervously asked one manager about my script. She looked annoyed, then found it on the floor behind her chair. She placed it on her desk as if it had a crusty coating of herpes and looked at me coldly. With one finger, she flicked it across the desk at me and said, "You're an actress; who ever told you you could write a screenplay?"

There are a lot of fear-based people in any business. You know them. They claim to want something different but when you give it to them, they shoot it down. While I'm not saying the screenplay was brilliant, at least I was trying to get a job, admittedly by uncommon and unorthodox means. At this point, it'd been over three years of trying to get acting jobs by playing by the rules. I'd tried to be a good girl. I did everything agents and managers had asked me for. I'd paid for new headshots, acting lessons, and casting workshops. I'd been banging my thick head against a brick wall. It felt like when I was trying to get cast in Second City Toronto by playing by their rules and auditioning, and ended up getting in by going onstage from the box office. That time I had stared at that impenetrable brick wall, then pulled a brick out and shimmied my big butt through it. But now, I was being chastised for not playing by the rules. And waiting. For what? I'd had years of that theater school teacher telling me I was too fat, and now agents and managers telling me I still was not enough for the roles that were out there: not fat enough, not pretty enough, not thin enough, not old enough, not young enough, not talented enough. I was never right for the part; I was never supposed to do anything but wait for that elusive job. Now I stood there holding my script, embarrassed to be told I shouldn't write because I was an actress.

I just couldn't be a good girl anymore.

I told the managers it'd be best if we parted ways. I felt pretty sure I had a real movie in my hands. It wasn't just brassy conceitedness. I had already gotten up onstage at comedy theater open-mic nights and read parts of it out loud—and people had laughed. Strangers found it relatable. They'd tell me afterward that it sounded like their own crazy families.

But I now had no agent, no manager. My phone simply did not ring with a job offer. So I called myself.

I realized if I wanted to perform, I could just get onstage and tell my family stories in the style I had seen Julia Sweeney and Jeff Garlin do. I sent the screenplay to the Library of Congress to copyright it, then turned the material into a solo show. With the money from my voice-overs and Ian's sitcom work, I rented a local theater. My set was a typical Greek living room: a couch with lace doilies on the armrests, and every other surface adorned with Parthenon knick-knacks. Then, I just walked out onstage and told the story by playing all the characters. First, just friends from my Second City days came to support me, which was really nice. I am grateful for my circle of actors and writers who actually support each other—we cheesily call ourselves The Core. (Believe me, we know how dumb it sounds and that's mostly why we like it.)

But I had ninety-nine seats to fill once a week. So I went to church and at the after-service coffee hour, I boldly handed out my show flyers. When I told my parents, they went silent at my effrontery. Then my mom said, "Did the icons weep?"

Well, those Greeks came to the show. A lot of Greeks. Then the Greeks came back with their non-Greek neighbors. And the non-Greek neighbors came back with their families. And the stage show sold out week after week. I was losing money on it. The theater rental alone cost over $400 a night. Add in the cost of flyers, posters, etc., and it's an expensive endeavor that never made money at ten dollars a ticket.

But I was creatively exultant. I was performing again. Sure, I idealistically hoped an agent would come to the show; then I could get the screenplay read by a studio, made into a film, and play a role. Since I didn't have an uncle who ran a studio, I needed an agent to get my script even read. I didn't know anyone in this industry who could help. (I didn't think to ask my lawyer, Jon Moonves, who to this day remains my personal friend and professional ally-attorney. Jon did my voice-over contracts and is such a gentleman, I didn't know then he is actually a high-powered super-hotshot.)

After a while of running the show, in 1997 I decided to try to make an income off it: if I could pull in mainstream Los Angeles theater-goers, then maybe I could expand the amount of nights I was doing the show. I took out an ad in the *L.A. Times*. It cost about $500 for an approximately two-inch-by-two-inch ad. Rita Wilson saw that ad the day it ran and called the reservation line. I answered. Our home phone number had always been on the poster and was now on that ad, so during the day, I used a different voice to take reservations. My point is, I knew she was coming that night and was thrilled. A while back, during an awards show, Rita's husband, Tom Hanks, referenced being married to a hot Greek babe and whenever he spoke of her in interviews, it was always with such joy. I had always hoped to meet her because she was a very funny Greek actress I admired.

That day I received the copyright for the screenplay in the mail. I looked at it. It seemed I had sent it in so long ago. I was zealously enjoying performing my solo stage show and now understood the reality of how hard it is to get a screenplay read, never mind made. You have a bigger chance of marrying a terrorist as you get hit by lightning on your fortieth birthday when you win the lottery or whatever the adage is. It's not that I had given up. It's just that by that point, many industry people had come to the show and called me in for meetings. It usually went like this:

The first thing they'd tell me is that no, they didn't want to read my screenplay, they wanted to just buy my story, have a "real" writer write the script, and change it all to Hispanic because there wasn't a market for a Greek film. I'd explain it was vastly important to me to keep it Greek because it was about my real family, never mind that I had written it so I could play a bridesmaid. I'd get a hot stare back. I'd then say no thank you to the offer and, harder still, no thank you to the money. One producer offered me $50,000. Ian and I were still struggling to make rent. But I said no thank you and went back to doing my little stage show.

There was other interest but I now knew the reality of how hard it would be to get the screenplay produced.

At the show on this night, Rita Wilson and her Greek mom, sister, and nieces laughed so hard that I had to pause and pretend to drink water a few times. I kept my composure, but inwardly, I was giddily enchanted that they related to my story. If the story had ended there, I would have been satisfied.

After the show, I walked out through the lobby and Rita was waiting for me. Her first words to me were "I love you." I was stunned. She is even prettier in person, and a beam of happiness seems to emit from her. She is vivacious and upbeat and kept hugging me. I was delighted by her and her warm family, very much like my own.

Rita then exclaimed, "This should be a movie."

We always say I then handed her my screenplay so fast her hair flew back. She was going to read my script!

The next day, I got a call on my "box office" home line. For the very next show, Rita purchased four tickets for the males in her family: her dad, brother, son . . . and her husband, Tom Hanks.

On show nights, my husband, Ian, would sit in the box office area of this little theater and take people's ten-dollar bills. The theater seating was first come, first served, but it was only ninety-nine seats, so all seats were good. But someone at the theater had heard Tom Hanks was coming to the show, so on this night they'd taped off four seats right smack in the middle. It was a small theater facing a small stage. I was the only one onstage. You could see and hear me from any seat, anywhere. You could've seen me from the lobby.

Anyway, on this night that Tom Hanks was coming, there were many Greeks at the show. And try telling a Greek they can't sit somewhere. I was standing what could technically be called backstage, but really was just behind a thin and fake wall. I peeked through a crack and saw hefty audience members gesturing at the taped-off four-seat area, as in, "Why can't I sit there? Why? Who are those seats for?"

I paced. I was worried. It was time to start the show. Ian came backstage and told me ninety-five ticket-buying audience members were in. Four patrons were missing. We stared at each other, not saying it: Tom Hanks was not there.

Ian ran outside to see if there was a problem. There was—the tiny parking lot was full. He then saw a shadow: running up the street from a parking meter was a small group led by . . . Tom Hanks. Ian gulped, ran back inside, got it together, casually gave them their tickets, and showed them into the theater.

I was on the other side of the fake wall peeking through the crack, watching the complaining Greeks—"But why can't I sit there? Who are those seats for?" And then, I saw their faces as they saw him walk in. Tom Hanks. Tom. Hanks. They realized those seats were being saved for the one, the only Tom Hanks. Suddenly that was okay with them.

The audience lights went out, the show music played, and I was in a tizzy. I stood backstage, not moving. At all.

I don't get nervous about performing—even in my years of improv, if a scene died, I could just shake it off and go back out there for the next one. But tonight was a ridiculous scenario. Here's the thing: to me, Tom Hanks had always been The One. He was always my favorite actor. I truly loved his work. I had watched his movies over and over. I couldn't even hear the theme music to *Philadelphia* without choking up at just the memory of his performance. I was about to perform for, never mind the world's greatest actor, but for my favorite actor of all time? A guy I now knew was cool enough to marry a hot Greek chick? I could hear a raspy sound. It was my breathing.

Then I told myself this: in seventy-five minutes I could either be really proud of myself or really mad at myself . . . it was my choice. It was in my control.

So I walked out onstage and purposely looked past the middle section so I would not have to make eye contact with the biggest and best movie star in the world. But I couldn't see any faces. I looked closer at the audience. There were no eyes. I saw just ears. All heads were turned toward those middle four seats. They were all looking at Tom Hanks.

I spoke the opening lines of the show and delivered the first punch line. Tom Hanks laughed. Loud and hard.

The entire audience seemed to realize at that point that there was a person onstage. They turned en masse and looked at me, like "uh-huh, go on."

And the show went on.

I talked about my family and how they reacted to my wedding to a non-Greek. Tom is not Greek and he married Rita, a Greek. Miles apart, Rita and Tom, and Ian and I both had weddings in a Greek church, where we wore head wreaths, and led by a priest we walked around an altar three times to seal our vows. In the show, I talked about the family members who first greeted Ian with suspicion and eventually accepted him with an assuring pat on his cheek: "You look Greek."

Like Ian, Tom had been enveloped and swallowed into a colossal and loving ethnic family. Like Rita, I had dared to bring a non-Greek, a *xeno,* into a fiercely proud family. On this night, as I told the story, I realized how similar our backgrounds were.

Then suddenly, the show was over. I was bowing and the audience was applauding and I ran off as usual. But they were applauding really hard. I looked through that wall crack and finally saw the face of Tom Hanks. I decided if this turned into a standing ovation I would go back out there. Suddenly, Tom leaped to his feet, the audience quickly followed in a standing ovation, and I ran back out so fast I'm sure I created a butterfly effect on another continent. I took another bow, looked right at him finally, and smiled. Just a "thank you for coming" smile. And Tom Hanks grinned back. Again, if the story had ended there, I would have been happy.

Two days later I received a letter from Tom Hanks. The letter says: "Dear Nia,

"I know you. You are one of those Greek girls who come into the lives of men like me. Men who are not Greek. Non-Greek men. We see you, then we work up the courage to speak to you, then we fall in love with you and ask you to marry us. Then you do, in one of those Big Fat Greek weddings where you walk around a table three times. And then us non-Greek men live happy forever."

Tom goes on to talk about the show, Rita, their family, signs it simply with his name and includes a P.S. "I look Greek."

If the story had ended there, I would have been . . . you get it.

Well, a while later Tom Hanks called me and asked if his new company, Playtone, could make my script into a movie. I always say it doesn't matter how many no's you get, you only need one yes. Here was mine. Rita Wilson had started it all by saying yes to reading my script. With Tom Hanks on the line, I gripped the phone receiver and breathed. Of course I was about to accept with boundless appreciation . . . but I went quiet. After years of struggling to get on-camera work, I really wanted to be *in* the movie. I yearned to be cast in any role, even the lump on Aunt Voula's neck. But I didn't dare make this request—this was Tom Hanks on the phone. Timidly, I began to consent, vacillated . . . then thought of the Laurel Thatcher Ulrich quote: "Well-behaved women seldom make history." I knew I was about to ask Tom Hanks, the best actor in the world, if I could play a bridesmaid. And what came out was . . . I asked Tom if I could play . . . the bride.

I was stunned at my audacity. I held my breath.

He said yes.

For Rita and Tom to get that movie made and subsequently released in theaters would be a complex and arduous process. This was problematic because I was a non-"name," and we were independently financed. Rita was always adamant that I must play the lead—we became very good friends over the course of the production and since. Both Tom and Rita treated me with the utmost esteem and truly like a peer. Gary Goetzman, an independent producer Tom was wise to partner with, forming their company Playtone, was incredibly respectful and caring. I tell everyone: Rita, Tom, and Gary treated me like gold before that movie made a dime. They let me be in on every aspect of the film from editing to mixing to marketing. I asked boneheaded questions and learned a lot. It was a protracted, laborious production to complete yet clearly turned out to be enormously rewarding. I broke into an industry that had told me loud and clear I didn't belong, and found success because I was tenacious, assertive, and obstinate.

During this entire time in Los Angeles and even during the filming of the movie, I was in the process of trying to have a baby. I'll spare you the gory details, but the miscarriages affected me deeply. I had never failed at anything before. I had moved to the States, gotten my green card and dual citizenship, written a movie, and played the lead role. How could I do all this but not make a baby?

This thought keeps repeating itself right now, as I white-knuckle grip my steering wheel. The rainstorm pounds and howls against my windshield. I dead-eye stare out and think about the stubbornness and determination that led me to getting the film made. It's the same tenacity that will ultimately not let me turn back now. I will keep driving through this frightening rainstorm and I will go to that fertility clinic again.

I guess I'm trying to explain the personality glitch that would make me put myself through these IVF treatments.

Thirteen times.

3

When?

More than a year later, I'm lying in a murkily lit room of artificial tranquillity, getting a headache from a cloying waterfall. Or maybe it's a mix-tape of fake waterfall sounds. Oh, here comes the Hindu chanting, which makes me think of passive-aggressive yoga people who bow "namaste" to the instructor then push past the rest of us out the door.

The ersatz waterfall's cacophony is drumming into the bone of my forehead. I'm supposed to feel soothed and lulled into relaxation, but it's hard to do anything but stare at the voodoo acupuncture needles in my stomach.

In addition to the fertility doctors, I am now seeing another recommended Eastern medical genius who guarantees he can make my eggs stronger.

It's all I do now—try to make stronger eggs. I am on IVF #9.

Oddly, I have it all in perspective. I refuse to cry. I don't feel sorry for myself. I don't consider my situation so tragic. I am almost ashamed that this is taking up so much time. Especially when I read the letters from nice people who tell me things such as *My Big Fat Greek Wedding* cheered them up when they lost their jobs, or they took the DVD with them when they were deployed. Or they watch it at night when they are caring for their sick parents . . . or since they lost a spouse.

I am astonished at the amount of pain people experience and how they have managed to go on. This is why I tell myself to buck up and be grateful I have the time and finances to do these treatments.

So I rest. I take vitamins. I drink daily jugs of toxic mud juice masquerading as "health tea." I try to avoid tension. But it's difficult to remain calm during this process that is not working, plus completely ignore anything to do with my career.

Every door in Hollywood has flung open. Opportunities for a sequel rush at me. I had signed a deal for a TV show before the movie was released, but now it feels as if I could cash in on the "Big Fat" franchise forever, with cookbooks to ethnic dance DVDs. I don't want to.

I can't work anyway. I just turned down a modeling piece for *Vogue* magazine because I am hiding the bruises the three-times-daily needles have left on my stomach and thighs. *Vogue*. Me. Me in *Vogue*. And I had to say no.

I just declined yet another acting job because it would require I be out of the country. I cannot be away from the clinic and the daily lab work and the monthly surgeries where they repeatedly remove my eggs, fertilize them, and implant the embryos to create a baby. I feel powerless. The doctors explain it's the drugs. I'll bet it's the glaring fact that this is not working.

IVF #9. How did I get here? I wonder if this will be my last. I wonder if this time will create a baby. I wonder how many treatments I will do.

The Eastern medicine doctor comes in, removes the needles, pats me on the back, and tells me to avoid stress.

I walk out of the clinic and find a parking ticket on my car.

A few days later, I have the surgery to remove the eggs. Then days later, as the fertilized embryos are being implanted into the surrogate, I look at her beautiful, kind face and sob with appreciation. I am very hopeful this one will work. Today after I leave the clinic, I buy green and yellow baby blankets. I bring them home, bury my face in them, and pray for an embryo to implant. I hide the blankets in my closet and wait.

Weeks later, I find out the embryos didn't "take." No pregnancy. Again.

A month goes by and I'm about to begin IVF #10. As I drive to the acupuncture clinic again I suddenly pull over. I sit here and ask myself how on earth I can start this next round and begin to do press for my second movie, *Connie and Carla*. But it's a small-release movie without a decent ad campaign, without even a billboard, opening against the juggernaut *Kill Bill*. Even though I am bloated and queasy from the drugs, I'm "old school" and feel I have to honor my commitment to do press. Without advertising, there is no other way for people to know about the movie. I'm proud of the script because of its small message of acceptance. Plus I got to sing in it. I love musical theater so much, I may actually be a gay man.

I look out my car window now and remind myself about all the good things that happened . . . from getting to host *SNL* to meeting people I admire, like Ellen DeGeneres, Nora Ephron, Katie Couric, Anne Bancroft, Callie Khouri, Elton John, Quentin Tarantino, and Steven Spielberg. Publicly, I've continued to fake it, plastering on a smile and pretending everything is fine. It's not. I feel sick and I have to start the press tour now, which means being on TV talk shows again. I don't feel well, I don't fit in clothes. I have to start the next IVF treatment now because it's timed to my cycle.

I've been under pressure before. As I've described, when I was in the cast at Second City, there was tension and conflict, and actors were fired if their material wasn't up to par. But I flaunted a carefree insouciance that got me through it. I handled it. What's the alternative?

My attitude might be the grace my mom taught me to carry myself with; it might be that I'm so immature I never face reality. But I can't deny this situation; this is very real.

I tell myself, I just have to get through this next round plus do press. There is no other choice. I assure myself in time this fertility stuff will be behind me.

A few minutes later, I walk into the acupuncture clinic and the first thing I hear is purgatory's bogus waterfall. I'm sitting in the lobby sipping tepid cucumber water when I spy the culprit—a wall-mounted tape deck.

I ponder if one of the lit incense sticks on this side table could ignite that tape deck.

A grown-up would never pick one up and try it.

But I do.

No one is looking, I fling a stick of lit incense up. It lands on the tape deck and I wait for it to catch fire and explode, thus terminating fake waterfalls forever.

The incense stick rolls off the tape deck, lands on my shoulder, and burns a pinhole in my shirt.

During the fertility treatments, I get the press interviews done. One hour before the premiere of *Connie and Carla,* I find out IVF #10 didn't work either. No pregnancy. I'm now standing on the red carpet, waving and smiling, with a concave dark hole in my chest. Someone—I think it's the *Entertainment Tonight* reporter—now asks on camera, "Any baby news?" I wish I could just walk away, then run as fast as I can. I don't want to be me anymore.

To further promote the film, I'm booked to be on *The Oprah Winfrey Show* again and have to fly from Los Angeles to Chicago with needles and medicine in my purse because I am preparing for IVF #11. I am standing at the X-ray machine, humiliated as I whisper, trying to explain my drug vials to Airport Security. Two of them are holding up my bag of needles and every traveler in line can see. My face feels hot. Finally, one security man takes pity on me and lets me pass. But not before telling me what an inspiration I am for writing my own movie but also that I've lost too much weight and look tired now. I smile wanly and board the plane, wishing so much I could be in bed.

Being on *Oprah* this time is vastly different from the first time I was on, with my real family, to celebrate *My Big Fat Greek Wedding*. That visit was buoyant and fun. This time, it feels as if the interview is all happening with an echo. I am so pumped up with fertility drugs, I can't think clearly. I try to remember funny stories to tell, and don't feel up to it. I sense that ever-omniscient Oprah Winfrey can tell I'm feeling off.

Afterward in the hallway Oprah stops, really looks at me, and asks how I am doing. I am completely aware I can't even make eye contact with her. Infertility has taken my confidence, drained the joy from me. It seems every day, women and men are stopping me on the street, at the mall, at a coffee shop to tell me how much they love my movie and how encouraging my success story is to them. But, truly, I now feel like a failure. I can't look at Oprah, but I murmur that all is good. She takes a moment, then lets it go. I am relieved—nobody wants to blubber all over Oprah. Pumped full of those hormones, I am always a breath away from blabbing out the whole sad story.

It's just not working. I am starting to get the huge hints I should stop the treatments. The anesthesiologist at the clinic had just told me his wife and he adopted an infant.

I call and confide in my best friend, Kathy Greenwood. She is still living in Toronto and is now a mom of two girls. She has been such a good friend to me through all this and listens patiently now. I tell her about the anger I am feeling that nothing has worked. I tell her I am so incredibly frustrated that I am still not a mom. Kathy thinks this over, then gently answers, "Giving birth is not what makes you a mom."

The next week at the clinic, the fertility doctor also has a quiet talk with me. He's been trying to suggest I stop treatments for a while now. I am resolute that I want to continue. He doesn't think it's sensible. I still want to go on. I ask him, "What would you do if you were me?" He sits across from me, smiles wryly, and tells me he has many adopted dogs and they've brought him more happiness than his children ever have.

It feels good to laugh.

I hear his message loud and clear. He thinks I should quit.

But I go back for more treatments.

4

Happy May Sucks Day

Blegh, it's May.

We all know on a certain Sunday of this month, overpriced flower arrangements will brighten homes, and restaurants will serve multi-calorie brunches. Reminders will be whispered, "Hey, be nice to your mom for a minute."

During the fertility treatments, besides abysmally gushy baby showers, Mother's Day is pretty much the worst day of the year for me. I avoid looking at Mother's Day TV commercials. Just the drug-store greeting card rack makes me pale. I loathe May.

In the spring, there are many social gatherings in Los Angeles, like this casual and large backyard home barbecue I'm at today. I shouldn't be here. The fertility drugs make me dizzy and very sensitive.

I am feeling particularly apprehensive because what happens next happens too often: with Mother's Day in the air, a mom blithely asks why Ian and I don't have children. This makes my throat close. Because yep, before I can answer, here it comes—other moms over-hear and jump in, exclaiming what a great father my husband would be, so why on earth don't we have kids? When I give a tight-lipped answer, "We're trying," they don't go mercifully silent. Oh no.

Their intention is to help—I know they want to and I value their kindness—but I don't want to get advice in this public setting. I think of the considerate friend who had learned of my situation last week and quietly pressed a prayer card into my hand. That I appreciated. But this open forum is not comfortable.

I feel my customary and dreaded upper-lip sweat beads from the attention. All I'd wanted was a snack and I'd dared to venture away from Ian to this food area. Now, crudité in hand, I am backed up against the appetizers table by chipper moms hip-bouncing their perfect, pudgy babies. These women are me, they're most of us. They're nice women offering information. So, I try to nod politely and accept the benevolence of these fine women's well-meaning stories of a sister who did egg donation, or a friend who found a baby in a Sears fitting room.

I hear a strident and shrill: "You should . . ." and my shoulders go up around my ears. I turn to see: sure enough, it's a beautiful woman who does not know when to stop talking. I love beautiful women and wish I was one. But some beautiful women's need to be heard overtakes many a social gathering as they fill the air with loud "You should" advice. There are lots of beautiful women who do not act like this. Most don't. No, only certain beautiful women have this affliction. It's called Beautiful Woman Syndrome. These BWS women, from the time they were young until recently, were the most beautiful woman in the room, so men listened to them. They somehow confused this result with being interesting. But now their men no longer listen to them. And they're still talking. At me.

This woman's finger-pointing "you should" advice now comes my way. I hate the phrase "you should." As in "You should have bangs." Or "You should talk to my sister about her genius doctor in Prague." Or "You should just adopt from China."

I *should* speak up, but I can't. I'm not good with confrontation. I get tongue-tied or worry I'll hurt people's feelings. I wish I was more mature and could articulate that this is a private matter. But I'm more likely to make a joke than instigate a moment of gravity that might suddenly whirl up into an awkward social tornado. So, I don't say anything. I just want to throw dip in the air and run.

Conversely, I don't blame them—before I was in this situation, I said dumb, dumb things to women about their baby plans. We all have. And I know all these nice women, including the one with BWS, truly want to help. Just as I get away from them, I hear a hissing sound and look up.

Oh, crap.

The group of unhappy women is looking at me. You know them. This is a worldwide club of not-nice-women who spew nastiness at other females. Membership requirements are merely a bitterness over the dissatisfaction with one's own achievements and the ability to curl a lip into an impressive sneer. I try to escape across the lawn but am encircled by . . . The Coven.

Since the days of my theater school teacher wanting to stab me for being a fat but happy girl, I have accepted there are some fractious people who just wish I'd explode. Plus, the good luck of my first movie has made me an easy target for the disenchanted. Guileless me wants to get out some pom-poms and shout: *But don't you see, when a geek like me finds success, this means the impossible is possible for us all?* But no, they don't see.

These members of the Coven now standing around me had, on previous occasions through skeletal taut smiles, already made it clear that they were perplexed by the fact that I, far less attractive and talented than they, was a working actress. I can't imagine what they want from me today. They look smug. Ah yes, they've overheard I am struggling to have a child, while these women are on their second and third—and they realize they have something over me. They can breed and I can't.

In the bright sun of this backyard, the Coven squeals at me about how "amaaaaazing" their pregnancies had been. Oh, her husband had looked at her with "awe" as she gave birth. Ohhhhh, breastfeeding is a "gift." I look into the eyes of one woman who had once taken a deep shot at me: upon hearing about my acupuncture fertility treatments, she'd snidely proclaimed she'd never had to do that because she was "perfect" and my body was "defective."

I am confused as to why they need to feel superior to me, and, yes, it hurts. Sure, I could ingenuously ask: "Did pregnancy hormones grow your monobrow or did you have it before?" But I don't. Not because I am so emotionally evolved and take the high road . . . no, no, I am scared of them.

Women like this are missing out on real female friendships. Sure, to some it seems as if it's just shoe shopping and cellulite talk, but we know what it really is and we value it. It's at times like this that I miss my sisters, sister-in-law, and cousins. My mom and aunts never pitted us against one another. I am extremely close with my funny cousin Nike (pronounced Nikki and the basis for the exaggerated version of a fun South Side Chicago broad played so well by Gia Carides in my first movie). I'm also still very close with my girlfriends from elementary school through my musical theater days, Second City, and my film career. I enjoy writing many funny female characters in ensemble films and TV shows. So I don't understand women of the Coven, and I am speechless at their need to put me down now when I am at my most vulnerable.

They finish their attack and leave me here, blinking back tears. As I watch these women cross the yard, I don't resent them for getting to be moms. Of course, because I'm not a saint, I wish they'd get hit by a random meteor or fall into a sinkhole. I watch and wait. No hot bolt of the Rapture takes any of them out. Damn.

I signal to Ian across the backyard. I feel terrible and want to leave. It's hot and my clothes don't fit. The sick irony of fertility drugs is they usually cause a bloating that resembles pregnancy, and I often get asked if I am pregnant. Even now, as I wait for Ian to disengage himself so we can go, I reach for an iced tea and because it's non-alcoholic, on cue a passing woman pats my tummy and says, "When are you due?" A small social guideline: don't ask a woman if she is pregnant unless her water breaks on your flip-flops, a baby arm dangles out of her vagina, and she asks you to cut the cord. Then and only then may you ask if she is having a baby. Otherwise, shut up.

I turn to the nice group, the well-meaning women who are waving good-bye to me. Taking a deep breath, I say, "Um, before I was in this situation, I too said things to women about their baby plans. Please don't. Instead, have some compassion, especially around Mother's Day. If you see someone without kids, don't ask them why they don't have children, why they don't just adopt, or if they are pregnant. Please just be quiet and pass the dip."

No, I don't. I just smile and wave good-bye.

5

"I Have Bad News"

I am staring at his mouth. It's as if I can see the words he's just said floating in between us. I want those words to unform. I want the letters to scramble, go back into his mouth, and come out as a different sentence. I want his face to go soft and then grin so I can know he is playing a joke on me. But he is not.

Something terrible has happened and I am trying to comprehend it. The embryo specialist, next to the fertility doctor, is standing in the doorway. The specialist now closes the door with one hand; his face is filled with anguish. I am terrified, and yet I can feel the palpable sorrow coming from his eyes. It's difficult to tell anyone something they don't want to hear. But he's not just telling us bad news. He is telling us he has made a mistake.

I am woozy and afraid I will faint. I feel Ian's arm behind me, keeping me upright. I have just completed yet another round of treatment. It was an especially difficult one. I am so bruised from needles I can't be touched. I'm bloated from the drugs and I feel sick all the time. Five days ago, Ian confessed he wants me to stop. He said it's just too much for him to watch me suffer anymore; he doesn't want me to continue. But I cannot stop. I have to beat this thing. I just have to. So I completed the round of needles, and the eggs were the healthiest the doctors had ever seen. The embryos divided more than they ever had and were very strong. So we came to this room and got ready for the next step. The kind surrogate was prepared, lying down and waiting to have the embryos implanted.

And a moment ago, the embryo specialist came in and said he'd made a mistake in the lab and my embryos had accidentally fallen into the incubator and been destroyed.

There is just no way to describe this black pit of silence. The absence of sound feels hollow and unreal. Everyone is still. No one yells, no one cries. We are numb as we try to absorb the news. This has never happened before. Ever. The embryo specialist hangs his head, and the fertility doctor comforts us. The embryo specialist now takes me into his lab and lets me look through the incubator with a microscope—there isn't any sign of my embryos. They're gone.

We silently leave the clinic.

Later, I get very upset. What else can happen? Why is this not happening for me? But this is not a story about anger.

Days later, I receive a handwritten letter from the embryo specialist. It chronicles exactly what happened. The letter surprises me because he has put the incident in writing and I am holding a beautiful and heartfelt apology. I keep reading it, profoundly sentient of the courage it took to write it. And I am fully and painfully aware that in this litigious society I am holding something that can be used in court. I could wreak havoc on that clinic; I could make them all pay for my years of anguish. But this is not a story about revenge.

Soon after, I am summoned to the clinic for a meeting with its panel of doctors. When I enter the clinic, it's quiet. The sterile fluorescent lights hurt my eyes because my entire body feels exposed and susceptible. I don't want to be here.

I round a corner and there he is—the embryo specialist. Without hesitating, we collapse into each other and just hold on. I tell him I accept his apology and more importantly I forgive him for what it was—an accident. This man has brought babies to so many people; he has given happiness to so many. He is a good soul and a kind person and I want to release him from any guilt for his one mistake. Standing here in this hallway, I feel intensely relieved that I can let go of the anger. I feel light. But this is not about mistakes and forgiveness.

It is a story about knowing when it's time to move on.

6

The Road to Adoption

It's 2:00 A.M. and I am on an adoption site, scrolling through the pictures . . . of Petfinder.com. I am taking that fertility doctor's advice and looking for a dog. I click on one picture of a magnificent yellow Lab. Brown eyes smile back, as if to say, "Pick me." To be honest, I can't say I feel anything. My heart feels dead.

It's been more than a year of trying to adopt.

At first, I did a lot of research. A barrage of unfamiliar terms had hit me. I couldn't see the difference between domestic infant adoption and private adoption. I didn't know if open adoption is what we wanted, or what it was, really. I didn't know if the statistics on drug-addicted babies were correct. I learned that in some states the birth mother can change her mind for up to six months. So I'd finally get a baby and then have to give it back, like in a Lifetime movie?

If you do an Internet search on "adoption," you get taken to sites that look credible. Many are. And many are not. Some have words that make you think, *Oh, this company is real,* but after getting on the phone with them and finding out they want a $75,000 retainer with no guarantee of a "match," ever, you start to wonder how the adoption process can be so unregulated. It was impossible to know which website might actually match you with an out-of-state birth mother and which one would lure you to a hotel room to harvest your kidneys. I'd stumble on sites that showed videos of babies playing in a crib. Cute babies in a foreign orphanage! It was so adorable it looked Pixar-animated. I'd watch for hours. I started to look into hiring an interpreter to try to adopt from Romania. But then a friend went there to be matched with a baby she saw on the website. When she got there, she was told that baby had just died. Just. Died. Of AIDS. She shook her head in disbelief at this very convenient story. Then they tried to convince her to go back to the States with a four-year-old boy. It took six weeks to go through the red tape and . . . she did it. Days later, she found out he had a nine-year-old half-brother. She took him too. They're both children with special needs. I admired her. I considered doing it. My family told me they'd support whatever I wanted to do. My siblings were all parents by then and I could tell in their sympathetic eyes they've discussed my situation and would support anything I tried. I got us on the waiting list for Greece, even though I was advised the wait from an orphanage was four years.

But nothing worked. Every site I registered with didn't pan out. I met several people who adopted Romanian and Russian children and had very good experiences. I took down the name of the agencies they used and got us on the waiting lists.

I was surrounded by positive stories of adoption, but of course the scary ones kept me up at night. And the media did a good job of it too. It's just human nature to pick up on the things that cause us anxiety. I could hear a hundred fantastic adoption stories in a row and then be stopped in my tracks by the negative one. There was always some story of some drifter who'd decapitated a store clerk because he'd once been adopted. Or wasn't adopted. Or something.

Googling "adoption" took me to strange places. It was all a late-night Internet search haze.

Ian and I had written our profile, attached a pleasant picture of ourselves, paid a fee, and registered with many domestic adoption agencies, in many states. I dug for info and found out "open" adoption means contact with the birth family after the infant is placed. "Closed" means the birth family does not know where the infant is placed. "Adoption Agency" means a licensed group who matches prospective parents with birth mothers. "Private" means parents and birth mothers are matched via an attorney. I learned the amount of time a birth mother has to change her mind varies from state to state, and, many people assured me, a birth mother taking her baby back is actually quite rare. But it happens, so I worried about it. Another thing I learned is that it's the birth mother who chooses the potential parents for her baby.

We'd waited a whole year for a birth mother to pick our profile. We then changed our profile picture, hoping we looked more appealing in the new one. We waited on many countries' adoption lists. We waited to be matched. We waited to be parents.

The phone rang a few times. We'd listen carefully to the case presented to us by the adoption agency: "This Illinois birth mother has two kids with the same guy, and he is in prison on a seventeen-year sentence. This last baby was conceived on a conjugal visit and she hasn't told him because she wants to leave him. So this baby is up for adoption. Do you want him?"

Uh . . . we asked if we could think about it. Privately, we admitted we were a little scared of a felon who would eventually get out of prison and find out about his youngest. It's not as if we thought our own eccentric families' DNA was so superior, but what was this birth father in jail for? And how about when that child wants to meet the birth father? The adoption worker called us back to convey they found out the birth mother lied about a lot of things, including who the actual father is and when the baby was conceived, and she'd also refused a drug test. To say we weren't relieved when the worker called back a few days later to tell us we were not matched would be a lie. A few weeks later, we found out someone we knew had been successfully matched via that same agency with a high school girl in Oklahoma who didn't feel she could keep her baby and go to college. That sounded ideal. We did not get a call like that.

The phone rang again. It was another agency in another state: "These two boys, aged three and eight, have been brought over from Germany. The adopting parents are now divorcing and don't want the children. Would you be interested?"

We said we were interested. But the story didn't make sense. I knew firsthand what it took to immigrate; why would two adults go through all that paperwork and neither take in the children? We asked more questions. The woman at the adoption agency told me "it happens" and I'd have to speak to her supervisor if we wanted to take the next step. We said we did.

We waited. During the two days we waited to get more information, we thought about the logistics of having two boys living at our house. We have nephews. Boys are fun. We thought our quiet house could use some madness. From all the visits, we had quite an accumulation of crayons and half-used bottles of bubbles. To be candid, adopting two boys whose language we didn't know wasn't the most prudent path, but we were frantic to be parents. We felt we could do it. Finally, the supervisor called me back: "The boys have a history of violence, and the older one tried to attack the adopting mother. The younger one tried to light the house on fire several times."

Ian and I are just two dumb actors; we're not equipped to take on two children with such intense psychological problems. I mean, of course we could do it and we actually wanted to. We were so desperate to be parents that we thoroughly discussed every case. We were willing to do anything. But on the phone with the supervisor, before

I could go on, she said the agency would only place these children with experienced parents anyway. I blurted out that made sense to me and couldn't get off the phone fast enough.

Having heard so many simple and successful adoption stories, I now wondered: Where's my call from a foreign country? Where are all the bubbly infants born to corn-fed North American college girls? I encountered people every day who had adopted infants in a beautiful and smooth way. They would tell me their successful story and I could visualize the women's-cable-network lighting of the scene. I kept thinking: How do I get my hands on one of those babies? Why are we not being matched?

I gave in and finally met with a Celebrity Adoption Attorney. I capitalize it because that's how he referred to himself. He said for a "Certain Fee" (yes, he air quoted it) we could have a "match" (yes, this too) within a very short period of time. A matter of days, he winked. I didn't fully understand. He said there's a list and if I paid the Certain Fee, I'd be moved to the top of the list.

Are you thinking what I'm thinking? That someone else who had been waiting would then be moved down a rung as I walked away with their baby because I threw a bunch of money down? Yeah, that's what I thought. I said his method sounded like human trafficking to me. That didn't go over well. He leaned forward, offering me a bowl of dusty mints from his desk, which can only mean one of two things: I had bad breath or he was stalling. Probably both. Anyway, I said, "How can you guarantee a birth mother who's been working with another couple would then switch—" He cut me off quickly, saying, "There's no guarantee. I never said there's a guarantee; I said you'd go to the top of the list." I thanked him for his time and left. And later found out a famous actress I knew had been on his Certain Fee list . . . for six years.

But there's something I felt about all these situations that intrigued me: I didn't feel right about any of them. I cannot explain this. None of them sat right with me. I felt like I was on the wrong path.

Another thing I know about myself is I need to talk things out. But at the time, I kept this all in, confiding in very few people. It's because it's a seemingly endless path of sadness without good news. I'm used to a more carefree and fun environment of laughing and good times. Inside, I felt like a drag. So I just didn't talk about it with Core or many people. Because nothing was working.

We quietly approached our super-hot friend Kathy Najimy (humble-brag alert: people think we're sisters) and her equally tremendous husband, Dan Finnerty, of the Dan Band, because they know Rosie O'Donnell, who I'd heard might be able to help. Plus Dan is adopted. Dan is a remarkably well-adjusted person and has a healthy relationship with his mom and his birth mother. I had watched Dan be in the same room with them both and it didn't seem exceedingly painful for anyone. That evening at their home, I didn't want to reveal much, but Kathy and Dan were excited to hear we were considering adoption. Kathy said, "There is something fantastic coming we could never imagine" and kept feeding us hummus and pita bread in her kitchen, knowing the way to get anyone ethnic to talk is through a full stomach. Dan kept jumping up and down, saying, "Do it, do it!" He pointed to himself. "You could get this!" I then asked Kathy to connect me with Rosie O'Donnell, who discreetly led me to an adoption counselor: a facilitator.

Ian and I sat on the couch in her small office and the facilitator started by gently asking what had brought us to consider adoption. I started to explain everything that had happened. Or hadn't happened. The miscarriages, the fertility treatments, then not one, but two surrogates, then not being matched through means that had worked for other people. I realized two things. First, I now knew why I was keeping it quiet: I couldn't talk about my experience without loudly snot-bawling. And second, I discovered that, interestingly, while I could see myself very clearly as a mother, I didn't necessarily see myself with an infant. The facilitator seemed intrigued by that vision and told me there were other options. This was the first time Ian and I discovered we don't have orphanages in North America. In the United States alone, we have over 500,000 children living in foster homes. Of these, 129,000 kids are legally emancipated. This means the parental rights have been terminated. And these children can be adopted.

The facilitator looked me right in the eyes and asked if I would be open to adopting an older child from the American foster care system. I didn't blink. That actually made a lot of sense to me. It felt like the right fit.

But I'll be honest—emotionally, I was a mess. Except in this office this one time, I had never taken the time to just face what I'd been through because I was afraid I'd sink into a funk. I kept it all at bay and tried to press on, hungrily pursuing adoption research, but never allowing myself to digest what had happened. From fertility treatments I had quickly rappelled into the adoption world because I was so afraid I wouldn't ever be a mother.

But any decision made in fear is a reaction, rather than an action.

On the way out of the office, I pondered taking time off to just think it all through. I wondered if I even wanted to be in a movie. I had said no to everything that came my way. I was so angry at myself for missing opportunities in films and on Broadway during the years of staying close to the clinic. But now I admitted I truly didn't feel like acting in anything. I thought perhaps I should officially take some time off. I wondered if I dared step back for a bit. And grieve.

Grief is an inevitable part of processing information. You can't push grief down and pretend it's not there. It will stay close by like an annoying sibling tapping you on the shoulder, saying, "Look at me, looooook at me." Until you do.

So I did.

What happened next was completely out of character for me. I stepped back from being an actor for a while. After years of making my living as an actor, I just didn't act in a film, put myself through clothes fittings, or pose on a red carpet.

I said no thank you to every invitation that came my way. No to films. No to attending any press event, from the Golden Globes gift suites to Oscar parties. I said see-you-later to the sparkly life for a bit. Now let's be clear—it's not like Scorsese called me and I said no. It's not like Sofia Coppola was a-begging me to be her muse. The roles I was being offered were not life changing, so it was pretty easy to slip away. The hilarious thing is . . . uh, no one noticed. It's not like TMZ was going through my garbage wondering, wait a minute, how come she's not acting? Nope. I just slipped under the radar.

One thing I really appreciated is that Core friends didn't ask questions. I never explained what I was doing or not doing because I needed respite from it all. I needed to just not be asked about fertility and adoption and what my next move was. It seemed as if we all had a tacit agreement that I was going through something and it was private. I appreciate that my friends, family, and representatives were supportive.

And I knew stepping away was temporary and necessary.

I was hired by several companies and studios to write, plus got to develop with Jonathan Demme. I opened my Final Draft and wrote six scripts—romantic comedies about unconditional love, dramas where things don't turn out okay, stories about women who dared to be happy even if they didn't achieve everything they wanted.

I highly recommend the checkout. It brings a clarity unlike anything I've ever known. I realized who my true allies are. I found out although it's nice to get a good table at a trendy restaurant, I didn't need fame. I'll be totally honest: I liked being a known actor. It's enjoyable to read friendly letters from all over the world, and receive gifts from clothing and purse designers, but I didn't go nuts without it. I just made my living by writing, hung out with good friends, and didn't act.

During my hiatus, I even stood up to that lifelong member of the Coven who made fun of me for getting acupuncture. Yes, the one who had called my body "defective" compared to hers because she could have kids. One day I called her up and told her to suck it.

But all this didn't bring a grounded feeling or some purr of inner serenity. When the phone rang, I jumped, hoping we'd been matched. It just didn't happen.

Grieving also means I finally let myself cry. A lot. It is truly embarrassing to let it all out like a bachelorette who didn't get a rose. I didn't want to feel sorry for myself when there are people with real problems. However, I told myself it's essential to mourn. So I grieved for my unborn children, my mortality, and for my ever-understanding husband.

It was the feeling of failure that I was getting over. This was difficult for me. As an intractable person managing to have an acting career against all odds, it was humbling to come up against Mother Nature and get a poke in the eyeball.

There's no way around grief. You have to go through it. You have to cry it out of your body, then wade through your own tears to the other side. Where there is cake. Moist cake. Have a piece. It will make you feel better. Have a second piece. Lick your fingers. You will feel better. I promise.

As time passed, I could now cope when a sweet stranger at the supermarket patted my cake-pudgy stomach and said, "Are you making a big fat Greek baby?" I didn't burst into tears. Well, not in front of her. In my car, yep.

Once you get over yourself, you feel everything. You cry for everyone, knowing full well they've got it worse than you. I cried for victims of the tsunami, victims of Katrina. Soldiers in Iraq. I cried for unloved children. Unwanted children. I cried for the incredible inequality that comes with geographical birth. I discovered what really helps when you're tired of thinking about you is that you think about someone else. I threw myself into charity work, donating and flying to cities to do fundraisers for rare diseases and Greek churches that sent money to the underprivileged. I recorded a lullaby for an album to get music into schools, taught screenwriting, mentored inner-city girls, spoke at AIDSWALK, and shot a magazine photo for the Until There's a Cure bracelet. Occasionally, I was photographed for friends' film premieres or charity events. My weight was up, my weight was down. I didn't care. Actually, no one did. No one noticed.

No one was concerned that on the night of my Broadway debut I was crying onstage. My good friend *SNL* alum Rachel Dratch and I were cast in 24 Hour Plays together—a charity event that benefits inner-city kids. This is a process that takes place within twenty-four hours—the plays are written during the night, the actors are cast that morning, and the play is performed that night. For Rachel and me, being from the improv world of Second City, its fun recklessness is challenging. But that morning, I was stunned when I saw the subject matter of the play I was cast in: adoption. Rachel was playing a mom who had once placed her child for adoption. I was handed my role—a mom who has adopted that child and is urging him to call his birth mother.

My eyes distorted the text as I flipped through the script pages. Right away, my chest pinged with that familiar ache. I couldn't look at anyone. All day during rehearsal, I kept a distance from the material. I learned the lines quickly and rehearsed them without emotion.

But then, that night onstage, I turned to an actor to say the lines and found that my face was soaked. I was weeping at how painful these words were and even though, sure, part of me wondered if I could get nominated for a Tony Award for this, I couldn't believe it was happening. It was really painful to play this role.

I got back to L.A. and kept writing screenplays and doing charity work. And after a while, the tears were gone. I just felt spent.

So now, it's 2006 and I'm on this Internet site at two o'clock in the morning looking at dogs. I look back at the friendly dog with the brown eyes and see he has been abandoned at the pound. Abandoned. On a whim, I fill out the form and press Send.

A few days later, a friendly volunteer brings the dog to us. She pulls into our driveway, opens the hatch of her car, and a big furry beast bounds out and pants up at me, like "I'm heeeeeeeeeeeere!"

I feel something go *spro-oi-oi-oing* in my chest. Like when you've swallowed a too-big chunk of bread and it's been lodged in your throat forever, and then it suddenly goes down a pipe. That's what I feel when I look at this yellow Lab with the giant paws. I love him. I love him immediately. Ian loves him, too, and we sign the papers and officially adopt him. We decide to pick a name for Ian's birthplace, Manhattan, and mine, Manitoba: so we name him Manny. Because nothing says yellow Lab like a nice Jewish accountant.

Being with Manny simply makes me happy. We go for long walks around the neighborhood and I beam with pride when people stop to pet him and tell me he's handsome. We get him only the healthiest dog food. Ian takes Manny into the shower and bathes him with special dog shampoo. He'd been left at a pound. We had our hopes for parenthood chucked under a bus. It's a second chance for everyone. We all have cartoon love hearts popping over our heads. Ian and I pet Manny, kiss him, and pick up his poop. We call him our "son."

He is. We are delighted with every trash can he overturns, every bone he chews.

And we are aghast to discover ourselves talking about him at parties. Yes, we've turned into Those People Who Tell Pet Stories. Realizing it's a slippery slope to a Christmas card with the three of us in matching sweaters, Ian and I make a pact that we'll stop each other at the next party, with any signal from a light press to the forearm to a taquito in the neck. This works for a while. But sometimes, I hide and show our hostess a few pictures of Manny. What I find sweet is how many women are patient with me during this period. They take the time to marvel over Manny's thick fur and sweet face. They let me ramble about his poop. I have nice girlfriends. Even if they are privately discussing an intervention, I appreciate their kindness.

My best friend, Kathy Greenwood, and her family come to visit from Toronto. As her husband, John, and Ian put their girls to bed, Kathy and I sit in my backyard and drink red wine with Manny at our feet. Point-blank, as only your best friend can do, Kathy asks me why I have abandoned pursuing adoption. I tell her I have not. But she makes me admit I have not worked on it. Because she knows me. Whether I'm hosting a dinner party or directing an indie, I work hard. I'll be up all night researching, investigating every fact, planning every detail. I'm not doing that with adoption. I've stopped checking in with any of the agencies. And Kathy says it out loud. We sip more wine and I am peeved on this summer night in the way you can get annoyed at your best friend. I tell her, "I'm done. Done. I cannot try anymore when clearly it will not happen for me." She asks, "So you're not going to be a mom?"

And I can't answer.

The very next day, I get a call from my mom. My niece has been born prematurely and we're terrified for the baby. It is an uncertain and helpless feeling for my entire family.

An eerie feeling starts swirling in me on this day. I start to think about a little girl. I tell myself it's just daydreams and thoughts of my premature niece. But, within a few days, I start to believe again that it will happen for me. In the next weeks I tell Ian I think we're going to get matched with a girl.

When I get to hold my new little niece who has passed the point of danger and is growing strong . . . I am now feeling something that could be described as both disturbing and insane. If you're going to make fun of me now, know that I'm already doing it for you: I have started to feel more certain that there is a little girl out there. A little girl with blond streaks in her hair. And, when I say it out loud, Ian stares at me as if I've lost it, and Kathy Greenwood tells me to keep it to myself in that way your best friend can tell you that you sound crazy. So I know it sounds deranged that I'm telling you now and as I write it, I'm pretty sure I'll cut it from the book before it goes to print. But then again, I kinda don't care because it's true.

By 2007, the grieving period is over and there's no denying that I am feeling more like myself, the buoyant upbeat idiot. I go to movies, out for dinner, on walks with Manny . . . it's better.

When Ian and I are sitting around with Manny, we talk about how we adore him as if he came from our bodies. We both know since we could love this furry animal so much, of course we would love a child who didn't come from our chromosomes. But we don't pursue it. It's just been too painful. It's a shelved project; the phone doesn't ring anymore. The system just didn't work for us, and I wonder if I have accepted it.

One evening, I go with a group to see our friend's daughter play volleyball at her school. As I sit in the bleachers, I watch these amusing teenaged girls interact and be good teammates on the court; they're so rambunctious and funny . . . and . . . ah, here it is . . . that anxiety creeps in. It's back. My chest hurts. I put my head in my hands and sigh. Watching these girls, I have to admit I just want a daughter. I just do. And, I know, I just know she's somewhere waiting for me to find her. I want to be a mom, I am supposed to be a mom. I can't deny it any longer.

I don't want to lose it in front of my friends, so I go outside to get some air.

I'm standing here outside the gymnasium wishing so much that I had just been watching my own daughter play volleyball. Just wishing so much that I had a daughter at that school. I lean against the railing and try to breathe. I want to take control of the situation. And I realize I can.

I decide right now to try one more thing: to learn more about the options that facilitator had told me about. I decide to learn about adopting from the American foster care system.

7

Almost There

Now I want to write that it gets really easy. But, no. No, it doesn't.

The next phase takes a while because the information on how to adopt from foster care just isn't out there either. I can't comprehend the term "fos-adopt" (sometimes referred to as "fost-adopt") because, like many, I think it means you foster; you take care of a child until they're reunited with their family. I admire the people who do that, but we've been through a lot. Ian and I don't want more loss. We want a family, forever.

Not sure who to approach, I go directly to the State of California. I know there are amazing social workers who work for their states, but I sure don't meet them today. Instead, I'm taken to a room without a chair, where a woman hands me a loose, ungainly binder called *Waiting Kids,* looks at my designer purse, and smirks, "You want to do this?"

There is nowhere to sit, so I lean against the wall and begin to flip through the heavy binder . . . and see the kids. Imagine several hundred faces looking at you wondering if you want to be their parent. I defiantly snap the binder shut and say, "Yes, I do," and that I am "open to any sex, age, and ethnic background."

Oh goodie, they goad, because they can place an at-risk multiple-sibling set in my house on a trial basis, and an adoption might come out of it after the parental rights are terminated in court in a few years.

My mouth goes dry. As in, just-licked-a-pumice-stone dry. That sounds . . . complicated. But I really, really want to be a parent. So I say, "Okay!"

I do ask about the 129,000 children I've heard about who are already legally freed and am told there is a process and I have to be patient. I explain I thought I would be connected with a legally freed child who is waiting for a home. Again, they explain I have to trust their procedures. Huh. We all know there is a certain type of government worker who enjoys his or her teeny amount of power. I now feel apprehensive, thinking I might get lost in yet another situation that won't resolve in a positive way.

At this point, it has been over eight years of trying so many methods, too many routes, of waiting on so many lists. Then I remember . . . when I was in the cast at Second City, we used to improvise in front of an audience. That's a trapeze without a net. In this same way, I feel I just have to jump in. So I repeat, "Okay!"

I am sent away with a thick packet of fingerprinting forms and a daunting Home Study kit. As I sort through the mounds of paperwork, I do more online research and find out about FFAs.

That's when things finally accelerate. An FFA—Foster Family Agency—helps individuals navigate the state system. The social workers (I like to call them super-pretty angels) at the FFA we work with are helpful, compassionate, and organized. I discern an FFA is a free service in every state to guide potential parents through the paperwork plus the necessary and thorough background screening process. I learn the fos-adopt route includes a child's full medical and health record. In terms of a child's lifelong medical care, full disclosure can help. American foster care welcomes families of all income levels and, unlike private adoption, is virtually cost-free. The fos-adopt system doesn't discriminate financially, on religious or ethnic background, or in any way—single parents, older couples, gays and lesbians—all may apply.

I wouldn't discourage or disparage anyone who goes outside their own country to adopt—of course every child deserves a home. So if you want to adopt from anywhere—any country, any planet—do it. I decide fos-adopt is the route I want to take. I'm feeling energized because the FFA social workers tell me they can connect us to the network of 129,000 children who are already legally freed and available for adoption. I tell Ian I feel like I have finally found the key.

We fill out the paperwork and take the parenting classes, which are interesting and valuable in terms of finding out what your spouse feels about bedtimes, religion, music lessons, etc. We must complete a first aid course too. Again, I see nothing wrong with these requirements and view it all as useful information. A nurse comes over to certify us in CPR, and Ian and I practice giving first aid to a bunch of dummies in our TV room. Even though I get an annoyed look from the nurse, I make sure to take several pictures of Ian doing mouth to mouth on a dummy.

Tonight, a Home Study social worker is coming over to evaluate Ian and me. As I've mentioned, I am not a grown-up. The more serious the situation, the more likely I will do something dumb. Even when I had dinner with the (name-drop) Queen of England, I had to push down my immature impulses. After I was first invited to attend the dinner to celebrate the Queen's Golden Jubilee, I received a call from a Protocol Secretary. He warned me there were guidelines I would have to follow. For example, I would have to curtsy in a certain way (eyes forward but lowered, one foot behind the other, hands at sides), then wait for the Queen to extend her hand before I extended mine. Also, to not speak until Her Majesty spoke. Wait there's more: do not bring up a new topic of conversation, no hugging, no fist bumps. I took notes, practiced my curtsy in the full-length mirror behind my bathroom door, bought a beautiful blue silk Alberta Ferretti suit and Louboutin slingbacks, and Ian and I flew to my hometown, Winnipeg.

Before the dinner, I waited alone but surrounded by six members of security in a corridor of the Parliament building. The Queen was arriving at any moment. My husband, parents, and family were in the balcony about ten feet away, watching me. I looked up at them, wondering if this was really happening when I heard the Protocol Secretary ask if I had practiced The Curtsy. I informed him indeed I had. He paused, then said, "May I see it?" With everyone watching, I had to do it for him. Of course I did it wrong, teetered, leaned on his forearm, almost fell off my slingbacks, was instructed to do it three more times, and . . . suddenly there was a hush in the hall. The Queen was announced and was walking toward me. Me.

As a Canadian, I was stunned at the sight of her in person. As the immature moron I am, I wanted to say, "Hey, you're the lady on our money." But I didn't, only because my mom was watching from that balcony. As the Queen approached, someone whispered my name to her. I curtsied, she held a hand out, I held mine out, and we shook once. She then asked, "Did you write the movie as well?" I said, "Yes. I wrote it about my husband and family. And they're right there." I pointed up to the balcony, and my husband and family smiled big, very big, and waved. My mom and I looked at each other and squirted the ethnic eyeball lotta-tears gush. The Queen smiled at them and then me and just like that, Her Majesty advanced into the room for dinner. The Protocol Secretary leaned in and whispered "good job" to me, but I didn't get a Milk-Bone.

Inside the hall at our dinner table, the Queen was warm and witty as she guided the conversation from fine wines to Manitoba bison. Again, I just acted the part of an upstanding member of society as I fought the urge to yank off her giant diamond brooch and bolt off just to see the look on her face and how far I could get. I mean, it was going so well, so well that I wanted to do something ridiculous. Something crazy. Because a small part of me thought the Queen would be amused by it too. Hasn't she had enough boring dinners? Surely she'd welcome a bit of wicked outrageousness. It's not as if I was expecting a high five for trying to steal her brooch, but I thought it would be entertaining. I really did. I wanted to do it so badly, I squeezed my hands together in my lap.

I looked over my shoulder to see if I could spot Ian and my family at their tables when I heard Her Majesty's voice. I turned back: I was being addressed. I leaned in to her, and she said, "Philip is Greek, you know." I nodded. Like an Irish person can recite the Kennedy family tree, all Greeks know Prince Philip was born into the royal family of Greece. Then the Queen winked: "He converted to Anglicanism for our marriage." And I winked back: "My husband converted to Greek Orthodoxy for ours. I guess with Prince Philip leaving and Ian coming in, it was sort of a Free Trade agreement." Then there was a pause. In that interlude, I knew the guards were coming for me. I knew it was over. I should probably snatch that brooch now since I was going to prison for treason anyway. Then . . . Her Majesty chuckled. Yes, really. I grinned back, then ultra-quickly looked at my hands in my lap so I wouldn't blow it. I knew if I kept talking I would say something stupid. I could feel her still turned toward me, but I wouldn't look up. Eventually the Queen turned to her right to begin a new conversation and I exhaled. So to this day I ponder if the Queen of England wonders if I blew her off, or am narcoleptic.

Okay, I got through that, and the whole experience was exhilarating bordering on terrifying. But meeting this Home Study social worker tonight at our home is even scarier than that, because she will determine if we would make good parents. And here's the thing—Ian is even more immature than me. This is a man who picks me up at the airport—standing among limo drivers who are holding signs with names of businesspeople—with his own homemade sign: Mrs. U-Smell.

We're both so immature; when we have to write a check for a parking ticket, we hide a tiny "C.O.I." within the loops of our signatures (it stands for Choke On It). So before this evaluation we have a gritted-teeth talk with each other about acting like grown-ups. We pinkie-swear: no poop jokes, no wife-swapping jokes, no stories about theater days when we stayed up until four A.M. playing poker and drinking. No jokes at all, we agree. But we say we will act natural, be ourselves. We nod and woodenly practice how real parents might act, as we keep changing our clothes. At first I try a dress—too fancy; the Home Study worker might think I'm full of myself, I decide and yank it off. Ian tugs off his tie, too. I ask him if he's got a vest, maybe? Somehow, I see the dad from *My Three Sons* as the prototype. As I flip through more of our clothes looking for what Mary Tyler Moore might wear, the doorbell rings. The Home Study worker is here.

I change quickly and run downstairs to greet her in the most prim and diffident "mom"-like manner I can muster.

As I put out refreshments I realize both Ian and I are wearing sensible black slacks and white shirts. I have no idea where we found these clothes but in an attempt to look respectable, we now look like census takers.

I am fake-smiling so hard I have a sharp pain through my right eye and suspect it's oozing blood. I have never tried harder to appear so normal. Anything Ian says, for example, "Would you like some wine?," makes me exclaim, "We never drink. I mean rarely. I mean, sometimes, but not a lot. I mean, what's a lot right, heh, heh . . ." Ian looks at me; what's with my fake laugh? I wish I knew. I keep "heh, heh"-ing and then we trail off into thunderous silence.

Later in the visit, Ian tells a fun story about a high school class-mate who got him in trouble, and says, "Oh, I coulda killed him." I pounce, "He's kidding! Ian does not have a temper, heh, heh . . . hey, do you like pizza? Look, I made us a . . . have I mentioned I like to cook? And home-make."

Home-make? Ian looks at me. I've never said this before. Or since. He knows it and I know it. His mouth twitches. Oh no, we're going to laugh and blow this, I just know it. We both quickly look away from each other and try to sober up similar to what we often did onstage to not laugh. I now think of terrible images like a sand-wich of rotting mayonnaise and writhing worms. It works.

The Home Study worker makes notes about us I cannot see, no matter how hard I bend over pretending to wipe the counter and "home-make." She then asks Ian and I what we see in our future as a family. We reply we see ourselves with a child. She asks us to be more specific. I want to be matched and say we are open to any sex, any age, any ethnicity. The Home Study worker waits, head down, listening. She is patient.

Ian then says quietly . . . he sees us with a little girl. I am sur-prised at this revelation. This is the first time he's admitted he has visualized someone too. I then loosen up and tell the worker about the girl I see, the girl with blond streaks. The worker smiles and makes a note of it, and I peek to see if she's checked a box that says "crazy." We are worried we won't be matched with the available waiting children, and we say again and again, we are open to any sex, any age, any ethnicity. We mean it. We want to be parents. We want to scream: we know there is a child out there that we could be good parents to. Just match us, dammit.

But we just smile hard, really hard, at her as the kitchen clock ominously ticks.

Weeks later, we get her evaluation. She has deemed us kid-worthy. We're ecstatic.

The social workers at the Foster Family Agency don't give us any special treatment because we're known actors. Their job is to help potential parents through the system. Even though we've advised our social workers we want to wait for a legally emancipated child, rather than foster a child waiting to be freed of parental rights, we still have to be cleared as a foster home first. It's not that we're heartless and don't want to only foster, it's just that we don't want to fight anyone in court for a child. Also, although it's rare, we'd heard about cases where a child is raised by foster parents, then placed back with a member of the child's birth family. Again, it's rare. But we'd been through a lot and aren't looking for trouble. We trust this FFA and the process. We know there are children in foster care who are emancipated, waiting for a family to adopt them, and that's the situation we feel drawn to.

The next step is to schedule a Home Visit with the two social workers. They have to be sure we have an available spare bedroom with a window and closet. They need to see if we've installed a gate at the top of the stairs. They come over, and Ian and I silently follow them around, watching them walk through our home with a checklist to be sure we've baby-proofed it. I don't feel it's invasive. I feel they're trying to make it safe and I appreciate their knowledge. They now say of course they don't know what age of a child we will be matched with, so they advise it's best to be completely ready. Because it could happen at any time, they say.

Any time. I get a shiver of anticipation.

We're sitting at our kitchen table with them now. I set out mugs for tea and they answer all our questions about the rest of the process. We have to get fingerprinted for the background check, and our Home Study could take two weeks to three months to process.

We all sit here quietly now. It's been so many years of hoping, then not hoping, and these women are so attuned to our feelings, so compassionate.

One of the women pats my hand and says, "You will be a mother within the year."

And I believe her.

8

Soon

I'm in a very good mood. I smile at the Starbucks girl so hard, I'm sure she wonders if I'm about to ask her out.

I've been in such a jovial state of mind as we wait to get matched via foster care, I'm even planning to go back on camera. A *Simpsons* writer, Mike Reiss, has written a script called *My Life In Ruins,* and my beloved friends at Playtone are going to get it made. If I'll star in it. I want to do this for two reasons. I have missed acting, and I'll get to film at the Parthenon.

Yesterday, I'd even done my first actress-y thing in ages. I had a skin-brightening treatment called Cosmelan. It removes brown marks and brightens up the skin. At the dermatologist's, a bright orange cream was applied to my face. She advised me they were manufacturing it in a light brown shade soon and I didn't know why she was telling me until she sternly warned I had to keep it on for twelve hours. I hadn't anticipated that part of the process. I furtively drove home with my oompa loompa face, relieved I hadn't run into an ex-boyfriend or a member of the Coven in the lobby. I pulled up to a red light and watched as a drunk man crossed the street. His clothes were torn, and he looked unwashed. I felt sad for him. I wondered what event in his life had made *him* lose control to get to this point. And what would it take to sober him up—at that moment he turned, saw my orange face, shrieked like a banshee, and ran off.

Now as I walk home from Starbucks I picture the guy at an AA meeting telling that story. It's a beautiful day and I'm thinking we will be matched at any time. It could happen any day, they say.

The social workers from the FFA have been in constant contact. They sent me to a website called AdoptUSKids.org and various state sites called Heart Galleries to see pictures of waiting children who are legally emancipated and available for adoption. One of the social workers tells me to scroll through and when I feel a connection to a child, to let her know the name and contact number of that child's social worker and she will see if we can be matched. It's that simple.

There is a little girl in one city's Heart Gallery. I don't know what she looks like. The picture is of her running across a beach. It's taken from behind her. Curious, I take down her number and inquire if she is legally available for adoption. My social worker says she'll get back to me with information. I'm wondering if this little girl is the one I've been envisioning. Again, as peculiar as it sounds, ever since that night of the heavy discussion with Kathy Greenwood, I am feeling there is a child out there. I dream about a little girl with blond streaks in her hair. But Ian and I continually ask the social workers to tell us about any child, any age, any ethnicity. Because of their composed and candid manner, I trust their process and who they think we'd be a good match with.

I get home now. Oddly, I feel queasy. This happens a lot. I often feel dizzy. I stand in front of our front hall mirror and take a good look at myself. Years of writing scripts has made me gain weight again, and not in a groovy *Mad Men* way. Nuh-uh. I am living in stretchy tights and an oversize white button-down shirt—my writer's uniform. It's dangerous because fat-rolls can form and tights stretch. With this dizzy feeling I think my thyroid medicine probably needs adjusting, which is why I've gained weight again. When I was filming *My Big Fat Greek Wedding*, I'd found out why my weight went up and down. First of all, I liked to eat. And second, I was diagnosed with something called Hashimoto's thyroiditis, which sounds like a Japanese Greek cousin but is actually an autoimmune disease that destroys the thyroid gland, which regulates metabolism. The telltale symptoms are feeling tired and weight gain from lettuce. Chronologically: I was 220 pounds during my theater school/Second City days. Then 130 pounds when I got married and moved to L.A. During the preproduction of *My Big Fat Greek Wedding*, my weight crept up to 170 pounds even though I was working out a lot. That's when I got diagnosed by an endocrinologist, went on the thyroid hormone, and during and after filming got my weight down to 130 pounds again. I felt well, but there were some residual symptoms. For example, oddly, my curly hair went completely straight. And infertility has occasionally been linked to the disease. Even though I take a human-made version of thyroid hormone, I have to work extra hard to control my weight.

So now there's no denying I'm up to 155 pounds again. I have not been exercising much and my screenwriting process would best be described as Write-A-Page-Chew-A-Snack.

I make an appointment to see my endocrinologist. He does lab work and a few days later in his office he tells me my thyroid meds are working. Dang. I petulantly ask him to check the results again and he interrupts me to say my blood sugar is dangerously high. Not good. I have diabetes in my family. I ask the doctor what I can do and he point-blank tells me to lose weight. He's a brave man. Few can tell a Greek girl to lose weight and live to tell that tale. I'm furious because now after everything I've been through, I'm a tired chubster again. And it's my own fault. I had once lost control of my body to fertility treatments and now again because of a lack of discipline. Anyway, I decide to try something that's worked before: I stop eating so much and I exercise. No surprise, I lose about twenty pounds.

I have energy again and more importantly, I'm feeling in control. Intuitively, I feel on the right path with the FFA social workers. Manny stays with friends, and Ian and I go to Europe to begin filming *My Life In Ruins*.

I rekindle my love affair with acting, adore my entire cast, and am having a great time. Before we go to Greece for the exterior scenes, we are filming all the interior bus scenes at a high-tech sound stage in Alicante, Spain. Making a movie on location is summer camp with alcohol. When I'm among actors, I'm at my happiest because of our shared joie de vivre (a fancy way of saying: drinking sangria and playing poker for one another's per diems). Our job is: we get to have our hair and makeup done in the morning, then we cram into a fake tour bus and act all day. We pull pranks, make jokes, sing dirty songs, and act like teenagers.

Ian and I hang with my assistant Marianne, a rare combination of hardworking and hilarious, and cast members such as always-delightful Rachel Dratch and the very hot Greek movie star Alexis Georgoulis. On the weekends we eat tapas at midnight, dance until four in the morning, and laugh a lot. It feels good to let go. I feel carefree again. I truly feel like a match is coming. We're all anticipating the second part of filming—in Greece. As just a little indie, it's incredible that we've secured permission to film at all the ancient ruins, including the site of the original Olympic games, Delphi, and the Parthenon.

Yesterday, Ian went back to Los Angeles to be with Manny. It's a day off and I am in my hotel room in Spain packing for Greece when I get the call: the little girl I had seen only from behind in that picture . . . has been placed with another family for adoption. I hang up and lean my forehead against the cool stucco wall. I feel a happiness for this child I have never met or even seen but of course I am devastated. I walk outside.

Now, as I slowly walk the boardwalk of this pretty beach, I realize I am crying so hard it looks like I've just been dumped by some hot Spaniard. I'm looking up at the clouds thinking this same phrase over and over again: "When, *when* will I be a mother?"

An eerie thing happens: a girl is walking toward me. She holds hands with her grandparents and is looking at me. She is about five years old, appealing yet somber as she holds my gaze. Her hair is brown and her eyes are very dark. We're staring at each other; we get closer, closer. Just as she is beside me, she grasps my hand. Her grandparents are looking ahead and they don't notice this. I am totally still as she continues to slowly walk past me, holding my hand and looking up at me. As I turn my body in the direction she is going, she squeezes my hand and gives me a very solemn look: soon.

I don't know how long I have been standing here watching her walk down the boardwalk. But I have stopped crying.

Soon.

9

Then, One Day...

I laugh, spitting vodka across this L.A. mod lounge. John Corbett roars victoriously when he sees my drink drip off my chin. John is both child and man so he delights my juvenile brain, and yet he is incredibly supportive when I'm in charge.

I make new friends with each film, but nothing compares to the closeness I feel to the second family of *My Big Fat Greek Wedding*. I truly love the cast and treasure my friendships with the producers, Rita, Tom, and Gary. Because I traveled with John and Gary for months and months on a fifty-city press tour, we became inordinately tight friends. We share that bond which can only be formed when you've had to ask someone to buy tampons for you.

Today John is having me do what he calls A Wobbler—he makes me move my face side to side super-fast so he can snap a picture of my cheeks G-forced out.

It's 2008 and we're about to shoot a script I wrote during my acting hiatus, *I Hate Valentine's Day*. Financiers gave us the green light if we'd both act in it and I'd direct. The budget is so low, there'll only be eighteen days rather than the standard month to shoot, but I get to cast new actors plus funny friends, including Dan Finnerty and Rachel Dratch again. My family and Core are supportive and tell me they just want to be there to hear me say "action." Three Core/Second City alums, Rose, Tracy, and Rachel H., will arrange to meet me in New York to do cameos. I am excited about attempting to pull off this experiment, because I'm looking for challenges again. I feel in a good place even though it's been several months since Ian and I have been cleared as a foster home. We're still waiting for that elusive match.

John looks me over and tells me I look happy. All in all, it's been over nine years of trying to be parents, yet impossibly I am optimistic. I feel the phone will ring.

As I drive home from my meeting with John, my cell does ring . . . and I receive the not-good news from our social workers about an older girl we'd inquired about. A panel determines she would not be "safe" with us, because a photograph of her could run in a tabloid magazine and her birth mother could find her. Again. When the birth mother is in this girl's life, the results have been disastrous. The girl has already been exposed to shady adults with criminal dealings. The panel feels it'd be better if this girl could lead an anonymous life. Although I agree with it, I am disappointed. The social worker tells me a relative will take the girl in and keep her whereabouts hidden from the birth mother. I shake my head and wonder once again about the unfairness for the ovarian challenged. The next week, our social workers check in and after some reflection, I admit I'm not shocked any of the matches didn't come through. Although I pursue every avenue, I am still waiting for something I can't explain or define.

• • •

A month later, I'm writing at my desk at home and the phone rings.

It's a nice man I've met who works to place foster kids.

He tells me there is a little girl.

She is almost three years old.

She'd been relinquished to foster care by a young couple whose relationship did not last the birth.

She is presently legally freed for adoption.

The man says he has contacted our social workers and they all want to know if Ian and I would like to meet the little girl.

I nod my head not realizing he can't see me. I'm not nodding yes to the meeting. I'm nodding yes because I know this is it. I know this is the match.

Running through the house, I find Ian and, gulping air, tell him about the little girl. I don't know anything about her background, but we can meet her tomorrow. I am jumping up and down, saying over and over "this is it." Ian tries to calm me down, so worried I will lose my mind if this doesn't work. But I know it will.

The next day is the exact date two years ago when we met Manny. As we drive across the city, Ian and I are completely quiet in the car.

The way it works with foster care is you have to have a chemistry meeting so everyone can determine how you get along. It isn't a test—they just want it to be a suitable pairing. That's why it's called a match. Wisely, they don't want the children to experience any more rejection, so the child is not told they might be meeting potential parents. The child probably just thinks it's more social workers, foster care workers, lawyers, etc. So today, this little girl is being brought to an office so we can all meet.

Ian and I drive into the parking lot of this office. As we park we see a small group of people standing in the middle of the lot. As we get out of the car, we see a little brown-haired girl in a social worker's arms. And as we walk toward the group, the little girl turns and looks at me.

At me.

And she smiles.

Everything goes quiet. I hear nothing at all.

All I think is, "Oh, I found you."

Because now I know who I have been waiting for. I know exactly why the other processes didn't work. I know I was supposed to wait for this little girl.

I put my hands out to her, and without hesitation she leans forward. As I cradle her I can't hear anything. I am looking at my daughter. Finally. And I feel a peacefulness come over me like I have never known. I waited a long time for her and she is worth every minute of anxiety. I am holding my little girl and just inhaling her scent.

She is apprehensive, not sure what's happening today, and she clings to me and hides against my neck. I kiss her and whisper in her ear that everything will be okay. I tell her I love her. I hold her out now and smile at her. Ian puts his warm hand on her and they look at each other for a long moment. He is smiling. The little girl smiles shyly. She is truly beautiful. And now I see she has little blond streaks in her hair.

Ten minutes later, we're all in the office watching this pretty little girl play with a red-and-yellow plastic toy train. She is dressed in a light shirt and cotton shorts over a cumbersome diaper. We can see she is very curious and imaginative as she takes each toy from a box and acts out scenarios without words. Her small face is fully absorbed in her playacting, but now and then I see her sneak peeks at Ian and me. She wants to know what's happening, but I see how calmly she takes in the situation. Actually I see now, she is not unruffled . . . she is pretending to be cool about it all. She gets it.

The social workers take us aside and are now telling us everything about her background. Following the protocol of foster care, there is a very thick file filled with information from vaccinations to birth parent health history. Some is positive information; some could be worrisome. The little girl, they tell us, does not speak. The social workers don't label her, but they indicate a doctor has said she should be speaking by now. They tell us she can be withdrawn, is not responding to her name, therefore renaming her would be a healthy fresh start for her. Ian and I don't even have to look at each other to know we want to move forward.

I'm listening, but I don't absorb very much. I'm watching this curious, sweet little girl. I look up at Ian—he's watching her too. I feel like I've seen this scene before. Is it because we wanted it so badly, or is it because it feels so natural?

The social workers now leave us alone with her. Ian and I look at each other—what should we do? Immediately, the little girl finds a metal pole and bangs it against another pole. It's loud. She bangs it again and again and now looks at us, with an impish expression: you going to try to stop me?

Ian and I laugh. We have spotted a personality we know well—mischievous and forceful.

The little girl now stands up, trips, and falls. On her face. With us—two supposed adults—only inches away, she has fallen on her face. This is exactly one of those moments when I realize I am not a grown-up because I don't know what to do.

But before we can get to her . . . she just leaps up, looks at us like, *That happened, huh?*, and shakes it off. She doesn't cry or make a fuss. She is capable. Tough. Determined. She's cool.

My husband and I have a niece who is the same age, so now we speak to this little girl as if she understands. We do what anyone would do: we get down on the floor and play with her for a while. Then we ask if she is hungry. She nods yes.

So we tell the social workers, and all begin to leave the office. The little girl is clinging to me again and as I carry her, I keep whispering to her that everything will be okay. Now I add that I will always take care of her. She leans into me, her body is so warm. Our entire group follows us down the hall, but I don't really notice anyone but this delightful, perfect child. We get to the next doorway and Ian now holds out his hands to her . . . she goes to him. Then she clings to his neck. Ian tries to shift her, but she clings hard as if to say "never let me go."

Ian's eyes fill with tears as we walk to the elevator. She is holding on tight. My eyes are so wet I can't see the elevator buttons. No one is speaking, they're just letting us have our time together. I run my hand up and down the little girl's back to reassure her. She is holding on to Ian, and looking at me. I nod reassuringly to her. My insides feel like soft pudding.

On the street Ian puts her up on his shoulders, and she grins widely, really liking it up there. I am beside them with one hand supporting, holding her up when Ian turns toward a plate-glass window so she can see herself. Our reflection stares back: we look like a family.

We get to a deli and as we all slide into chairs, Ian and I now indicate to the adults, shaking our heads, that they not speak about this situation in front of her because it's clear she understands. One of the men who works closely with foster children is touched by this and says, "You're parents already." Honestly, although we don't know how to be parents, Ian and I feel very protective of this little girl.

We all eat lunch. She plays with the spoon and napkin but doesn't speak or eat. She's withdrawn but listening, trying to figure out the situation. I keep a hand on her back or hair; I can't stop touching her.

Later, as we walk back to the parking lot, they inform us this is when they have to take her away. They've told us the process: the state will determine if we're the right fit for her. The little girl is living with a family as the system works to permanently "place" her. They've told us legally we have twenty-four hours to think it over. We tell them we don't want the twenty-four hours. We want to take her home now. We don't want them to take her. We already know we're her parents.

In muted, hushed voices, they firmly tell us we *have* to take the required twenty-four hours and they *have* to take her now. I'm upset. This is hard, beyond hard. I just found her; how can I let her go? But I know she is taking her cues from me so I relax my body, keep my voice low and subdued, and say to her, "See you soon." I gently give her back to a social worker. I feel my insides crease as she is carried away from me.

I follow them.

As they put her in the booster, I lean into the car and say, "Bye, sweetie."

She has not spoken one word all day but now turns to me with a small wave and quietly says . . . "Bye, Mommy."

No one moves. Everyone heard it. No one can make eye contact. The car drives away, and Ian and I stand here for a long time.

I say, "Did that just happen?," and Ian says, "Yep."

We call the social workers when we get home and try to say yes, but they insist we follow protocol. So we pace for the twenty-four hours, then say that official yes. We now have to wait for their match. We are in constant contact with the social workers, who keep us informed of the slow process. Two days later, we find out the first step: we've been wholeheartedly approved by their office to be this little girl's parents. But we still have to wait for the official State stamp of approval for the match.

Ten days later, in the early evening the phone rings again. It's a number I don't recognize. I answer and it's the social worker calling from her cell.

And she says the words I have been waiting a very long time for: "You've been matched."

Just like that, I am a mom.

I think I hang up the phone. I am now on the floor but can't remember lying down. I can feel the hard wood under my head as I breathe in and out.

I'm a mom.

Ian is working; he won't be home for hours. I can't just leave him a voice mail with this huge news.

I am a mom.

I'm trying to sort my thoughts, to think clearly. I had asked: "When is she coming?"

"Tomorrow," she said.

I am a mom.

Ironically, it is nine months since I met with the FFA social workers.

I now have fourteen hours to get the house ready for our little girl.

Our little girl.

I am a mom.

Ian is a dad. He doesn't know.

I text Ian: "Can you call me after work?"

At 11:00 P.M., he calls and says, "Hey, want to join the cast for a drink?"

I tell him the news. I tell him we're parents and he goes silent. I know, even though he will kill me for telling you, that he's bawling. He gets home so fast there must be a zip line across the city.

It's almost midnight and we tear apart the guest room, wondering aloud if the down comforter is too heavy for a toddler; are the pale-green walls kid-friendly enough? Manny is panting, running around, wondering what the late-night excitement is. We tell Manny that he's going to have a little sister. He wags his tail because "sister" sounds like "snack."

Luckily, wall sockets are already covered and glass vases have been removed—everything has been baby-proofed because of the social workers' walk-through. Still, we move the bookcase away from the window. Additionally, we're worried about her rolling off the adult-size bed, so we dismantle it and put a twin blow-up mattress on the floor.

I run to my closet and dig out the two blankets I had bought so many years before—the green and yellow fluffy soft blankets. I gently lay them across the little bed.

Now, Ian and I wordlessly take in this room. Tomorrow a little girl will be living here. We are in shock. We barely sleep.

The next morning, I make a long list and Ian flies out the door to get diapers, milk, bottles, and food. He comes back a few hours later and I can't see him in his Prius—just a part of his face is visible in the front seat. The car is completely packed with pink things: quilts, sheets, pillows, toys, blankets. And one giant red Elmo doll.

We keep looking at each other, trying to get grounded, to be sure this is real—I suspect this is the alarm all expectant parents feel. Am I doing enough to prepare?

We quickly drag everything from Ian's car into the house. We don't know what a child of preschool age eats or plays with. I pull a T-bone steak and a teething ring out of a shopping bag—which one is appropriate? Will this jack-in-the-box toy scare her, or—it suddenly pops up in my face and I leap backward, bouncing off Ian. We keep running past each other putting toys and snacks out, then away, then out again—we're completely freaked.

We run to take showers. Just as we throw on clothes, the front gate buzzer rings.

Fourteen hours after that phone call, I run down the stairs. I hear a rushing sound in my ears of my accelerated heartbeat pushing the blood through my body.

We sprint outside and immediately stop short on the front walk, trying to look as casual, just as friendly as possible. Where is she? I can't see her in the back of the car. I'm dreading that they're here to tell us they've made a mistake.

Then, surrounded by social workers, lawyers, foster care workers . . . I see her. There she is, our little girl. They're taking her from the car and I see the sun's light envelope her beautiful head as if to say, look at this shiny present.

The lightest of breezes makes my arms feel warm and yet chilled. I ache to run across the lawn and scoop her up, but I make myself take it slow. Ian and I are smiling at her as we slowly walk toward the car. I can smell jasmine from the bushes across the front fence as they bring her closer. I can hear a light buzzing of people talking, greeting each other. But I'm looking only at my daughter.

She's here.

A social worker puts her down and without hesitation, she just walks through the front gate, toward us. She is so brave.

In the front yard, Manny intercepts her. He gives her a sniff, then licks her entire face. She doesn't flinch at the big furry dog tasting her. Instead, she giggles.

I take her hand; it's warm and so very, very soft. I want to cry, but I make myself keep it together. I want to be composed for this imperturbable little girl. Ian and I gently lead her toward the front door. She is calmly exploring the front walk, so we now let go of her hands and let her take her time. Then, she looks up at the house and casually walks in as if she's lived here her whole life.

She spends the entire day walking around, exploring everything. She goes into every room, opens every drawer, every cupboard, and just looks at everything. We just let her do what she wants so she feels comfortable.

Finally, the social workers, lawyers—everyone—leaves. We're alone. Ian and I are not sure what to do—feed her, bathe her, watch TV? I'm not sure what we should be doing.

This sweet little girl is still looking around, and she won't eat. She is too inquisitive to stop moving. Like all children, she arrived without an instruction manual. But this child walks. So we just follow her around.

I start to worry that we don't know anything about her habits— Does she nap? When does she sleep at night? In the bag that came with her are two diapers and a change of clothes—no note. Again, like with an infant handed to new parents, there are no instructions on habits and sleep patterns. We're on our own. We don't know what she likes to eat, if she has food allergies. We assure ourselves that the social workers and this process are so thorough, surely we would have been informed. Ian and I keep offering her things like cereal or a cookie and she shakes her head. We now know she knows four words: *Mommy, hi, bye,* and *no.*

We talk to her as if she can understand. She does. We realize she's just too excited to eat. She keeps exploring.

I'm relieved when she finally does take a bottle of milk. She can hold it and keep moving on her discovery tour. We now find the crayons and paper left over from niece and nephew visits and she sits at the kitchen table and lets loose with a drawing of an explosion of colors. I put the date on it so we can frame it for her room.

We decide to take her upstairs; she explores some more, and we now show her her new room. Her beautiful brown eyes take it in. Again, it's as if she understands. She seems to be accepting this new situation.

It's now nine P.M., so we take off her clothes. I marvel at how soft her skin is as I put her in the bed and cover her with the new pink quilt. Her little face is very serious now. As I start to move away, she holds my fingers to stay. This literally makes me want to weep. I try to relax my face for her. Of course I'll stay. I bundle her in the green and yellow blankets and pull her into my arms. Manny lies on the floor, Ian turns out the light, and we all just go quiet for a moment. I'm rocking her. Ian is stroking her hair.

And that's when she starts to cry.

She is so scared, but we don't know what to do other than reassure her over and over again that we love her and she's safe with us and we will take care of her. She doesn't ask for anyone. She just lets out heartbreaking plaintive wails through the night. She is terrified. Who wouldn't be? We keep giving her bottles of milk, continually changing her diaper. At midnight, she is so exhausted, she finally sleeps. I run a cool cloth over her tear-soaked face. Ian is dozing, stretched across the floor.

I get up, let Manny out, and go to our room to send an email to the family that all is okay. Earlier in the day, I had called to let them know we were suddenly parents. The shock in their voices was only exceeded by my own. I'd asked for suggestions on what to feed an almost three-year-old child. I now see so many emails: my parents and siblings are going crazy with excitement, and my mom lets us know she's on her way from Canada. I'm thankful for this. I need my mom. I mean, I'm elated but truly not sure about the best way to help our daughter adjust to her new home. She is scared. So am I.

The lawyer stands over me and shrieks, "Wake up, Nia, you're a mother now," and I bolt up. I have fallen asleep on my computer keyboard and the lawyer, of course, is not in my room. It's my daughter's screams I'm hearing. She has woken up at four A.M. in this completely strange environment and is frightened out of her mind. I run to her room and Ian is trying to comfort her and she's petrified of him. We take turns trying to soothe her until six A.M. My body shakes with my own impotence as she cries and cries. Finally, thinking a change of scenery might help, we take her downstairs. Our daughter cries harder as she peers at the sun coming in the kitchen window. Ian makes coffee. Manny steps forward and licks her feet. She sniffles now and takes a long look down at him. They hold each other's gaze. His soft brown eyes say, "So how long you staying?"

I hand her a bagel. She starts to chew it. She stops crying. We all exhale.

10

Getting to Know You

It's the afternoon of Day Two and I have discovered my daughter has a temper. She is screaming and kicking and angry. You know what? I get it. We're strangers to her, she hasn't slept well, and now she is so mad her eyes roll back in her head. Yes, really. I try to comfort her and she stomps me on the ankle and runs. I'm afraid she'll fall down the stairs, so I hobble after her. For five chilling minutes, I can't find her anywhere. I can feel my hair going gray from the roots to the splitting ends.

Unexpectedly, she jettisons from behind a living room curtain and now bolts out through the patio door and into the garage I stupidly left open. Lamely trying to pretend it's a chasing game, I emit a brittle laugh that sounds like a donkey getting hit by a bus. When I get to her, she takes my hand . . . and bites my finger. Hard. I'm talking eye-wateringly painful.

Now she roars at me. Like a demon-lion roar. I'll admit it—she looks possessed. And, because her head will soon turn around on her neck as she vomits pea soup, I take two steps back to give her space. She has barely slept, barely eaten, and she is really angry. At Ian and me.

She's acting out to see if we're going to reject her. So we decide (mostly because we're afraid of her) to just let her do what she wants. We let her stomp through the mud in the garden, sleep if and where she wants, and eat anything that isn't poison. We stay close to make sure she doesn't jam a crayon into Manny's eyes (again) and decide we'll figure out rules another time. My mom is flying in today. I cannot wait.

Later she calms down, sits on the couch with Ian, and watches the Mickey Mouse clubhouse. I run to call Kathy Greenwood, who just lets me blab and blab. I email her a picture. Kathy does exactly what a best friend is required to do: she tells me my daughter is beautiful and looks like me.

The social workers call to check in, which I really appreciate. By law they will have to do six impromptu visits to see how we're all doing. I'm sure they hear my voice crack now when I say, "All good." They tell me they know it's not good and that's okay, which is a relief to hear. But doesn't help in the slightest.

They'd said re-naming her might help her see this all as a fresh start. As I worry it might hinder her acclimatization, they ask if we've chosen a new name yet. We have not. We call her "girlie," "sweetie," "honey," and now as she naps on her face on the cold tile floor (her choice) of the TV room, Ian and I hide in the kitchen and go through names in a baby book. We decide "Cujo" might be too ethnic.

The beauty of adopting a child who is older than an infant is you can get to know the child and pick a name that fits. Since we don't know her that well, we decide to not choose a name right away. Really, at this point, I'm just trying to keep the dog alive and my fingers uneaten. But no matter how many things she throws, how many times she scratches and punches us, we already love her so much it's ridiculous. She is bold and fierce. I admire this little creature's courage just walking into her new home. I marvel at her volcano of anger when she realized she doesn't actually know us. She is so small, and yet an actual person. When she sucks on a bottle and holds our fingers, she is sweet and the depth of the vulnerability in her eyes makes my knees wobbly.

Ian and I grin, albeit maniacally, at each other. We are *so* off our game. This situation is baffling, invigorating, and completely daunting. We are intrinsically aware that the two of us are responsible for keeping this person alive. We don't know what we're doing. With Manny, we could go to a movie for a few hours and leave him alone. He was okay if we left the TV on. But this little girl is an actual human who needs constant monitoring because so far her hobbies are: running as fast as she can into hard surfaces, diving off the stairs, and emitting ear-shattering wildebeest squalls in the front yard. Ian remarks that this little spunky, opinionated kid is exactly who the two of us would make. He says it'll take a little time for us all to get used to each oth— A banana smacks into the back of his neck. She's awake.

We run to her and she takes off out the back screen door.

The phone keeps ringing—the friends of Core want to come over and we keep saying no. This is not the norm for us. We love having people over, we love parties. I tend to cook large vats of wine-soaked pot roast or bake a stuffed turkey with sides of yams bobbing in maple syrup. Ian serves cocktails and we throw raucous dinners where friends sit around our long dining room table and tell hilarious psycho-dating, fired-from-work, or bad-audition stories. Everyone is witty and self-deprecating, and we all love a good loser story. Many summer weekends there is a pool party at our place. I make arugula salads, Ian grills, friends bring side dishes, and the parties go so long that someone will yell what's said on a movie set in overtime:

"Second meal!" Then we pull out pizza fixings or someone throws sausages they brought onto the barbecue. John, married to afore-mentioned Rose, has named me Mixie (a nickname I love) because I grab random ingredients and throw together second-meal dishes I can't ever re-create again: sauces of leftover ingredients, or shredded chicken chili topped with a delicate and fragrant aioli (okay, okay, it's just Parmesan cheese and garlic flakes in light mayo).

So of course now our friends want to come over and meet our daughter. Our families want to come visit. The phone keeps ringing with relatives congratulating us. Ian and I are so touched at how thrilled everyone is for us. It's nice that everyone wants to meet her. But instinctively, we know this is not a good idea. We want this little girl to feel safe. The last thing we want to do is put her on display. I mean, we actually want to get a banner made of her little face and hang it off our roof—but we know that'd be all kinds of inappropri-ate. She's just getting used to us; we have to give her some time to adjust and trust her new surroundings. We don't want to overwhelm her. Plus, like any kid who's sleep deprived, she's not in the greatest mood. She's Tasmanian Devil whirling around the house, tearing everything apart that comes in her path.

She clomps around the house now, picking up objects and throw-ing them at walls and at me. She waits, expecting me to get mad at her. The social workers have cautioned us: this is a test to see if I'll reject her. So I toss my head back and emit another of my forced wheezy cackle-laughs in a feeble attempt to be a cool mom. She's not buying it. I look crazy.

I give her the new toys; she plays with them for a few moments then chucks them at my front teeth and stomps around some more. I open a cupboard to find some colored paper and see a bottle of bub-bles left over from a family visit. I blow one bubble. She looks up . . . and it's as if her entire head smiles.

Ian and I look at each other: bubbles! We've found something she likes. We run outside with her and spend hours blowing bubbles, replenishing the supply with dishwashing liquid. The grass is now slick and will probably never recover. But it's worth it. Because my daughter is chasing bubbles and laughing the most beautiful tinkling sound I've ever heard. We look like a Church of Latter-day Saints commercial.

I'm now smiling like a baby with broccoli gas remembering it in slow motion as I wait for my mom at the airport. I scan the crowd at baggage claim. There she is. My mom and I see each other and weep through another episode of *The Ethnic Sloppy Tears Show*. We hug for a long time and then she exclaims, "Where's my granddaughter?" I am so touched at how my family has embraced my situation. They don't even know this child, and they already love her.

Here's the thing about my mom, Doreen. She is unflappable. She was a stay-at-home mom who was always driving us somewhere yet found time to volunteer-teach Sunday school, fundraise for our church's charities, and still visit the elderly. After we all moved out, she worked as a bookkeeper for my dad's business of real estate development. And yet, she somehow kept a freezer full of baked goods at the ready for any drop-in guests. Although I based Lainie Kazan's mom character in *My Big Fat Greek Wedding* after my mom's personality of never-ending patience and acumen, my real mom doesn't have an accent. She was born and raised in Winnipeg, but let me be clear—she is Greek. Both sides. Full Greek. Here's why I stress this point: like many actors, there have been many wrong items or gossipy stories written about me and, yes, that's annoying. But unloading my grievances to my mom really helped me get over the injustice of that aspect of being a known person. She would help me laugh it off, even when someone at church point-blank asked her if I was having an affair with Colin Farrell. Her attitude would show me the bizarre humor in the tall tales some less scrupulous members of the press would make up about me and our family. She was right; those who knew us knew the truth and the rest didn't matter. Except this once—a publication erroneously reported my mother was not Greek. And she got furious that her full Hellenic lineage wasn't respectfully represented. She called me up and said, "Get on the phone with them and tell them to check their facts!!"

Now, on the car ride home, my mom asks me questions about my daughter and I tell her the truth: she's wonderfully perfect and I'm so happy, but it's going to be a rough transition and I feel helpless. My mom assures me every new mom feels this way. I'm silent in the car because I cannot express how much this simple statement means to me. My mom has become a grandmother seven times before this day. I know my mom's heart ached every time she'd see me admire all the school photos. Ian and I would visit Winnipeg and hear our nieces and nephews running into my parents' home yelling "Yiayia and Pappou, I'm here!" Of course I was happy for my siblings, but I also wanted my own child yelling and running around my parents' home. They all wanted it for me.

My mom knows what I'd been through. She was always supportive and told me to keep trying. On this car ride home, it feels surreal how suddenly those unsure days are over and replaced by new anxieties as I try to figure out how to help my daughter acclimate to her new surroundings.

My mom and I get to my house and as we walk in the door, I realize this is the first time I've come back into my home since my daughter arrived. It feels different. There is a vibrancy, almost a hum, even though the situation teeters uncertainly between a shrieking abyss of chaos and the blissful placidity of those two-minute naps.

My mom puts down her purse and sees a little girl across the backyard, standing with Ian. My daughter turns and gawks at us.

My mom instinctively knows what to do. She walks out, smiles and waves, and just sits down on the patio step. Because of my mom's wisdom and years as a parent, she knows not to run toward my daughter, arms outstretched yelling, "Come 'ere, ya shrimp." That would send this little being into shock. My mom waits on the patio step, just smiling. Slowly my daughter meanders over and sits beside her, curious. They both sit there quietly. Then my little girl looks up at my mom inquisitively, as if to say, who are you? My mom gently touches her granddaughter's cheek and says, "I'm Yiayia." And my daughter leans into her.

A few hours later, we're all in the house and Ian wheels in the suitcases. My mom asks him to put the biggest one on the TV room table. Our daughter watches as my mom unzips it and pulls out Tupperware container after container of baked goods, including a fresh batch of Ian's favorite cookies. I exclaim, "We just told you yesterday, when did you have the time to bake this?" My mom shrugs, "Last night!"

My mom is consistently unruffled in that, like most moms, she can make a meal for fifty out of a handful of beans and leftover Halloween candy. Like all the women in my family, the best way to flatter her is to ask for the recipe. Also like all the women in my family, if you make the dish better than her, she'll be happy about it. She is so good-natured and loving and now completely embraces her new grandchild. And now that my mom is here, everything starts to get better.

Yiayia cooks things that our little one actually eats, like lemon-chicken, and not-sweet milk-dunking biscuits called *paximathia*. Our house smells delicious.

There is almost imperceptible progress. On Day Three, to show she's hungry, our little girl pulls my hand to lead me toward the pantry. I give her two *paximathia* and she takes them with a small nod, looking me in the eyes. Later, when she's drinking water, she then hands the cup back to me and lets me stroke her cheek for a moment.

At the end of the day without warning, she calls Ian "Daddy." I look up, fully expecting to find only a puddle with Ian's eyeballs and a shoe floating in it. My husband has a look on his face that would best be described as a hot mess. This is the first time I have seen him at a loss for words. It's a big moment. And "Daddy" suits Ian. Interestingly, up to that point, I had not referred to him as "Daddy." This came from her. Like on that first day, when she called me "Mommy." We're keenly aware our daughter chose us as her parents. Even if she's sometimes trying to kill us now.

Yiayia's presence in the house is soothing and calming for our little girl. Together we bathe her and comb her hair and try to snuggle with her. Sometimes it's allowed, and sometimes my daughter pushes away and will barely look at us. Sometimes, she keeps her head downcast. Her eyes stay hooded. She is confused. It's understandable. She is pale and guarded. Sometimes she just wants to watch cartoons for hours and doesn't want to engage. We decide to allow it and simply sit beside her on the couch. We just want her to get used to us. Sometimes, when she has a bottle of milk, she'll lean into us. But she mostly stays away. She's not whiney or clingy. In fact, it's quite the opposite. She is competent and independent. She's sending the message that, if she could figure out a way to get that milk out of the fridge on her own, she wouldn't need us at all.

She still sleeps for only a few minutes at a time. We've bought a stroller and have discovered she will fall asleep if we push her around the neighborhood. But when she wakes up from that nap, she cries. And when I try to console her, she usually kicks me in the face.

She cries at night before she sleeps for those few precious minutes. My mom gives me good advice: sometimes kids just need to cry it out. So we hold her and soothe her and tell her she's safe.

I'm holding my daughter now in her room, rocking her in my arms, trying to get her to sleep. I can feel her body giving in to the swaying. Delectable smells are coming up the stairs. My mom, in that seemingly bottomless well of mom energy, is making Greek meatballs at nine P.M. Whatever Ian doesn't devour when he comes home from work will be frozen for another meal. I wonder if everyone has these emotional buoys to cling to when they adopt? Does everyone have sisters, a brother, sister-in-law, brothers-in-law, and a dad calling and giving advice and encouragement? I hope everyone has a mom who fills their freezer with baked delights and full meals in Tupperware containers. She tells me my siblings have already mailed gifts, books, and clothes. I am so lucky that I have this foundation under my somewhat shaky legs. I whisper in my daughter's ear now "So many people have been waiting for you. So many people love you. You'll meet them all."

Within a few days I have to go to work. Yes, really. It's not like I can call in sick and believe me, I tried. With almost no sleep, I get to the set and although I feel light-headed—okay, I'll say it, almost high off the thrill of my secret—I don't tell anyone that I am a mom. I can't explain why I keep it quiet, other than I am still processing it. Also, in my haphazard plodding trek toward motherhood, after so many things falling through and not working out, I am fighting back illogical fears she'll be taken from us. Yes, even though I am sure she's my daughter, plus she is legally emancipated. But truly, I think I don't say anything because it feels so special. To say it out loud almost feels as if it would ruin the delicate beauty of the story. I just want to keep it to myself for a while.

I have barely slept; I am saying my lines in a haze and only thinking about my daughter at home with my mom. I can't wait to get home. Later, I just lie down beside her in bed and inhale her scent of chalk and shampoo, even as she does elbow me in the ribs to get away from her. I breathe her in: she's real.

. . .

This hazing of no sleep isn't good for any of us, so when I finally have a day off filming, Ian and I leave our daughter with my mom so we can go to an appointment we really need. Our friend Tamara, super organized and well read on this mom thing, recommended a site called SleepyPlanet.com, which has connected us with a children's sleep therapist.

This therapist is sympathetic and within minutes reveals she used to work with kids in foster care. We describe how our daughter will not let us hold her but will clutch our fingers as she sleeps. When she does wake up, she hastily checks her surroundings. If she can't see us in front of her, she screams in terror. Yet she fights sleep, trying so hard to keep her eyes open. The therapist explains why our daughter is sleeping for only a few minutes at a time: she is afraid to wake up and find she's not with us anymore. This breaks my heart. Now we know as much as she's pushing us away, she doesn't want to leave us.

As strenuous as it's been, this information makes my daughter even more impressive to me. She doesn't know us, so her survival tactic is to stay awake and keep an eye on us so we can't try out a demon-worship ritual on her. She simply won't let herself relax and sleep. She's like a vigilant soldier in a foxhole, keeping one eye on the enemy at all times. The lack of sleep is taking its toll on her. Sometimes there's just no reasoning with her. She careens around the house like your drunk college roommate who won't give up her car keys.

The therapist gives us little tips such as setting a routine timed to the minute, the same every day. As in: bath from 6:00–6:20 exactly; read books until 6:35; bedtime at 7:00 P.M. She tells us TV is not good for any of our brains before bed because of the beta waves. Most important, she advises us to do the opposite of letting a baby "cry it out." She says to do anything we can to make our daughter feel as secure as possible. She counsels us that it's okay to rock our daughter to sleep and to give her as many bottles as she asks for. Most significantly, she advises we don't sleep in the same bed as her but rather to put another cot in the room right beside her bed. And no matter what—to never leave her alone in the room at night. This way no matter when our daughter wakes up, she will see one of us there in the exact same place we'd been in before she nodded off and this may help her anxieties lessen.

We take the therapist's advice and begin to set a routine. But after so many days of no rules, it's not easy. So we try to make it all fun. Everything becomes a singsong game. I am now in her bathroom singing, bouncing, and flailing around like a clown with no bones, "time to get out, time to get outta the bath." I stink at this; nothing rhymes.

She's okay with that as long as I clap. She likes the clapping and dancing and singing. She allows me to hold her and lightly swing her around the room, as long as I am singing.

We literally move into her room. This evening we put her to bed at 7:00 P.M., and I am lying on a little cot, surrounded by magazines, books, and a bottle of water. I tell her I, or her dad or grandma will be right here all night. Sure enough, our daughter wakes up every two minutes to check if I'm really here. I am. When I need more bottles of milk or to use the bathroom, I text Ian so he or my mom can take my place on the cot. A pattern emerges: our daughter bolts awake but sees one of us there in that extra bed. So she falls back asleep. She goes through six bottles of milk a night. We keep giving them to her. Sure enough, over the next few days, the two-minute sleep intervals turn into twenty minutes, then slowly into an hour at a time. She is visibly becoming more trusting.

This is why I described getting back my energy before filming *My Life In Ruins*. There is no way I could have done this when I was feeling weak: every night, I swing her in my arms for as long as it takes for her to feel sleepy. This segues into a list of everyone who loves her. I tell her all her new cousins' names, her aunts, uncles, friends. All the names become a singsong mantra of how many people love her. Her eyelids get heavy, but she keeps them open. She fights sleep as hard as she can. Sometimes, this takes hours and my arms ache. No matter how fit I thought I'd become, this is hard because we didn't have a seven-pound baby to begin with, to work arm muscles up to carrying the weight of a toddler. I am immediately rocking over thirty pounds, and my shoulder muscles rip from the weight. But to see her slowly relax and her mouth form that angelic pout is worth it.

On this night she is really fighting sleep and now pushes against my shirt. My buttons are too pointy. Without hesitation, I rip off my shirt and rock her against my chest. The skin-to-skin contact calms her. I feel like a cavewoman standing here rocking my baby without my shirt but . . . oh yes, she is sleeping.

We're slowly introducing her to a few friends. As I confide to my cousin Nike and close friends, such as everyone of Core, plus Sean Hayes, Rita, Tom, John, and Gary that I'm a mom, their cheerful, bordering-on-ecstatic responses surprise me. I become conscious of how much they all knew I needed this but hadn't pried.

Some days are great. We see progress in every way. Some days are steps backward. We try to not worry, and we try to be patient even though she is still not speaking. Plus, she still doesn't sleep for longer than an hour or so.

Today our friends Rose, Tracy, and Suzy come over and as I open the door with my daughter in my arms, I have to fight back the urge to scream, "Isn't she cuuuuute?" Instead, I calmly say, "Sweetie, these are your aunties." Rose gives her a toy. She chucks it at Rose's chin.

Oooookay, not a good day. My girlfriends assure me they understand. I can see they do and how excited they are to see her. But, yeah, the lack of sleep would make anyone incorrigible.

It gets worse later that afternoon. She keeps throwing things, testing us again to see if we'll get mad, if we'll reject her. A sharp toy car glances off my shinbone. It is taking every bit of patience I have to not throw that toy back. I just pick it up and ask her to not throw things. She stares up at me, daring me to get mad. She doesn't speak, but I know she understands. I tell her I'm sad and show her it hurt. She decks me once again and runs away. I'll admit it—this is hard and I wonder if it will ever be less chaotic. Am I going to be defeated by this three-foot holy terror?

The doorbell rings; it's Kathy Najimy holding a cute stuffed teddy bear. She, Dan, and their sweet pre-teen daughter, Samia, come in, beaming beatitudes of exuberance which illuminate my own mental fatigue. Our daughter shyly peeks around the corner. I see her through their eyes: she is naked except for a diaper, her eyes are curious, and even though she just punched me in the crotch minutes before, she is truly perfect. I can hear Kathy and Dan's voices are thick throated, but they keep their tone even and just say, "Hi, how are you?"

And my daughter breaks into a stream of gibberish, complete with gestures and arm movements. Using sounds like *ha-ka-bakakakabah* that are not words, she tells them her whole story. It really seems as if she's saying, "Okay, I lived somewhere else, right? And people took care of me." Kathy perceptively says, "Uh-huh, and then what happened?," and this little creature responds with the *ha-ka-bakakakabah* sound, her own language, and it's got the cadences of, "And then I met these two people, see them, one is a lady and one is a man, that's them, and now we all live in that room, that room right there! And did you know I have a dog?"

The expression on Kathy's and Dan's faces is as if they're witnessing a miracle. We all take in this charming, brave little creature standing here effervescently telling us her whole life story. This little doll in the diaper is so sublime we all have to blink to be sure she's not a hologram.

The next day, I tell the social workers everything, not worrying about being judged, and overall how it's going better. Now they advise we take the next step in letting our daughter know this is permanent. It's time to name her.

11

What's in a Name Anyway?

After a few weeks, our daughter is simply not as mad at us anymore. She is sleeping better and eating well, making eye contact and smiling more often.

Plus, she is funny. Her response to humorous things is explosively joyous. She turns the handle of that new jack-in-the-box toy and of course the creepy clown pops out at her face. But she thinks it's hilarious and now gets our visiting adult friends to turn the handle, reveling in their startled expressions.

Sure, she plays typical kid games like peekaboo and hide-and-seek. But she also has a very mischievous side. When Ian is calling Manny to go for a walk, she covers the dog with a blanket and makes a face, pretending she doesn't know where he is. She likes to hide behind the curtains and pretend to scare me. Her eyes light up when we laugh.

We read her a book called *Good Night, Gorilla*. At the moment the zookeeper's wife realizes all the animals have escaped from the zoo and are in the bedroom with her, all together, we make an "Ehr?!" sound and do a double take. She knows it's funny.

One day Ian was walking toward her but tripped over Manny, slip-sliding in his socks across the hardwood floor and finally landing on his thigh with a loud *thunk*. We've been married a long time so, yes, I laughed. I was surprised to hear another laugh. The kid. She knew it was funny to see a grown man go down hard, and she really cracked up, rolling backward onto the couch and kicking her feet up.

For my entire marriage, there has never been a cold drink taken from the fridge by Ian or me without it first being put against the back of each other's neck. If I see Ian looking the other way when I have a cold drink, I have to do it. I can't help it. His startled reaction to the icy cold on his neck is even better if he's been sweating.

So today when Ian sees me facing our daughter, my chest puffed up like an old country yenta as she slurps the chicken soup I have lovingly made her from scratch, does he revel in the tender moment of mother and daughter? No way.

Instead, he takes a cold water bottle from the fridge and of course puts it against the back of my neck. And of course I jump. Well, this delights this little girl. De-lights her. She thinks it's the funniest thing she's ever seen. So Ian does it again, and she laughs and laughs 'til I have to stomp hard on his foot to signal him to cut it out.

So two minutes later, when I am facing the other way getting her a cracker, she presses her cold milk bottle against my arm. I am not acting. It's cold. I jump, then turn and see her laugh. She is pretty pleased with herself.

Ian and I look at each other. We saw it that first day and there's no doubt now. We recognize a kindred spirit—we may have a class clown on our hands.

So we're all getting used to each other. But we can't call her "sweetie" forever.

For that reason, as she finishes the soup, I look at Ian . . . now? He nods "do it," and I oh-so-casually lean into her.

"Evelyn?" I murmur.

Evelyn was my beloved grandmother's name, and I am trying it out on my daughter to see if it's a fit. But my daughter doesn't respond. I try it again.

"Evelyn . . ." Now my daughter sharply looks up at me. With a really dirty look. She does not like this name at all.

Ian tries one. He leans in with a name he likes: "Bella?" She now looks at him and shakes her head no. As in "no way, sucker."

Even though the social workers and therapist recommend we rename her, we're not sure we're doing the right thing. But we'd been informed she'd been right beside a kid with the birth name she'd been given and whenever that name was called, our daughter didn't look up or respond in any way. She is telling us all this is not her name.

Ian and I have scoured baby name sites. We avoid the obvious our-same-three-letters choice of Ani because it'd be so insipid our friends might club us in the head. We try many names just to see if we can get a feel for what suits her. As I said—this kid is opinionated. She gets what we're attempting now and really lets us know we are not on the right track with the names we're trying out.

"Clio?" gets a "don't even think about it" face.

"Dolores" gets a "get real, weirdos" chin-upturned sniff.

We try "Vera," "Ava," "Harlow," "Eugenia," "Antonia," "Arden," and many other names. And the minute we say each, we realize the name doesn't fit her. Plus, she doesn't like any of them. She lets us know with that face.

Then I come across a name in a book that means something in Greek that actually suits her personality. It means "something that is joyous and funny." Ian and I agree to try it out.

It's the next day and our daughter is playing in the backyard with my mom. Ian and I lean out the door and I call out the new name: " . . . Ilaria?"

My daughter looks up and her expression says, "Yeah?"

She is smiling.

Just like how she chose us, she chooses her name.

And Ilaria suits her. She nods her head as if to let us know we did okay this time.

So I say, "Is your name Ilaria?" and she nods again and grins. Immediately, we all start calling her Ilaria and she really likes it. It is a fresh start for her now more than ever. Things begin to change even more around here: Ilaria is now letting me hold her more, and she is even climbing into Ian's lap as she drinks a bottle.

The fascinating thing about California law is the state will re-issue Ilaria's birth certificate with her new name and us as her parents. I see how adoptions were able to be kept a secret. However, based on the advice of Dan on his own adoption at birth, the social workers, and our own common sense, we don't keep her adoption a secret from her. She's almost three years old, she will remember things. When the social workers advise me to begin to re-apply for the birth certificate, this should allay my fears that something will go wrong, that she will be taken from us . . . except they inform me I can't actually complete the process until I have the official "finalization day" certificate of adoption. I don't know when that final court date will be, but I start to fill out the forms. I take out Ilaria's birth certificate and see her birth date.

Even though many keep their schedules electronically, I still use a Ye Olde Time day planner because I like to write things down. I've used the week-at-a-glance Moleskine brand for years and kept them all as journals. So I dig out my day planner of the year of her birth to see what I was doing when she was born. I look up her birth date . . . dang . . . creepy . . . the evening I'd had the heavy discussion with Kathy Greenwood about whether I had given up on being a mother . . . Ilaria was born later that night. The same night her cousin was born prematurely. And, yes, it was that next day I'd started to believe there was a little girl out there waiting for me. I know, I know . . . cue *Twilight Zone* music.

I put Ilaria's original birth documents and all the documents that came with her into a manila envelope. We're going to give everything to our attorney to keep for us so there aren't any secrets in the house. This way when Ilaria is ready, we'll open up the entire file and learn about her birth parents together. If Ilaria decides to contact her birth parents, we will completely support it because it will be healthy for her.

As I fill out the application for the new birth certificate, it is surreal to list Ian and myself as her parents. It's actually happening. I am her mother.

I write the name we've chosen: Ilaria, which as I've described can be translated to mean something fun and joyous. I now add the second name she also has chosen—Isadora—so she can be named after my ever-supportive mom. My mom's name, Doreen, is derived from the Greek name Dora, which means God's gift.

Her name is Ilaria Isadora.

After years of us praying to be parents, this little miracle simply appeared.

Ilaria Isadora translates to: a funny gift from God.

12

The Ritual

Of course there isn't a baby shower. It's not just that there isn't time for one, it's because I hate them. I have left one too many stuffy houses on a Sunday afternoon with a throatful of egg salad and an empty aching uterus to inflict this same abuse on others.

Again, kids are not for everyone, yet the friends in Core have become amazing aunties and uncles to Ilaria. They're all professionals with busy lives, but they make time to come over and hang with her.

In these first weeks, I watch Suzy and Ilaria lie on their tummies coloring with crayons. Jackie comes over with little handmade gifts; Jenna and her daughter bring homemade cookies for a tea party on the monogrammed set sent by Johanna. Tracy and Rose hide toys in their purses for Ilaria to find, and help her knead Sculpey into cows who live in Popsicle-stick barns; Dave has funny grown-up "talks" with her. Renee and Brian gently teach her how to swim while she splashes Kate . . . and to make Ilaria laugh, John walks into the pool wearing all his clothes. Although they may have privately discussed my situation, none of them expected this. I shocked everyone by revealing my hidden need to be a mom by suddenly introducing Ilaria, and I am grateful for how they've all acclimated to this new situation.

Everyone takes pleasure in the fact there's this new little creature around. My mom has gone back to Winnipeg and she'll be back with my dad soon. My sisters and brother are now preparing their visits to meet their new niece. All our nieces and nephews have sent gifts and cards from where they live—Toronto, Winnipeg, and Australia. Without even planning it with one another, the kids had written heartfelt letters to their cousin welcoming her to the family. They're all framed in Ilaria's room—we read them to her and show her pictures of her new cousins until she can meet everyone.

Of course, Ian or I still sleep in the cot beside Ilaria's bed. We rock her to sleep, give her as many bottles as she asks for, but she is sleeping in two-hour increments.

Our environment has become a hectic, noisy, and fun kid house. We blow so many bubbles that the yard grass is a yellow and soggy bog. Pastel sidewalk chalk graffitis the driveway with kid gang symbols. We gingerly step around the booby trap of Playmobil pieces on every floor surface. At three A.M., a tiny remote-controlled car zooms on its own through the living room. A Big Bird electric toothbrush in a drawer "whirrs" us awake at dawn. There are toys, books, and stuffed animals everywhere; it looks like a Toys "R" Us barfed into our house.

I embrace this new thing called parenthood. I'm getting wrinkles. Not from stress but because I smile so much; I have laugh lines around my eyes. There isn't a word for the elation I feel. The weekends are unplanned and gloriously lazy because one errand now takes half the day. We live about a five-minute walk to a street of shops and cafés. Over the years, I've walked the few blocks thousands of times. But with Ilaria it takes forever. There isn't a "there" in a kid's day. She stops to inspect every tree trunk, every flower, every rock. Now in my sleep-deprived-bordering-on-hallucinating haze, I notice that vine twisted around that tree trunk actually looks sort of enchanted. I perceive my neighborhood completely anew, as if fairies are fluttering around, sprinkling glitter. I see blue shutters and clay roofs and red doors and neighbors I had never noticed. When Ilaria picks a beautiful purple flower and gently holds it out to me, I realize I have never been precisely still before, completely present, not wanting a moment to ever pass.

While I once spent my evenings perusing the adoption sites, I'm now on the computer buying out Pottery Barn and Crate and Barrel as if I'm goading our business manager to call and scream, "Leave some for other parents!" The pretty white furniture arrives and we all decorate Ilaria's new bedroom—it's like a remake of *Yours, Mine And Ours* to messily stick flower decals on the walls while laying out that furniture on top of a new pink rug, as Manny lies on and licks everything.

I am delighted by Ilaria: every facial expression, every tantrum, every small thing she does is fascinating and fantastic. Mornings are now a flurry of juice spilling, tiny clothes washing, and frenzied kid-chasing. It is thrilling to not know what's going to happen next. Even though she's still not speaking yet, Ilaria is happy and relaxing more and more. She's not frustrated and on guard as much, and her tears have been replaced with the sweetest of smiles and a hilariously gurgling laugh. She seems to have begun to accept this is her home and we're her parents. She gets it all. Sometimes we just look at each other and laugh for no reason.

She sits in my lap as we watch YouTube videos of kitties playing. Now, being from Canada, the image of even a nun slip-sliding across ice slays me. So I gladly click on the many compilations of *America's*

Funniest Home Videos of people falling. Ilaria and I laugh so hard at old people bouncing and falling off trampolines, I'm not sure who is the parent.

She now does many things to see if she can make us laugh. When I turn away to get a napkin, she puts ten straws in her mouth and waits patiently for me to turn back and laugh. She eats a bag of animal crackers, then holds the bag out to me, in the "want one?" gesture. When I reach into the bag and discover it empty, she breaks into peals of laughter.

Ian notices she is not giggly about it. It's more like she's sly and ironic, wryly trying to outsmart us. Sure, I'm describing typical kid behavior, but I mention it because Ian and I laugh a lot, and our house is loud and fun. Ilaria is adapting to her environment.

I'll be honest here. As I described earlier, because things went wrong for us so often on this path to parenthood, I'm still holding my breath. Obviously, I'm having fun, I'm enjoying myself, but often an uneasy feeling washes over me. I tell myself it's probably the lack of sleep.

I stare at Ilaria. I love her so much. I need this placement to be finalized.

One evening we attend a casual Greek fundraising picnic event hosted by our church.

Our priest, Father John, meets Ilaria, promptly understands the situation, and does not ask questions. He only kindly asks if he can bless her. I explain I'm nervous because her adoption isn't finalized. He gives me a wise nod and tells me then he should definitely bless her.

So that Sunday we head to church. Our daughter silently takes in the chanting and the smell of incense as the sun shines through the stained-glass windows. It can be daunting, but she finds it alluring.

After the service, the congregation leaves and Father John subtly gestures for us to join him at the front of the church for the additional ceremony. As we get to the altar, Father John opens a book and begins to read. But this isn't a standard blessing I'm hearing. This is new to me. It is a special prayer for . . . adoption.

The words and ceremony are a beautiful acknowledgment that some families are created in different ways but are still, in every way, a family.

The priest now says these words, "Today you have given birth to your daughter," and, yep, here it comes . . . the ethnic gush. But this blubber session is quickly followed by a quiet gratefulness.

I hold my daughter in my arms and thank God for bringing her to me. If the standard route of creating a family had worked for me, I wouldn't have met this child. I needed to know her. I needed to be her mother. I know now why all those events happened. Or didn't happen. So I could meet this little girl. She is, in every way, my daughter. I am carrying my Funny Gift from God and all is good.

I am curious as to why we humans seem to need these rituals to get things into our skulls. There isn't just one reason we want these rites. Perhaps it's essential we witness, or we require catharsis to process information and emotions.

Ah, maybe that's what the baby shower is—part of the mental preparation for the expectant mother. Although I find the opening of tiny onesies followed by a group "awwww" so irritating, and am not comfortable watching grown women dance with a hat of gift bows unless vacation tequila is involved, I now perceive that the ritual is part of how we process life's milestones. Okay, okay I get it now.

I thank Father John for the ceremony and we head down the aisle. And I realize while I have walked into the church many times . . . on this day, it is the first time I am walking out as a mother.

13

Waiting to Be Finalized

"Gloria?"

"Ilaria," I say.

"Lara?"

"Ah-LAHR-ee-ah," I say, aware that I am speaking loudly.

The grocery store clerk smiles down on my daughter, sitting in the cart, looking up at him.

"Spell it?" he asks.

Ah, jeez. I have saddled my daughter with a tough name. I myself loathed my odd name growing up. I wished I was a Jane or a Heather. On top of it, no one correctly spelled or remembered my name. Even now, the most ardent admirer has trouble with it. They'll run up with pure love in their eyes, screaming "big fat Greek girl" or "Come here, fat wife!" or if they like *My Life In Ruins,* it's "Poopi-kisser!!"

They hug me, quote lines from my movies, then say, "What's your name?"

I answer, "Nia." And they squeal, "Yes, Nina!"

Now I see my daughter watching the clerk but her expression is puzzled, as if "Ilaria" is the most common name in the world. Somehow, I know this kid will not see her name as a burden. She doesn't lack confidence.

Grocery shopping today is one of the few times I've ventured out with her beyond our neighborhood. Yes, I'm still edgy about the placement being permanent. The way it works with North American foster care is the child is placed in the home for a six-month period before the paperwork is finalized. Even if the child is legally emancipated, this juncture during transition and social worker visits is still called fostering. Thus the confusing name fos-adopt. Typically, initially there are more parent-child visits, then a trial sleepover or two before a child is placed in a home—but every case is unique. All indications have shown our placement is permanent, but I still worry something will go wrong.

We load the groceries into the car and as I click Ilaria into her booster seat, I get a call from my publicist Heidi Schaeffer: somehow a member of the press has found out about Ilaria. I try to keep my face calm for Ilaria, but my insides screech like a howler monkey and cave in. Heidi tells me Marc Malkin of *E!* News called her and while he doesn't have the details correct, he does know a lot and wants confirmation. I keep my face composed and reach back to hand Ilaria a sticker book as Heidi tells me she leveled with him. She told Marc if he goes public with the story, he could ruin the permanency of the placement. Heidi is also my friend and a mother and knows what had happened with other adoption panels feeling we possibly couldn't provide privacy to a child from foster care. She asked Marc to please not run with the story out of the goodness of his heart. And . . . he agreed. Heidi tells me Marc saw the humanity at stake and did the right thing.

I exhale, hang up, and look back at Ilaria as I start the car. She's happily ripping apart the sticker book . . . I want this adoption to be finalized. And soon.

Later that day, the social workers come over to our house for an official visit. They walk around and check things, such as making sure any medications are in a lockbox and that all second-floor rooms have a rope fire ladder. We don't see any of it as an intrusion. I don't feel like they're spying or judging us. I feel they're there to help. They do.

They assess how we're doing and answer our questions about the process of finalizing our adoption. I gasp as they give us our court date. It's still months away. By law we have to wait six months from the day Ilaria was placed with us to finalize us as her parents. The judge will require six months' proof of social worker visitations and placement evaluations. It seems like an awful law and a long time to wait and I am having terrible nightmares some unknown birth relative will come forward and Ilaria will be taken from us. I find myself waking up in the middle of the night to reach out and make sure she's still here—like she does to me.

Just last night, I woke up and discovered her already awake, looking at me. In the dark, we both smiled. She tentatively reached out and put her fingers on my cheek. I did the same and stroked her face until she fell asleep. It seems strange to me now that we'd asked our social workers to only match us with a legally emancipated child. It's because we simply weren't seeking trouble then. But now there's no way I'm giving up Ilaria. If a catastrophe occurs, Ian and I will fight for this child.

However, I'm not taking any chances. We don't go beyond our neighborhood because we live in Los Angeles, and there's a scourge in my industry: paparazzi. I'm not talking about photographers. There's a vast difference between legitimate members of the press corps and paparazzi. Sure, some paparazzi are passable individuals who merely want a celebrity picture to sell to magazines. I understand that trade-off of my industry; in a way we're all krill. But it's terrifying when that other kind of paparazzi jumps out at you at the park—these scum want that sellable shocked, angry expression. I don't want Ilaria to get scared, plus I don't want a picture of her in some tabloid. Not only do I want to keep her safe, I don't want anything to jeopardize her placement with us.

So I tell the social workers everything I'm concerned about in terms of Ilaria being taken. Once again, they listen with such respect, such kindness. They assure me that once she was placed with us, we needn't worry. She is legally emancipated. They soothe my fears about a birth family member coming forward and claiming DNA rights. They explain that all the paperwork is done and fully vetted to confirm a child is legally freed. This was all done before Ilaria was placed with us, and now even if an unknown relative shows up, the law is on our side. I don't want to fight anyone in court, but as I said, I would. Actually, I've decided I'll just take her and move to Switzerland.

As I've explained, there are 129,000 kids who are legally emancipated and living in foster care, waiting to be matched with parents to adopt them. There are also 350,000 kids living in foster care whose parental rights have not been terminated. These kids live in foster care or group homes as they wait for their birth parents to get it together and for a judge to grant the parents the right to get their kids back. These kids are also hoping to be fostered in a loving home, and if their birth parents' rights are terminated, they can be adopted into a "forever family." I marvel at the people who choose to foster and wait through a legal process to adopt that child. If you're thinking of the ones who do it for money and are mean to kids, those are the rare individuals and, of course, the ones the media has told you about. I'm talking about the people I've met. There is a whole world of foster parents and social workers who run group homes who just want to do good. They just want to give kids a good life. And they do. When I was checking the adoption sites, I saw images that stay with me. I saw some kids with Down syndrome or cystic fibrosis or who were severely handicapped and in wheel-chairs. Months later, on their profiles it would say, in large letters—ADOPTED.

Many people adopt this way via foster care; first they foster and then they get to adopt that child after the parental rights are termi-nated. There is an event once a year that is truly staggering to wit-ness. It's called National Adoption Day. On this one day, in every state a courthouse is donated and lawyers and judges work for free—you heard me, for free—to finalize adoptions. Adopting via foster care is free. The children's medical and dental expenses are covered until adulthood. I didn't know about any of this. When Ilaria was placed with us, because she'd been relinquished to foster care, she was immediately covered under our insurance. We donated her medical and dental rights back to the state.

As the social workers explain each step of the process that will happen over the next few months, inwardly I encourage myself to stop worrying. However, I will still make sure my daughter is not photographed.

Let's be clear, Ian and I don't really live a hip Hollywood life-style. It's not like we have paparazzi following us around all day try-ing to get that risqué, incriminating picture. We're not thin enough or famous enough, plus we're boring. As far as I know, neither of us has done cocaine off a stripper's butt on Sunset Boulevard, so pa-parazzi couldn't even get a lucrative shot of us.

But lately, there have been paparazzi at our local outdoor mall. We've even noticed them in our neighborhood. We know two actors with a new kid is a sought-after picture.

So, since Ilaria loves being a kitty-cat, we have the solution: we face-paint her. Now, with whiskers, a black nose, pointy eyebrows, and a sun hat, she is unrecognizable. So every time we go to a public place, we have our little kitty and no one gets a clear picture of her. I keep the kitty-cat makeup in my purse in case we make an impromptu visit to a place known to have paparazzi. Luckily, like a lot of kids she enjoys having her face painted. We didn't have to go as far as Michael Jackson did with his kids' veils but you know what? I get that, now. I am so protective of her, I will do anything it takes. Until the adoption is finalized, we want to be cautious so a judge won't rule our lifestyle isn't safe for the private life of a child.

So if we see paparazzi, we make it a game. Ilaria knows only family and friends can take pictures of us and if anyone else tries, she gets to hide her face. When paparazzi do jump out at us, she doesn't get scared because we've made it a contest. It's an amusing challenge for her to play peekaboo and incredibly satisfying for us to see an annoyed paparazzo give us the finger while we feel her giggling breath on our necks.

Ian and I have always been appreciative of anyone who has seen our work and asks for a photo with us. It can be embarrassing to ask for a photo and be rebuffed. Before I was a working actor, it happened to me. I asked a famous person for a photo and was rudely rebuffed. Quite brusquely. No, I'm not telling you who it was (without a martini in me), but my cousin Nike and I will never forget the sting of embarrassment we felt. Minutes later, we met John Stamos too—far more famous and good-looking than the first guy. Nike simply held out her camera and John said, "Of course!" Sean Hayes, John Corbett, Tom Hanks, Rita Wilson, Jewel, and most actors I know are like this too. They appreciate that being courteous in public is part of the job.

As John Corbett once advised me—once you're a known actor, there's no day off. My theory is if I don't want to be approached by admirers, I don't go out. So I never rebuff people. Not even when that lady snapped my picture after my spa massage. I didn't enjoy it, but she didn't know it was invasive to snap a picture of me all oiled up like gyro meat in a robe and shower cap. On this topic, if I ever meet Stockard Channing again, I owe her an apology. Before I was a known actor, the two of us were alone in the changing room after a workout class. As she was changing her clothes, I realized who she was, blurted out my sincere veneration, and touched her bare leg. She was nice but as I gushed, it dawned on me I might have chosen a more opportune time to stroke her thigh.

I've noticed and value this about the people who like my work—they're nice. I think they're nicer than the people who like other actors' work. Yeah, I said it. Because I once heard a reporter say something like this about one of my scripts and think it applies to all my films—they play best for an audience that does not hate themselves. My movies are unabashedly affectionate so the people who like them are particularly kind. And I genuinely appreciate their good-heartedness.

But now, I have a child. A daughter I want to protect, especially when we're in public. Most people, when they see me with my daughter, just nod and grin, or yell "love your work," which makes my head crack open in a smile so wide, I look like a Pez dispenser.

Sometimes taking photos requires a bit of creative thinking. One day at an outdoor mall, a group of fabulous gay men screamed "Connie and Carla," my drag queen movie, and I was delighted as they came running at me, quoting the line, "Your voice is giving me mono." They beseechingly held out their cameras. I pointed down to my daughter, indicating I couldn't take a photo. Ilaria and I headed for the food court with the gaggle of gay men in hot pursuit. Ian was getting us ice cream and they squealed at my "bear" husband and snapped his photo. Then Ian watched Ilaria while the boys and I walked over to the fountain, took photos, hugged, and said good-bye. I loved those guys for understanding I couldn't be a mom and a parade float at the same time. Ilaria did not ask what *Connie and Carla* was. No secrets. If she asks, I'll tell her about my movies. But it's very clear and important to me that to my daughter, I'm solely her mom.

But when I got back to Ian and Ilaria, the hurt expression on my daughter's face stopped me in my tracks. I realized I'd made a mistake. She didn't know why I left to take pictures and, actually, neither did I. She is my primary concern.

This actor/parent thing is new to me. I appreciate anyone who has ever enjoyed my work, but my biggest priority is helping my daughter feel secure and safe. After much discussion, Ian and I assured Ilaria that we will no longer take photos when we're with her. We all call it our Family Promise. We soon see that when we explain to film and TV enthusiasts that we don't take photos when we're with our daughter, and that it's a Family Promise, people get it and are sincerely understanding of our request.

So if you don't mind, let's make this agreement—if we meet when I'm with my daughter, you can tell me anything you like about my movies, I get to tell you you look cute in that shirt, we shake hands and move on. Deal? Thank you.

14

Move That Cot

For these first two months, every day there is progress. Ilaria is wak-ing up about every two or three hours and upon seeing one of us on that cot near her, goes back to sleep.

More and more, we can see how secure Ilaria feels: a cookie handed to her is immediately broken up and shared. Before you think it's all a Hallmark moment, she's still throwing toys at our faces. We respond with reason. We show her where the toy hurt us. We see her thoughtfully take this information in. Sometimes she wants to make it better by rubbing the bruise (ow).

When we go for walks, she stops doing that toddler thing— running away—because we make it a game. We practice—she gets to run down the sidewalk until we yell "stop." When she hears that word, she gets to run back and tag me. Yes, it's usually a shin-punch, but it counts.

I'm trying to accept that for now, while we're in this transition, our house is a mess. I really like a clean and tidy house. I'm very organized to the point where I get overheated at those stores that sell boxes you can store stuff in. That's porn to me. But now my house looks like Dr. Seuss closed his eyes while he made green eggs and ham. Some of it is necessary: books and clothes. There's just so much stuff a toddler needs.

I haven't figured out how to shop and watch her, but really I don't need anything because gifts keep pouring in. Our friends bring so many toys over that I have to beg them to stop. The couch is buried in an avalanche of delivered presents. I am so touched by the generosity and spend many mornings just writing thank-you notes. One day I sit down to attack the thank-you notes again and the Leaning Tower of gift cards has gone missing. In our sleep-deprived haze somebody must have chucked the big pile. If I have any regrets about this whole situation, this would be the only one. I only sent out half the thank-you cards. I have no idea who the rest of the gifts are from. The polite Winnipegger in me is wholly discomfited by this. I worry people will think my mom raised a heathen. If you're reading this and I never sent you a thank-you card, um . . . thank you for the dress/socks/boots/quilt/books/shorts/jacket/pillow/lamp/shirt/tea set/fruit basket/hat/peaches/barrettes/guitar.

On their next visit, the social workers bring parenting books (I have a thank-you card written before they can get out the door) and ask me how I am doing with the angst that something will go wrong. I know Ilaria will do better if I am steady in my conviction this is a permanent situation. I am trying. The social workers had offered the good advice: to be sure we never refer to this as her "new life." The best thing they say today is "don't treat her like she's adopted." This makes a lot of sense. Maybe she isn't conversing in formed words because she isn't ready. Maybe it has nothing to do with her parenting situation at all. I find this an enormous relief. Before the social workers leave, they give Ilaria a tiny pink T-shirt to wear. On it is printed: Worth The Wait.

We take their advice and continue to ask Ilaria questions about her other living situations to help keep her memories alive. We ask her if she had a bedroom and toys, just to keep reminding her that her past is still a part of her. This is not her new life. She's the same person, in a new situation. Simple questions like "Did you have a dog before?" can get a happy stream of the *ha-ka-bakakakabah* gibberish. Ilaria is a good communicator, willing to talk about anything, and has many opinions. We are starting to understand the babble language.

She is smiling, laughing, and making eye contact. The guarded eyes-downcast stance is gone. She is still a bit rough and tends to hit or scratch when she is frustrated. We're working on it.

If she is angry, we allow her to express herself as long as she doesn't hurt herself or anyone. She takes every pillow off the couch in the TV room and chucks them, checking to see if she's in trouble. I remember something Kathy Greenwood had told me she did in the middle of her youngest's tantrum and I try it. As Ilaria is screaming today, I hand her a juice box and say, "You must be thirsty." That stops her cold. She takes the juice and drinks it. Within ten minutes, she helps me put the cushions back and we move on from the incident. It's good advice: don't make everything a teachable moment.

Often, she still won't let us kiss her. We don't want to force it. We try to figure out ways to get close to her just to establish body contact that won't scare her. When she's watching TV, we try to hold her and kiss the back of her neck, but she mostly squirms away.

One morning, we're all lying in bed languidly deciding what to do today, but Ilaria won't let us hold her. Manny jumps on the bed and Ilaria pets him and rubs her cheek against his furry back. I remember that since most kids comprehend that frosting is legal heroin, Ilaria enjoys helping me bake cupcakes. We put them in our hands and shove our whole faces into their warm deliciousness. So I blurt, "Let's bake a Manny cake!" I pass her pretend cups of sugar and she "pours" it on him. Then, she "cracks" an egg onto his furry back. Ian passes her the flour. As we add each ingredient, we are all lightly touching and massaging Manny's furry body. Then I yell "Mix it up, mix it up" and with gusto now, we all knead his tummy and back. We pretend to pour him into a pan and then push him under the quilt, which is the "oven." I yell "ding" and we pull him out and descend on him, "eating" up the Manny cake, really just nibbling or nuzzling his face and body, which he loves.

Ilaria goes nuts for this game. Now we do me. We make a Mommy cake. They all descend on me, "eating" me all over. And then . . . we do Ilaria. As Ian and I are pretend-chewing her, we lightly nuzzle her hands, tummy, and neck, which is ticklish and fun for her. After a few days of this game, we gently shift into kissing her neck. And her face. We do just a little bit. Then more. And after a week . . . she's letting us kiss her. And she's kissing us back. Within a few more weeks, on a whim she is grabbing our faces and kissing us. Yes, her soft kisses are amazing; they melt us. "Baking" each other is working. We now see her "baking" her stuffed animals and dolls and eating/kissing them.

It's been almost three months now and we're getting ready to go to a friend's house. I ask Ilaria where a stuffed toy is and she explains it's in the garage behind the big boxes.

Ian and I stare at her. Because it wasn't the gibberish plus five words we've come to expect and understand. It was a full sentence. Of many words. Followed by more. She's now telling us that she put her toy there for a nap because he was grouchy but she'll go get him right now.

Just like that, Ilaria is talking. And just like me, she never shuts up again. Poor Ian.

This is a good lesson for me to just trust and wait for my daughter's own readiness on her development. On the next visit, when the pediatrician hears her talking in actual words, she simply nods to me, as in *See, all good.* The doctor had never been worried and didn't attach labels. Ilaria just needed a bit more time. She quickly advances with words past her age, and, seriously, has not stopped speaking since she started.

She tells us things about her prior living situation. Some may be real memories, some may be dreams. For example, she tells us she had "Twenty-nine brothers and sisters" (her favorite number). Sometimes it's "Twenty-nine dogs." We listen and ask questions as if everything she tells us is a real recollection. She is infinitely assured by this validation and in time we notice the stories become more ingenuous and factual.

But there still is a trust issue. She trusts us, but not the situation. Even though she's more affectionate and seems to be relaxing, Ilaria has started saying she thinks she has to go and doesn't want to leave. When we reassure her that this home is not temporary, that she is our daughter forever, she has anxiety still and says this heartbreaking sentence: "I don't want to leave my big yellow house."

No matter how often we soothe her fears, she's not sure this placement is permanent. I understand her anxiety because of my own worry—it's hard to let go of unease when it's been with you for so long. I reason with myself that, for Ilaria, I have to put aside my own concerns and be stoically steadfast.

One evening in her room, I take two of her dolls and pretend-play that one is the mom putting the girl doll to bed. As the mom doll I whisper, "I am your mommy forever. I love you and I will never leave you; you are staying here forever." I repeat the same with another doll as the dad. The dad doll tells the girl doll he is her "daddy forever and we are your family forever." I don't look at Ilaria to check if the message is getting through. I just start to read her a book, then tuck her in and lie in the cot beside her, holding her hand as usual. The next night I do the same thing, saying the same words. Ilaria's big eyes take it all in. One week later, we're in her room, I duck out to hang up her wet bath towel and when I come back, I see Ilaria holding the mom and dad dolls and whispering to the girl doll, "You are staying here forever." Then she has the parent dolls gently kiss the little girl doll.

I just pick up Ilaria, gently rock her, and whisper into her ear: "I am your mommy forever. I love you so much and I will never leave you."

Then . . . she slowly pats my hair and says, " . . . okay."

I tell myself: if this little creature can relax and trust the system, so can I.

We're all pretty exhausted. Like most people with a new baby, there isn't much sleep. But we have a toddler who doesn't sleep and knows how to punch you while you're passed out. It's going better though. Ilaria is now sleeping just over three hours at a time. She still wakes up for the bottles of milk. She still needs six bottles a night, often reaching out for one in her sleep. I'm lying in the cot now, looking at her sleeping. She's actually sleeping. The peacefulness on her face was hard-won. I think about how her sleeping was achieved by giving her control—she wakes up, see us in the cot, feels in control of the situation, and goes back to sleep.

Suddenly, something clicks. In those first days, when I'd see Ilaria just looking at us with her hands on hips, I'd think, *Wow, she's defiant, stubborn, and focused. Huh. She's me.*

Is this why Ilaria was so familiar to me when I met her? We are alike. Consequently, this is what I realize now—I knew how I felt when control of my body was not exactly mine during those fertility treatments. Now I realize everything that has worked with Ilaria is because we gave her the control. From sleeping in the cot, to baking each other for kisses—she was in charge and let us know when she felt it was safe to proceed.

So we make it her decision to gain control over the six-bottles-a-night situation. Ilaria had told us she was annoyed that she kept wetting herself through the night and didn't want to wear a diaper. She also didn't like getting woken up when we changed her. Ian and I explain that the milk or water in the bottles turns into pee. She seems fascinated by this simple fact. We make it a game: on the first night, we line up the six full bottles and say, "Let's see if you can drink only five bottles instead of six; let's see if you will wet a diaper."

She loves the game. Of course she wets many diapers with five bottles. So we all then propose to try to see if four bottles would do it. Of course, four bottles yields wet diapers. Ilaria loves the challenge of this game and slowly, through impressive willpower, gives up a bottle at a time so she can stop wetting that diaper. Soon she is not waking up so often to ask for a bottle. She'll still wake up, but often can be comforted with just hand-holding. For every night she gets through the night without a bottle at all, she gets a star sticker to put on a chart. Soon she no longer needs to wear a diaper to bed. Plus she's sleeping four hours at a time.

I report all to the sleep therapist, and she advises we now remove the afternoon nap. She says Ilaria's little body will get used to being awake for longer periods, as opposed to four-hour increments. She says she will fall asleep more easily at night and her body will naturally go into REM sleep, which we all need to be truly rested. But she says when we remove the nap, we should get ready for an explosion of anger again.

Actually, it goes okay. Because we make it her choice, and Ilaria decides she would rather not nap. She also likes the control of choosing what we do instead of the nap. We spend the afternoons in the park, or swimming, or playing her favorite game—kitty-cat. She still loves, like many three-year-olds, to be a little cat, purring up against us, and lapping up milk from her own saucer on the floor (which we hide when the social workers visit). Now without that nap, she does fall asleep more easily in the evening. As she sleeps, there is movement under her eyelids, which we find out means she's probably in REM. After just a few months without a nap, she is sleeping around six hours a night. During the transition, Ian and I shake our heads in awe when something works. It's all trial and error and trying again. I am amazed at how alike we all are. Ilaria is coolly laidback like Ian, and goal-oriented like me. Ian and I often remark if there was a child we wished we would have made—it's Ilaria.

Our daughter is easing into a feeling of belonging. One day, we visit our friend Ann to play with her two daughters, both a few years older than Ilaria. Watching Ann parent is a lesson in composure. She laughs, she enjoys herself, even when a toy is chucked or cupcakes are not shared. Inwardly, I call it nonjudgmental parenting. Ann never goes silent or locks eyes with me when Ilaria or her daughters do anything that might show a lack of manners or development. She just laughs. Sometimes our girls are model citizens, sometimes not. Ann's lack of attitude makes me feel at ease. This does not mean I felt judged on other playdates. All the moms were welcoming and warm. The nervousness I felt came from me. I'd enjoy anything outrageously funny Ilaria did in the privacy of our own home, but for the first few playdates, I worried she might kick their dog or push a baby under a wagon and be banned for life from further visitations.

But watching Ann parent, I realize most moms know—kids are kids. All children have moods, good days and bad days. If a kid doesn't say thank you, it doesn't reflect badly on how they're being raised; it doesn't mean the parents are trash. I see now that I can just let Ilaria be. I can just let her have fun on the playdate and, again, not everything that happens today has to be a teachable moment. So when I hear Ilaria ask Ann if she can keep the yellow princess costume she's borrowed, I don't cringe. Instead, I choose to see it as a representation that Ilaria feels so loved and accepted here—which is a wondrous emotion for a child to experience.

Okay, *fine*, yes I cringed. The Canadian in me is horrified that my daughter asked for a parting gift. But I let it go. I even try to smile with indifference. Ann tells Ilaria, yes, to please keep the dress. We leave and I don't lecture Ilaria in the car. I just talk about our fun day and inwardly marvel at Ann's calm parenting skills and demeanor. I'm really glad we went there today. (And I held my breath until we were invited back.)

Over the next while, I relax even more and we do quite a few friend playdates and have a steady stream of visitors at the house. Ilaria has become more sociable. We often go to the shops close by, but are still worried about taking her out to public places like a street fair, not just because of paparazzi. She is flagrantly fearless and still tends to disappear. She moves so fast, I call it pulling a Houdini. I have never seen anything move as fast as a toddler can disappear. I'd seen this happen with my nieces and nephews; they're just suddenly not beside you. Ilaria isn't afraid; she is really independent. When we walk around the neighborhood, she walks ahead and almost forgets I'm there following. She is attaching to us really well, she is really sociable, but she's not fearful; she just tends to be fine on her own. She's like a little capable island. We have many talks with her about not taking off. We reason with her, try to teach her about safety and responsibility. That's not working. This is another thing it takes me a while to process. Sometimes you just have to tell kids something 20,072 times before they get it. Every time I have to tell Ilaria something again, I want to call my mom to apologize for being such a jerk.

But to be candid, what we try works or doesn't and we'll try something else. Ilaria is developing at her own pace. Sometimes, she's behind her age group and sometimes she's ahead on certain issues.

For example, a colleague who has never seen Manny sends us a stuffed dog who actually looks exactly like him. Ilaria is delighted and calls him Baby Manny. He now goes everywhere with her and when she sleeps with him clutched against her chest, she looks like a Norman Rockwell painting. But a parent has never known cold dread down the spine like that moment when I realized after we got home from a playdate that the stuffed best buddy did not make it with us. The cool thing about Ilaria, however, is, sure, she has her toddler meltdowns now and then, but she is remarkably adaptable. She responds well to reason. Rather than flip out, she decided Baby Manny was on a sleepover for this one night. Ian and I notice when we explain things to her, she accepts facts and moves on. Is it because she had former living situations? We're not sure.

This applies from sleeping in her own bed—we say she'll get a better night's sleep and have more energy for playing—to why a sundae in the morning will make her hyper—we explain what sugar does and she accepts the logic of it. It's amazing to see how reasoning works with her. Sometimes. Often, it's like trying to talk politics with that naked guy at Burning Man.

The sleep therapist hears our update and now tells us this is why we were not supposed to sleep in the same bed as our daughter—it's time to move the cot.

I don't wanna.

Things have been going so well, why would I upset everything now? I tell the therapist, we're just going to continue sleeping in the cot for the next ten years, all's good. She holds my gaze. Actually, she tries to make eye contact, but my head juts sidewise from the isosceles angle of my one neck muscle that still functions. I gotta get outta that cot.

"Two inches," she tells me. She advises we get Ilaria to help push it toward the door, two inches at a time. Okay, so we make that a game too—in dissonant and inharmonious song we dance around her room as we all push the cot. We tell Ilaria she gets to choose which stuffed toy will sleep in that space on the rug left by the cot. She takes it pretty well.

Really. She thinks it's superb that her stuffed animals line up on the floor in that wider and wider space left by the cot.

Three times over the next month, we move that cot two inches at a time toward the door.

By now we've gotten her a permanent toddler bed and there isn't a lot of room to step around the extra cot. I tend to underestimate the width, step on a bouncy corner, and, arms a-flapping like I'm in an English farce, career backward until a hard wall stops my fall. I'm bruised and tired.

But tonight, Ilaria says she doesn't want to move the cot any farther because that would mean it's headed for the hallway. She knows what we're up to and flat out tells us she's afraid to sleep alone.

A few days later at breakfast, I make up a story about magic super-round sleep kitties that protect children. Then, Ilaria and I go to the toy store and just happen to find the toy I'd scoped out before I made up the story—a big super-round stuffed kitty. Ilaria squeals when she sees the kitty I'd described. We buy that toy and she decides he protects her. We slowly move the bed two more inches away so it's now halfway out the door (so now when we trip over it, we ricochet off the clothes dryer).

But here's the thing. Ilaria is sleeping. Still only about six hours a night, but now without the cot jutted up against her bed. She wakes up and calls out to check that one of us is there in the hallway. We are. But she's resting.

The social workers come over and I actually see them do a double take. Ilaria looks different. She is beaming, and it's as if a sparkly light has gone on in her eyes. Her skin is caramel colored and her hair is ethereal blond wisps around her pink cheeks. To overdo a flower analogy 'til you groan, yes, she blossomed—truly bloomed—into a happy little girl. As we all watch her running around, I want to make a joke that I'd put her in a tanning bed and highlight-foiled her hair but since the social workers have DCFS on speed-dial I just don't for once. The cot still has to move a few more inches down the hall, but all these nights sleeping on it have been worth it. Because the social workers now say, "Wow, she looks happy."

I see the glow flash from their eyes. They're so happy for this child. And us.

I wonder if these social workers know what an honorable profession they're in. I hope they look in the mirror as they brush their teeth at night and think, *Hey You, nice going today.* Do they high-five themselves at night before they sleep? I really hope so.

I am in such a selfish industry of often needy and recalcitrant people . . . while these social workers find homes for children. They make people parents. I wish the media would do more stories on them rather than the occasional rotten social worker that's out there. I've never encountered more selfless people in my life than social workers and foster parents. This experience has profoundly changed me in so many ways. As I watch the social workers smile at Ilaria, I start to think I really want to blab about these people. I'm not sure how I'm going to do it, but I'm thinking at this moment that one day I plan to talk about them.

Finally, about six weeks after we started, the cot is a little farther down the hallway, about halfway to our bedroom. Ian and I take turns sleeping on it but as noble as this sounds, we don't mind. Because . . . we like to be close to Ilaria too. Our house is set up so her bedroom is down a long hall from ours. So, as much as the damage to our necks is quite permanent, I'll say this: When she calls out . . . I like it, because I love to provide comfort to her. The reason she's blossoming is because she is loved, thoroughly and unfailingly loved by us. I wanted to be a parent and I accept this side of the deal. That time of a full night's sleep is gone. That's okay.

Now that she's sleeping better, it's time for the next step: I have to get Ilaria accepted into a preschool. This is going to be more difficult than moving any cot. •

15

The Kids Are All Right

It's been an emotional week for us. Just getting to take Ilaria to buy her first Hello Kitty lunchbox is a thing I never thought I'd get to do. So I bought two. Okay, four. I used to avert my eyes from the kids' department at stores. Now that she's not taking off anymore at stores, I cannot stop buying her little clothes. I cradle her mini-sneakers and wonder, will I ever get used to this parent thing? I hope not.

Ilaria starts today at a little preschool called the Sunshine Shack. None of the kids can pronounce the name.

There aren't many preschools we could have gotten into and we had trouble finding one with better security than Do Not Cross police tape separating it from the liquor store. In Los Angeles, the exemplary preschools have waiting lists and a kid's name is put on at birth. Since we didn't have that benefit, we couldn't get into a good preschool. We tried everywhere to no avail, and were panicked Ilaria would be missing out on vital aspects of socialization. When we'd just been advised to make a hefty donation to a sought-after preschool plus buy the owner a fancy gift (yep, really), we heard about one spot being open at the Sunshine Shack. This is the only pre-school we could get into.

On the drive over, I'd sung and clapped out a little song with Ilaria: "No hitting, no biting, no scratching, no fighting." We still try to make everything a light-hearted game. She's doing so well, but because she can still play a bit roughly, I worry about what's allow-able behavior at this age. I wonder if it's normal to worry your kid will get expelled from preschool and become a social pariah.

We walk in.

We're warmly greeted by Sara, the owner of the school and also Ilaria's teacher. She is very pregnant. Ilaria stops to touch Sara's round tummy and now asks her if she is going to keep her "baby or give it to someone who needs it." I shoot a weak smile at Sara and pretend to get fascinated by some paintbrushes.

All the parents are looking around the adorable little playroom and there's a scream—two little girls engage in a knockdown fight. Phew, it's not my kid. Ian and I raise an eyebrow at each other, re-lieved Ilaria hasn't punched anyone. Yet. It's not that we don't trust her; it's just that we're still working through some issues. When we applied to the school, we did not tell them we've only known our daughter for a few months. Yes, Ilaria did hit, *like toddlers who are not adopted*. But it's so infrequent now, we don't want to mention to her new preschool that she has a mean right hook.

To be honest, we like how tough she is. We like how she takes care of herself. About a month ago, we were at a public playground. As Ilaria was about to go down the slide, we saw a big rough boy about eight years old, climbing the wrong way up the slide. His clompy feet were about to stomp on Ilaria. We ran toward the slide while looking around for his parents. The dad was across the yard, texting. You know those parents. Smoking, oblivious, looking else-where as their brute steps on your small child. Ian and I called out and started up the slide to help Ilaria. But she didn't need us. She didn't even look for us. She just kicked the crap out of the boy. She kicked him hard. Six times. He slid back down so Ilaria could take her turn. She did. Ilaria is capable. She can handle herself. I admire her.

I tend to work with the same talented people because of our gratitude of the good fortune of our lives. Similar to hosting a party, I like my film sets to be happy places where everyone has a good time and knows they're not going to get yelled at. Many people in the entertainment industry feel the same way, but then . . . there are some real whiners. I really have seen the ultimate cliché—a dieting actress scream at an assistant because her seaweed-wrapped tofu lunch wasn't cold enough. I truly have seen a crabby crew member, wearing shorts and no shirt, rage like a baby about the hot weather as he sucked back an iced coffee. While here's my baby, with new parents in a new home, and she's doing just fine. So I had low tolerance for petty gripers before and even less so after meeting my daughter. She's just cool. And the bravest person I know.

I watch her boldly greet her new classmates with ease. We see no need to tell the preschool right away that Ilaria is adopted. It's not a secret; it's just that we want them to get to know her as her. We don't want her to be endowed with any preconceived notions.

Of course Ilaria knows she's adopted—she remembers. She'd pointed to Sara's pregnant tummy because like a lot of kids her age, she knows where babies come from. She'd asked us and we just never lie to her so we told her. Yes, we told a sanitized version of the gruesome facts; no need to freak her out. Because like all kids want to know about the night they were born, she wants to hear and rehear the story of how she met us. We tell her: a man had a seed and a lady had an egg and they put them together in the lady's stomach and Ilaria was grown. Those people loved her but couldn't take care of her, so she got to choose new parents and she chose us. She is immensely satisfied with the story. One night she asked us how we found Manny and when I explained he'd been at a pound, she sat up in bed, hugging him and squealing in her helium voice, "Manny, you're adopted too!"

So it's all quite open. But the subject of adoption is not something we bring up all the time to everyone we meet. For example, when someone at a playground tells us Ilaria looks like Ian and me, we just agree. We do look alike. (Yes, I sat her in my lap at the hairdresser's so I could get her highlights I covet.) We've decided we don't have to blurt out "She's adopted!" every time to strangers. There's no need to make it a part of her identity. It's a part of her past but not something that needs to be discussed ad nauseam. We make sure she remembers everything she wants to talk about. We make absolutely sure she knows she was not abandoned. We make sure she knows she was not a mistake. We explain when she was born there was a different plan for her. We make sure she knows the birth parents tried—they really tried—to have enough time to take care of her. To put it simply for her, we explain they were too young to be parents.

I sometimes think about the couple who placed her for adoption. I admire them and feel a kinship to them for saying, "Hey, I can't do this." I now know there's no shame in admitting you're not able to do something, to acknowledge when it's not the right path for you. I get that now. Again, it's about taking control.

One day we are in my car, Ilaria is looking out the window and quietly thinking. Then she says, "I love them." I ask who, and she says, "My first parents." My lungs collapse as I pull over, turn to her, and manage to say, "I love them too, because they made Daddy and me parents." She is very satisfied with that. Ian and I do love these two strangers who got together to make Ilaria. I hope they know they did the right thing in letting us be her parents. They were not ready. We are. I hope they don't have guilt; I just want them to live good lives, and maybe we can meet when Ilaria is an adult. We will thank them. I know all this sounds naive and a tad earnest. I'm just saying, when you go through something like this, you kind of lose your cynicism.

I wonder if I am doing everything correctly. I presume I overprotect Ilaria and am overly sensitive to the situation. Perhaps I do it because we humans say weird things.

For example, one time we were at a play center when Ilaria was still exhibiting rough behavior, again *like a lot of kids who aren't adopted* . . . she yanked a toy from another kid's hand and the kid started to cry. I rushed over to help them work it out and the other mom got right in Ilaria's face and rudely said, "You're tough." She looked up at me and snarled, "Hey, tame your kid." Imagine if we'd announced Ilaria's adoption in the press. Imagine the vitriol that might have spewed from that woman's mouth. In front of an impressionable child. My child. I might have shoved that toy into that woman's nostril.

There was another man who could've benefited from a scholarship to Couth School. We were at the swing set at a park and he'd heard from a mutual friend that Ilaria was adopted from foster care. He asked, right in front of my daughter, "Aren't you afraid she's damaged?"

Truthfully, this man's only crime was saying such a dumb thing within my daughter's hearing range. I actually don't judge the question because I myself once had these same prejudices about kids adopted from foster care. I worried they'd been through so much that they might not be affectionate or would have trouble bonding or would be violent. It's ironic that we'd all be more likely to bring a stray dog into our homes than a child. A stray dog has fangs and can eat our faces as we sleep. An innocent child just needs love. I've done adoption fundraisers and have met children from abusive backgrounds who were raised in loving foster homes—the kids are doing just fine. They're well adjusted and doing average things like you and me—graduating from college, getting married, holding down jobs. Many of them become social workers and help kids much like themselves because they were raised by kind foster parents who treated them with the respect and kindness all children deserve. Sure, many kids live in not-great conditions in foster care and group homes. But I've met inspiring families: parents who adopted kids from terrible backgrounds. The kids then became happy, well adjusted and do well. Loving kids, providing them with comfort and safety, is what it takes. Plus a lot of patience. And so many people do it. So many adults have changed kids' lives. You will rarely hear these stories portrayed in the media. But I have met them at the many adoption fundraisers I get to be a part of now. I have met adults who were willing to get into these kids' lives and let them know they're loved. They're the most valiant people I've ever met. To be honest, they're also quite average. They're not superhuman. They're just people who stepped up and said to a kid: hey, you deserve better. So no, the kids are not damaged goods. They're just kids looking for guidance and love—like all of us.

Most of us have been around kids from many varied backgrounds. We've seen that ten-year-old boy who stomps toys into pulp. We've met that six-year-old girl who eats snot. We've known that fourteen-year-old girl who entertained the football team behind the bleachers. Were any of those kids adopted? No, they're being raised by their biological parents.

Additionally, I see now in preschool all the kids are going through something, from hitting to learning disorders to anger issues, to shyness to crying fits to overassertiveness . . . because kids are kids. The lack of labeling is my favorite thing about Ilaria's preschool. It's fortuitous this is the one that had a spot for us because it is so nurturing and gentle, and they know kids go through phases. We all did. I'll just say it out loud—I was weird and so were you.

Yep, we're all kind of strange. Can any of us really be defined as normal? Nope. Therefore, I'm not afraid my daughter will display issues *because* she is adopted. She may have issues, sure. Just like any kid. Just like I did. Just like you did. Uh-huh—yes, you did. And so did I.

The fear of the unknown can be a powerful deterrent from anyone adopting. Again, I am not suggesting parenthood is for everyone, so if you feel it's not for you, I agree your life will also be wonderful without kids. But if fear is stopping you, please don't let it. I'm wondering why as a society some of us are afraid of what an adopted child might do to us, when it was the Menendez brothers who shot and killed their biological parents. Not adopted. Shot their parents while they slept. Shot them. Sleep tight, everyone.

But I am not judging anyone for the questions and concerns about adopting. I had fears too, and it's one of the many reasons I want to tell this story. When it came to adoption, I'd read the bad stories too. As I told you, I was scared. As was my family.

Before and after we adopted Ilaria, my own family was worried about saying the wrong thing. They worried that saying Ilaria looked like us might be too shallow. As if that mattered to them or us, which it didn't. They worried about giving books, gifts, and advice, as if that implied we didn't know what we were doing. They worried if they didn't ask about her past, it would seem like they didn't care, but if they did ask, it would come off as nosy. I am touched by the sweetness of these concerns from my siblings and parents and think it's better they said something, sent too much, cared so much, than did nothing at all. Our family and friends handled it all perfectly. It's as if they were all waiting, catcher's mitt out, letting me do my thing but still there for me. None of us was looking for drama, none of us wanted trouble in our lives. We were all scared of what this situation might be. Then this bright little toddler made it all okay.

At social gatherings, Ian and I meet many people who have adopted their children. We all tend to gravitate toward each other with a dreamy expression in our eyes, as if someone just whispered to only us that there's actually no fat in carbonara. There is an immediate understanding among us of our shared providence, as varied as our stories are. We convey ways to deal with dim queries, such as, "Who's her real mother?" (Uh, me.)

We disclose to each other that occasionally we find the questions invasive and don't know how to respond. The thing is, anyone who has ever played poker with me knows I am a terrible liar. If I have a good hand, I get overly chatty and players quickly fold. My friend Tracy has pointed out even if I am trying to cover up information, my neck grows. I cannot lie. It's also not my thing to make anyone feel awkward for asking. So "I dunno" is my new suave mode of vanquishing the Marauding Inquirers. Now any question from "What was her name before?" to "How much do you weigh?" gets an "I dunno," which is middle-child Canadian speak for "None of your beeswax."

By the way, the only term I disagree with some on is "adoptive mom." Why the qualifying adjective? Why not just "mom"? I've been introduced on talk shows as "*adoptive* mom Nia Vardalos." Um, once you've wiped a butt, you're a mom.

Anyway, we all confide we feel so lucky that we got to be parents against the odds. Many parents feel we were chosen for this unique path. Many divulge they always knew they were going to adopt.

I felt this way. Before we got married, I told Ian I wanted to adopt. Of course, I thought we would have biological children first; I didn't know I would have fertility problems. By the way, contrary to what a member of the Coven had once insinuated, I didn't wait too long to start a family. I'd started trying at thirty years old. I always find that the most sexist thing that can be said to a woman is, "Tsk, tsk, you wanted a career first when you shoulda had a baby." That's a bizarre thing to imply. I suggest if any woman is worried about biology fighting them later on, just freeze your eggs now. Smash through that glass ceiling at work and have your kids later. I think egg freezing should be offered as a free option to women at their college graduations.

Because biological motherhood was dodging me like the popular boys at prom, I am grateful for every minute of parenthood. Yes, even the time Ilaria had a fever and threw up all over me, from my bottom lip to my swollen ankles. And Ian, upon walking into the room with the fetched thermometer and seeing me covered in a kaleidoscope of puke, ran out of the room so he wouldn't laugh in my face. Now I don't feel that oddly unsettled feeling I felt when I was in the pursuit of motherhood. When I met Ilaria, as I've described, it all went quiet. That whirring in my head is gone, like that moment you turn off the stove fan and realize that sound had been getting on your nerves. That's what it feels like when you meet your kid.

The other thing I've noticed is that people who have not adopted congratulate me, while whispering out of the sides of their mouths about "those other celebrities who get foreign kids." I get many kudos and commendations that I adopted an American child. People turn up their well-manicured noses at "those celebrities" who have adopted from other countries and I get a "good for you" that I got "one of ours." I try to not blanch when I am applauded for what amounts to Buying American. Every child deserves a home, fer chrissakes. So if you're interested in international adoption, follow the laws of that country to adopt from an orphanage. Or sign up with a credible agency to adopt an infant from your own country. Or to adopt via foster care, talk through your fears with a social worker at your local FFA. The social workers provide professional support services for foster parents, including crisis intervention, advice and counseling, liaison with schools, and referrals for everything from respite care to family counseling. If you feel your child is out there, go find her. Or him. Or both. Go find them all.

. . .

A few weeks in, I see things are going well for Ilaria at the preschool. I found out they teach using the Reggio technique and Googled it so fast I chipped a nail. It is a unique process of kid empowerment. For example, the teachers understand Ilaria needs to talk a lot. But they don't admonish her for it. They give her time to express herself, then help her "leave room for other people's words." I'd like to bring the Reggio technique into some studio script meetings.

I feel so lucky to have met Sara, the school owner and Ilaria's teacher. Over the first weeks I see she has endless patience and sunny humor with all the kids. But this afternoon when I get to the school, she asks me about something I feel is disquieting her. Sara seems to be searching for words to describe how Ilaria got all the kids to gather all the dolls, then play a game where they put babies into an oven, bake them, and eat them.

I trip over my words, I turn beet red. I cannot explain fast enough that it's a game we made up and that baking and eating each other was a way to kiss her. It doesn't come out right. I almost pass out as I realize it's Yom Kippur.

Sara placates me . . . the explanation seems all right with her. She just wanted me to know.

I give Sara a pallid grin and hastily head to the playground. I hang out a lot to observe the language they're using so we can mirror it at home. Today, one of the kids throws sand in Ilaria's eyes and she's upset. The teacher calls the other girl over and asks her merely to look at Ilaria. The other girl will not do it. The teacher and Ilaria wait. Finally, the girl looks up. She sees Ilaria's eyes are red from the sand and her face is tear-stained. I see the empathy immediately flush across the other little girl's face. She blurts out that she's sorry. Ilaria accepts the apology. The teacher now asks the other little girl if she wants to check if Ilaria's all right. The other little girl wipes tears from Ilaria's face and says, "Does it hurt?," and Ilaria nods that it does, and then adds that it's better. The teacher asks them to hug only when they're ready. They hesitate. They wait. Then they do hug. They mean it. And it's over.

It's an astonishing thing to witness. There wasn't recrimination in the teacher's voice. It wasn't punitive. It was simply about realizing you'd hurt a friend and taking responsibility. I wondered if maybe there'd be fewer lawsuits in my industry if people just had to face each other and say, "Hey, you stole my TV show idea." Maybe they'd get back, "Yeah, sorry, here's some money." Maybe my industry would be less litigious if we'd all hug it out, get a snack, and take a nap together. Oh, wait, that actually is Hollywood.

One thing I discover during all the time I spend at preschool is how hard teachers work at herding all those kitty-cats. Their job demands an inordinate amount of serene fortitude. Another thing I realize is I am sticky all the time. In fact, that's how I would describe motherhood. It's dirtier than I thought. When I decided to write this book, I vowed I would stay away from the typical full-diaper stories. So that's not where I'm heading here. But honestly, I never imagined my bra would be filled with so many crumbs. I never thought I would find a Tootsie Pop stick stuck to my arm hair as I walked into a studio meeting. There are other adjustments. The most appalling transgression being my TiVo didn't record *Mad Men* because it was filled with ten million episodes of *Willa's Wild Life*.

I can see what an influence the preschool is having because Ilaria is flourishing. She is calmer, more gentle. The crunchy-granola Sunshine Shack's groovy hippie ways are helping. One evening, I am combing Ilaria's hair and when a knot snags and pulls, she turns to me and somberly says, "Please respect my body."

We use the Sunshine Shack expression at home—*safe hands*. As her vocabulary increases, Ilaria uses her words, not her hands to express herself. She is gentle and loving with the other kids, as are they. To be honest, I thought preschool was day care, but now I think of it as college prep. The kids are learning the two most important social skills I wish some adults had: politeness and chewing with their mouths closed. The Reggio technique is being used further to encourage Ilaria to be the leader she is and also help her understand to be open to a game someone else suggests. It's allowing her to be the individual she is by nurturing her natural abilities and strengthening other facets to help her develop further. I love this environment and enjoy watching the kids interact. This morning, I read a book to Ilaria's class and afterward I stay for a bit to watch the kids play. I should leave. I have so many pending work deadlines— commitments I made before I became a mother—but I write at night so I can be here during the day to watch them all play-act animal rescue scenarios and zoom around on little tricycles. Their energy and innocence is acutely and tenderly poignant.

Sara joins me at the edge of the sandbox and we chat for a bit. She tells me she feels simpatico, an affinity to Ilaria. She is truly amused by Ilaria's huge, funny personality and her stories about her home life and how she starts morning circle time by imitating Manny barking at squirrels. I can see Sara truly gets her.

So, right here, I decide to tell Sara our story. I confide that we're in the process of adopting Ilaria and it's been a tumultuous and chaotic five months and how I feel such relief that Ilaria is adjusting to the transition with us. Sara gives me a sage look as if she now understands something. She pauses . . . then softly tells me she herself is adopted.

I don't know what to say. There have been so many coincidences in this entire experience, I am no longer surprised at anything. I just feel comforted by it. We both turn and look back at Ilaria running across the play yard, the sunlight glancing off her hair like a million smiles.

16

Firsts

Here's the thing about parenting: no one tells you how tired you'll feel all the time. No one tells you you'll forget to brush your hair and even your teeth. And no one tells you how much fun it is. Actually, they do tell you all these things, but you don't listen because no one likes a lecture.

When we'd first talked about adopting a child older than an infant, some friends, family, and even we were concerned we'd miss out on "firsts." But there are still so many firsts. Even though Ilaria wasn't an infant when we met, we get to do things like potty train (no details, you're welcome), have that first dentist visit, and the best thing of all—we get to introduce her to Santa Claus. Now, as I've said, we don't lie to her. But Santa is very very real, so be quiet, Scrooge. She comprehends the concept of Santa right away. Within days, someone in our neighborhood screeches car tires and runs a stop sign. Ilaria's body goes indignantly rigid as she points a finger and screams, "You're on the Naughty List!!" On Christmas Eve, I'm in bed with her talking about the reindeer and just as I say they might be landing on our roof at any moment, Ian goes under her window and jangles a set of jingle bells. Ilaria squeals, "They're here!!!" and dives under the covers.

After she's asleep, Ian and I get to do the other fun things: eat the cookies left for Santa and leave a boot footprint in the fireplace ashes. Honestly, I am not sure who enjoys all this more—Ilaria or us. I now know Kathy Greenwood and my siblings and friends must have been holding back on all the cute kid stories all these years. Daily, I try to not bore everyone, from the magazine stand guy to a studio executive, with the cute things my kid says. My own mom dutifully listens when I call to describe everything from the six peas Ilaria ate to her sighing to Ian one morning in the car, "Oh Daddy, I just want to find a good guy." My mom listens endlessly. That's actually one of the firsts you get to do—testing your own mom's patience with the cute kid tales.

Here are more firsts we get to do. . . .

Birthday parties: It doesn't matter what age you start at, planning kid birthday parties is fun. However, Ian and I share a dislike of all torture devices in the trampoline family after years of seeing some kid roll out of the bouncy house holding her friend's front tooth. But good luck talking your own kid out of a bouncy house. We've so far managed but only by trading a princess. For a fee an actor playing a Disney character will show up at your kid's party and entertain with games and magic. Added bonus: the revealing Ariel costume is an inch away from coming with its own stripper pole—but it's worth it to not have that inflated bouncy house in my yard. Plus it's fun to watch the dads pretend to not look at her bedazzled navel.

Books: From the first week we meet Ilaria, we get to introduce her to books and we read a story every night. She loves the pictures, loves the stories, and loves to sit in our laps to turn the pages. We get misty-eyed re-reading all our old favorites like *Green Eggs and Ham* and *Everybody Poops*. We also experience an extraordinary moment during a barbecue with Core when Ilaria is three and a half years old. At her bedtime, in her bossy way Ilaria gathers everyone into her room to "read" to them. The book she chooses is *Are You My Mother?* It's sweet to see various Core adults squatting all around her room among the stuffed animals and princess tiaras. Although she can't read yet, Ilaria has memorized the book. As she flips through each page to tell us all the story, she asks, "Are you my mother?" It comes out as, "You ma mudder?" and Ian and I look around the room at our friends . . . everyone's soft and kind eyes are saying, "Yes."

Ice cream: Very early in our relationship, I get to see my daughter's face when she discovers ice cream. We're at the mall and I hand her a strawberry ice cream cone. I can see from her expression she doesn't know what it is. I wait. She looks it over, sniffs it, then licks the creamy perfection that is ice cream. The delight on her face is pretty cool. She loves it.

So now I have a secret weapon—ice cream. Since this is in that time period when she would wake up from her stroller nap and kick me in the face, I hatch a plan. Now after she's asleep, I quickly run that stroller home. When I see her begin to wake up, I zip to the freezer, rip the wrapper off a Fudgsicle, and throw it into the stroller like raw meat to a lion. As she licks it, I see her look me over and decide to not drop-kick me. Progress.

Haircut: One day as she naps, I do the quintessential new mom mistake: I trim her hair. With her head hanging at that Sleeping Pope angle it just comes out catastrophically wrong. When she wakes up and moves her head, I see I've given her a bona fide Monster Truck Rally mullet. As she sits up and stretches, I see actually the bangs hang not unlike Hitler's. I try to fix them. The bangs get shorter and more crooked and are now in a style that would best be described as Trendy Meth Addict. Ian comes home, takes one look, and pries the scissors from my hand.

Professional haircut: I take her to a place that caters to kids. Balloons hang from the ceiling and the kids sit in giant chairs that look like airplanes. The lady trims and fixes Ilaria's haircut, sprinkles sparkles into it, and affixes a multicolored glittery barrette. My daughter now looks like a demure little girl. We walk out, and, feeling victorious, I dig for my camera to record this mommy-daughter moment; but Ilaria yanks out the barrette and chucks it across the street.

Embarrass your mom: One day we are in an elevator at the medical building, and it fills with people in business attire. I look down, lock eyes with Ilaria, we nod as in, *yeah, this would be a good time for our new trick.* She takes my forearm and blows the biggest fart sound ever heard. The people in the elevator gasp. Ilaria and I laugh our heads off. As people give me a "grow up" look, it occurs to me that someone might recognize me and this story might be retold in a less-than-flattering manner. I guess I should think of these things before I teach my daughter that a loud flatulent sound in a close space is funny. But it just is. Then, she keeps doing it, over and over. I move my arm away and tell her to stop now. Nuh-uh, it's funny and she knows it. The elevator stops at many floors, new people get on. While I look at the ceiling, Ilaria grips my calf, blows farts, and waves her hand past her nose, wailing, "Mom, did you have a burrito?"

Christmas gifts: After months of appealing to our friends and family to stop spoiling our child, Ian and I completely lose our minds at Toys "R" Us over a toddler-size pink Barbie convertible. Upon discovering this pink jewel under the tree on Christmas morning, Ilaria immediately gets in, turns it on like she's sixteen with a learner's permit, and drives it straight into the living room wall.

Easter: On our first Easter together, I'm explaining my somewhat limited knowledge of the Easter Bunny to Ilaria. Greek kids don't receive a basket full of chocolate ears to bite off. Our Easter celebration consists of fasting for a week while attending nightly church services after school, then feasting on roast lamb on Sunday at one A.M. after another long church service. Sunday afternoon is another church service in another itchy dress, then a day of getting kissed by itchy-cheeked relatives only broken up with the excitement of clacking the shells of dyed-red eggs against your cousins' to see whose is strongest. Not exactly the same as waking up to a giant basket of sugar. Determined to give our kid the North American Easter experience, Ian and I organize a hunt on our front lawn. When I try to explain to Ilaria there is chocolate out there, she looks skeptical. I ecstatically bleat that the Easter Bunny hides kids' favorite thing: chocolate eggs! But she's not buying it. She gives me a wily wink and says, "So for you he hides new purses?"

Halloween: As I've described, like a lot of kids, Ilaria likes being a cat. Therefore, all three of us are cats on our first Halloween. We have matching fuzzy ears and tails Ilaria and I made out of itchy boaish material we bought at the fabric store. Ian's scalp sweats under the man-made fiber ears, and we affix the fluffy tail to his jeans. He's not quite feline—he looks more like Head Bear of the Gay Pride parade. We're sitting out front of our house with always-game Core dressed in outlandish costumes, handing out candy. Manny menacingly paces behind the gate, barking at werewolves. Ilaria isn't really into trick or treating. She'd rather stay out front of our home with all the adults. As each person goes by, Ilaria pours candy into their baskets, then lustily shouts, "Thank you for coming!" as if she's hosting Halloween.

Going out: Anna has been our sweet housekeeper and friend for ten years. She is a mother and grandmother . . . of sons and grandsons. She absolutely adores Ilaria, and the feeling is mutual. So naturally Anna becomes our babysitter. Anna urges Ian and me to go out for dinner for our anniversary. We're hesitant to leave Ilaria, but we read her a book, tuck her in, and after she falls asleep, we get in the car and try to decide where to go for dinner. I mention that Ilaria needs sneakers . . . so we detour to our local mall first. We walk the aisles of the kids' store, filling our cart with teeny T-shirts and socks. Ian and I never get to dinner, but we do manage to stay out for ninety minutes.

First play: Ian is traveling so I look up weekend things to do and find out there's a new kids' play in a local theater. I call up to reserve tickets and the man assures me it's recommended for preschoolers. Ilaria and I get there—it's a nice theater and the smell of the musty upholstery is very familiar and comforting to me. I'm thrilled to be able to share this experience with my three-year-old daughter for the first time. As the play progresses she looks around at the heavy curtains and rows of seats, then back to the stage, and giggles at the "dog." A guy in a costume is doing a very good job of scampering—wait . . . something's wrong. Ilaria is agitated, and I am not sure if what I think is happening is actually happening . . . oh yes, yes it is—in this story the dog dies. Dies. In a kids' play. Ilaria flips out. I comfort her that it's just make-believe but she keeps saying, "Why did the dog die?," and I'm pretty sure I could choke the person who decided it's okay to kill a dog in a kids' play. It ends soon after and we wait in the lobby for the actors to change their clothes and come out. I walk straight up to the guy playing the dog and, not unthreateningly, tell him under my breath he must show my daughter he played the dog and he is actually alive. I firmly request he get down on all fours. He does. It works. Ilaria believes him and is relieved he's okay. I think the actor is afraid of me because he lets her pet him for about twenty minutes.

Concert: Ilaria, Ian, and I are dancing our butts off surrounded by other parents and preschoolers packed into chic Club Nokia on this Saturday afternoon as the Imagination Movers rock the house. They're a group of nice guys who teach kids life lessons through creativity and song. And they're hot.

Movie: I'm with Ilaria at a matinee of our first-ever movie. We're sitting here waiting to see *The Pink Panther* and I'm really excited to bring her to a movie. As the lights are going down and the previews play, she is covering her ears, saying how loud the sound is. It dawns on me—surround sound is deafening to a child. Plus it's very dark in here. She doesn't like it and I try to calm her. Beside us the cranky octogenarian who smells like varnish, after spending the last ten minutes loudly crinkling open a bag of from-home popcorn until I wanted to tear it open and feed it to her, complains about my "crying kid." Now first off, Ilaria isn't crying. But second—I've been in a movie theater and been annoyed by kids whining to their parents that they didn't want to be there. Clearly, Ilaria doesn't want to be here. My big clue is she keeps saying, "I don't want to be here." So what am I doing here? I gently pick her up and we walk out. And the look of relief on her face in the lobby is so worth it. We smile at each other and I tell myself again and again—good things come when I listen. Now I hear "Miss?" and a nice manager is leading us to the side. He has seen what happened and is now refunding our tickets. And Ilaria's eyes record the entire event. I can see the lesson in her expression—"If I speak up, I will be heard." It's a good message for both of us. I spend the money on concession candy and we go home.

Ladies' day: I take Ilaria to our local salon for her first manicure and pedicure. Across from me, I can see her modeling the stance and behavior of the other ladies in the chairs. She is self-assured and chatty as usual. The manicurist leans in to begin on her hands and asks, "So this is your first manicure?" Ilaria shakes her head side to side and assures the woman, "I give myself a manicure every day. Do you know how? I pick it!"

Lost tooth: I get a call from the preschool. When I see that number come up on my cell phone, my hair goes gray and I get a chin zit. What, what could it be?? I answer and Sara tells me Ilaria has lost her first baby tooth. My throat aches as I race for my car. It had been loose for a week. I'd been lucky because I had seen Ilaria's face the moment she'd discovered it loose. She'd bitten into a cob of corn and sheer delight crossed her face. I was overjoyed that she excitedly looked right at me as she gripped her bottom tooth. She wanted to share this moment. This was huge news at our house. Everyone in Core cheered her on as she went right to work on that loose tooth wiggling and jiggling it for days. This morning, we could see it hung on a promise but she didn't want to yank it out or let Ian or I do it.

Now it's out. My mind is a jumble of thoughts as I get to the pre-school and as I run up, Ilaria bolts out of class. Right before she throws herself against me, I see the look on her face: triumph. She is so proud of herself because she's not a baby anymore. And that's why I can't stop crying.

17

Adoption Day

Now, though it's a while before that first lost tooth, I have another reason I'm a blubbering fool. The day is finally here. It's been over six months and as of today, Ilaria's adoption is going to be legal. It won't change anything in our family dynamic. But it means a lot.

I go into Ilaria's room. She's still sleeping and as I watch her from the door, I think about how loved she is, completely embraced by a family who has really let her know how welcome she is.

The day my dad met her, he was tossing a beach ball to her and when she ran on her sturdy little legs to get it from behind the couch, my dad immediately crossed himself to thank God for her health. I would say that pretty much encompasses how my dad feels about the events in his children's lives. I saw him cross himself before he walked my older sister, Nancy, down the aisle, and when my younger sister, Marianne, got her doctorate. I saw him cross himself at my brother Nick's daughter's baptism. And I saw him cross himself as the end credits ran at the premiere of *My Big Fat Greek Wedding*. He was not praying for it to be a success; he was thanking God for giving me the experience. My dad grew up in a poor village in Greece and really did come to North America with eight dollars in his pocket. His success as a businessman and family man probably exceeds his dreams. He and my mom took it completely in stride when they were with me on *Oprah*. I chose this profession, yet I thrust my parents into the spotlight and they handled it with ease. Also, my dad has a great sense of humor in that he knew everyone would think he was the "Gus" in the movie. Maybe because his name is Gus. He was baptized as Constantine but, like a lot of Greeks, acquired the nickname Gus. But the real Gus is not anti-education or anti-women's rights, nor does he have Greek statues on the front lawn. But, yes, he used Windex as a cure-all for everything. I know for years he and my mom worried about me going through life without a child. He'd suggested I try to adopt from Greece and was comforted when I was on the waiting list. When he heard we wanted to adopt from foster care, he was worried. As I've explained, I don't blame him—those negative stories seem to be the only ones we all know. But when he met Ilaria, everything he worried about melted away. He kisses her and thanks God for her every day.

My older sister, Nancy, met Ilaria when she came to New York while I was there making a movie. She later told me that one evening she and my mom were bathing Ilaria and were so in awe of this perfect girl with the caramel skin that they cried into the tub. I love the image of two weeping Greeks salting that bathwater as if they're making a good brine for feta cheese. My sister is the mother of three teenagers so is the definition of irony and patience. I saw how tender and sweet she was with Ilaria in those first days when she held her. I know she was remembering her own children being that age. Nancy kept stroking Ilaria's soft cheeks and long fingers, looking at me and smiling. I saw her thoughts in her eyes. My sister is so happy I now have this person to love, the way she loves her three children.

My younger sister, Marianne, a university professor, timed a visit with her two young kids while I made a film. Because we all have the gift of our mom's multitasking, Marianne spent the time writing her syllabus while cooking and watching over the kids as they played "tigers in a tree house." Every night, when I'd get back she'd stop marking her students' papers so she could gleefully report all the earnestly sincere, innocent things the kids said and did: "The three of them are getting married, living on a wild island, and protecting tigers. Oh, by the way, your daughter might be telling you tomorrow about walking into her grandparents' bathroom and seeing 'Pappou in his panties.'"

My brother, Nick, had emailed a video for my birthday. Ilaria's hands gripped the computer screen with delight and she replayed the video over and over—because her uncle Nick burped the song "Happy Birthday." So, when she met Nick, she already knew he was like her dad, a taller kid with a hairy chest. As Nick held her in his arms, he burped Ilaria's name, which swiftly made him favorite uncle. Before Ilaria came into our lives, Nick and I had had two serious discussions where he urged me to investigate every adoption angle and not let nagging fears get at me. Those conversations felt like a vague sepia-toned memory belonging to someone else when I saw my daughter in Nick's arms. My daughter.

My sib-in-laws—Dimos, Anas, and Lexy—upon meeting Ilaria, squished her with the kisses she now allows. Ian's parents and family, our aunts, uncles, and cousins, showered her with presents and affection.

I am particularly touched by the sweetness my nieces and nephews displayed at meeting their new cousin. Adoption is a new thing in our family, but kids are naturally kind. The teenaged cousins swooped her into their arms, holding her high and hugging her hard. The younger ones were at once curious and tender with her.

Since Ilaria has a cousin with the exact same birthday and they're a lot alike, they call each other Twin Cousin. We all fit in together so well. One day when the family was visiting, Ilaria ran by us all energetically yelling to her cousins to "Waiiiiiiiiiit up!" and I marveled to my family, "She's the daughter I always wanted." My sister Marianne wryly said, "With the highlights you always wanted."

Ilaria has come a long way in six months. We all have. I can't believe the finalization day is finally here. Still, I am apprehensive, I won't deny it. Even though I'm not a nail-biter by nature, my fretting concern of a birth family member contesting the adoption remains unabated. I just want today to go smoothly. I am looking forward to this process being over.

Has it been only six months? I can't remember what my day was like before I was a mom. I can't remember the years of the powerlessness of trying to be a parent. My girl has plugged the black hole in my psyche with blobby and chewed pink bubble gum.

Ilaria wakes up and I gently remind her: today is a very big day for us. We're going to court to finalize her adoption. We've made it very clear that even though we will sign official papers today, she was our daughter the minute we met her. I explain this is just so the judge can see her and how well she's doing. She's excited.

Later, I hear Manny downstairs running around showing off for Core life-member Brian, video-ing this day for us. I can hear Brian, Ian, and Ilaria laughing. I'm in my closet.

I change my clothes three times. I want to look respectable. I don't want the judge to deem Ian and me foolish actors (I mean, we are but . . .) who will be negligent when levied with parental obligations. Also, I want to wear flats in case I have to run away with Ilaria.

Downstairs, I try to be buoyant for Brian's camera, but inside I'm delivering a monologue to myself: *Stay calm, nothing is going to hap-*

pen, she is legally emancipated, the parental rights were terminated, nothing can go wrong, she is my daughter, she is my daughter . . .

As we walk outside, I'm so preoccupied I barely notice the weather or time. Ilaria happily sits in the backseat and Ian drives, with Brian following in his own car. I smooth my gray dress, take in that Ian is wearing a respectable suit, and try to stay positive. I look back at my daughter in her white dress and sparkly, glittery red shoes (yes, the colors of the Canadian flag)—she still seems excited about the day.

The courthouse for juvenile cases can be an ominous place. This is where foster kids see their birth parents show their clean drug test results to a judge. This is where events reach a point where birth parents' rights are terminated and foster parents get to adopt the child. And this is where we get to finalize Ilaria's adoption. As we walk into the courthouse we're met by the social workers and our adoption attorney. I watch their faces as they see Ilaria, so bright and animated— they're so pleased. Not with themselves. For us. Once again, it is remarkable to witness such selflessness. It puts me at ease to be in the company of true kindness. Everyone is jubilant and that joy rubs off on me.

Ian and I take Ilaria's hands, and we enter the courthouse. She happily presses all the buttons in the elevator. But when we enter the courtroom, she gets nervous. Maybe she remembers courtrooms as sad places. I can see she thinks something bad will happen.

All of a sudden the hearing begins, and the judge is speaking: he proclaims we're on the record and is asking the attorney to announce the case.

Our adoption attorney is responding and saying he represents us. He states our names and the case.

Now the clerk asks Ian and me to raise our right hands and we're sworn in. The judge asks a question . . . and Ilaria starts crying.

I actually dare to interrupt the judge. In this moment, I don't care if he thinks I'm an obnoxious actor, and I don't even look to see if birth family members have improbably shown up. I care only about my daughter's welfare. I stop the proceedings and Ian and I carry her away from everyone. We sit in the back of the courtroom and just talk to her and soothe her fears, telling her nothing bad will happen. We explain today is a good day. She tries to understand. She nods bravely. I am impressed and touched, once again, by how she never wimps out. She rises to the occasion like a child much older than her years.

When she's feeling better, we all return to the front of the room to try again. But I see it's not a tense atmosphere. They're all patiently waiting for us. They all want Ilaria to feel comfortable. This is infinitely consoling for us all.

The courtroom clerk gives Ilaria a choice of teddy bears. She chooses a bright pink one, whom she quickly names Addie the Adoption Bear.

The clerk gives the attorney the Adoption Agreement form and then, as a formality, the judge asks the attorney to explain the Adoption Agreement to us. Ian and I are taking turns holding Ilaria, trying to concentrate on the legalese.

But this, we understand: the attorney now asks us to swear to the oath questions. He asks questions such as, "Do you understand that by signing the Adoption Agreement, you agree to treat Ilaria as your own lawful child and provide for her health, welfare, and educational needs?"

Ian and I answer "yes."

"Do you understand that by adopting Ilaria, you agree that she shall enjoy all the rights of a natural child of your own issue including the right of inheritance?"

Ian and I answer "yes."

"Understanding these responsibilities, do you wish to adopt Ilaria?"

Ian and I have waited a long time for this question. We quietly answer "yes."

We solemnly swear that Ilaria is our daughter. She watches Ian and me now sign the documents that will make it legal. As if we need any of this. We became a family when we saw each other, but soon nothing can change this. Soon. I waited through so many "soons," and now I am holding my breath waiting for this next step.

Our attorney then turns to the judge and says, "Your Honor, I am submitting the Adoption Agreement to the court."

The attorney hands everything to the clerk, who gives it all to the judge to look over.

We wait. Ian and I hold Ilaria's warm little body and whisper in her ear. We reassure her and we all wait as the judge reads over our file to make sure everything is in order.

Then . . . the judge signs the Adoption Order and announces our daughter's full name is Ilaria Isadora Vardalos Gomez.

Everyone claps, and I feel like I'm levitating.

Ian and I hug and kiss Ilaria. This is it. It's legal now.

The attorney gives us the certified copies of the Adoption Order and the Certificate of Family Membership. We all thank the judge, take pictures, and leave the courtroom.

Then we go completely nuts in the hallway. We run outside the courthouse and dance and jump around with Ilaria, singing "Adoption Day, Adoption Day!" We put Ilaria on the ground to join in the dance, and she jumps up and down. I laugh and laugh. We're done.

We go home and celebrate with Core and an Elmo cake.

At the end of the night as I tuck her in, I breathe a sigh of relief.

Because it all went smoothly. The system worked. We'd been matched, we had six great visits with the social workers, the cot is far down the hall, and Ilaria is sleeping about nine hours a night in her own bed.

Most important, of course no one showed up to contest the adoption. All my neuroses were for nothing. Even a few months beforehand when Ilaria choked on the hard candy—that turned out okay. I tell myself to relax. I tell myself I am Ilaria's mom. She is my daughter. Nothing bad will happen.

However, a short time later, something does happen.

Luckily, it doesn't happen to Ilaria. But it happens to me.

18

That Stupid Class

I'm driving home in the evening. Ian's filming is going late. In the days since the adoption was finalized, I feel light and carefree and this is the first night I left Ilaria through bedtime with Anna.

I'd turned in a script before the deadline to the studio, and to celebrate I'd gone to the mall with Tracy and Rose, had dinner, and did some shopping. I feel decadent. It has been quite a while since I've had time with the girls, and it was a big step for me to not be home for bedtime.

Now, it's dark as I pull into my driveway. I get out of the car and check the street like I always do; I have always been careful to the point of paranoia. This might be because my grandmother Evelyn warned me during my puberty that most men are perverts. So I've always been very cautious, especially at night.

I see the street is empty.

I hear something. It's the sound of sneakers running on pavement. And after years and years and years of checking this shadow and that creak and that weird noise and it being nothing . . . this time it is something.

A man is crouching behind my fenced hedge. There really is a stranger on the sidewalk in front of my house. I can see the top of his hooded sweatshirt just above the bushes.

My front yard is dark. The street is dark. There is no one out here but him and me.

Years before, Kathy Najimy had convinced me to join her and a few friends in a self-defense class. I hated the class. I found the scenarios terrifying. I was petrified of the instructor in the attack suit. I didn't want to be at that stupid class. But in these next few minutes, I will use everything I learned.

The instructor had told us in the event of an attack, to not freeze up and to make as much noise as possible.

So I yell, "Hey, what are you doing!"

He quickly stands. He is big. He jumps over the hedge toward me. He is coming right at me. And I punch him in the face. I'm screaming as loud as I can. He pushes me hard and gets me on the ground, and I know the terrifying reality that now no one can see me. The hedge is high and my yard is very dark. No one can see me on the grass.

He is on top of me but isn't saying anything. He is so heavy and my chest feels crushed. And I fight. I kick and scream and somehow work my right leg up under his chin and I kick him off me. I keep screaming for help.

I can hear my dog going crazy, barking inside my house. I want Manny to help me. I'm screaming for someone to help me. I try to get up and he pushes me down and gets on me again. I am fighting so hard. I kick him off me again. Now he pulls at a tote and the bags of new clothes.

I scream, "Take it!" and he grabs these things and jumps over the hedge toward the street. I stand up and am still screaming.

Now Anna opens the front door and Manny tears out and tries to jump over the hedge and get him. The man runs to a waiting car and takes off. We can't see the license plate. I'm still screaming as Anna pulls me inside the house.

I'm so angry. I feel dirty and sick and furious. My neighbor calls to tell me she heard me and her husband has called 911.

I run upstairs to check on Ilaria. She's asleep and safe. I grip the wall and try to not throw up.

The police come within a few minutes. The policeman walks around my front yard while his female partner asks me questions in my front hallway. I give a detailed description and I am staring at the floor when I hear her tell me I did everything right. It's small consolation, but a lifetime of checking over my shoulder paid off because I was facing him when he jumped.

The police tell me he probably followed me home from the mall. I realize that's exactly what happened. There isn't a lot of crime in my neighborhood. But being followed home from a mall is common everywhere. I had heedlessly walked to my car in a mall parking lot while carrying a bunch of purchases and a designer tote. I was followed home and robbed. I can see Anna feels awful as she repeatedly tells me she could not hear me screaming because Manny was barking so loud. She didn't know what was happening. Manny barks at squirrels, passersby, other dogs. Anna says she only opened the front door because he was throwing himself against it.

Manny. I bury my face in his fur.

I run upstairs again to be with Ilaria. I sit on her bed now and try to calm myself . . . I can't stop looking at her eyelashes, so soft against her cheeks.

When Ian comes home, I tell him and I feel sorry for him. I know how powerless he feels. I'm sad for him and sick from the adrenaline of being knocked around.

Now it's four A.M. and I'm lying in bed, shaking. A physical attack is horrifying to replay in hindsight. My hands are bruised. My throat aches. My neck hurts, and my muscles are stiff from the sheer force of being attacked by a man. The synapses misfire through my body, seemingly unable to sort out that I have been involved in such a visceral exchange with another human being. I am thinking of the dark-hearted monster who would do this to a woman, and I wonder if he even has given me a second thought.

The next day, I'm weak with fear. The doorbell rings and my shoulders go up. I can't have anyone standing behind me without feeling nauseated. I'm weeping uncontrollably and of course hiding it from Ilaria. We've never kept things from her, but this is far too adult. So I have to tell her I don't feel well. It's true. But she knows something is wrong because children see through artifice.

Ian calls a friend who does landscape design, and together they completely change our front yard—within a few days the hedge is gone; there is only a see-through iron fence now. There are enough front yard lights to land a helicopter. It's a safe place.

But I don't feel safe at all.

In the next few weeks, whenever Ian has night scenes to film, many members of Core just come over. The house is full with Tracy, Rose, Suzy, John, Brian, Renee, and Jackie hanging out night after night with me. I'm afraid to be alone.

They're all downstairs now, watching TV, eating dinner, waiting for me to join them. I am in Ilaria's room, lying beside her as she falls asleep. And I am shaking in the dark. I can't drive at night. I can't be alone. This is not getting better.

Both Kathy Greenwood and Kathy Najimy tell me I have to talk to a professional, and Rose sends me links for victim-of-a-crime counseling. Suzy, Tracy, everyone urges me to do it. They're right. I need help, so through my medical doctor I find a psychiatrist.

This is where it just gets ludicrous, which is probably why I get better. Yes, I'll tell you now, despite this woman's idiocy, I really do restore my sense of well-being.

For the first session, I walk into a nondescript room that could be anything from a dentist's lobby to a quilters' clubhouse. I observe she's a female therapist in her forties and seems to take herself ultra-seriously. She purses her lips and peers at me over her collegial glasses. I ponder if she's cognizant she looks like an animated version of a psychiatrist. I mean, does anyone really peer over spectacles unless they're trying to appear authoritative? So this immediately strikes me as faux and not an honest greeting at all.

She is not smiling or funny. That's my next clue that this is not a good idea. I tend to gravitate more toward people who have a sense of satire. This woman writes notes on me as I sit down . . . and I wonder if I'm perched normally or what? A few moments go by and I wonder if I'm supposed to speak, or . . . ? Now she asks me what I'm thinking. I want to ask if she's ever treated Tony Soprano. But I don't.

The atmosphere is so staid and grim that I only want to make a joke. But I know that won't help me get better, so I follow her lead.

She asks me to tell her every detail about why I'm here. I talk my way through the story, and when I get to the part about him pushing me to the ground, she interrupts and says, "What did you think?" And I said, "Uh, that I couldn't move." And she says "And?" And I reply, "And that scared me."

She asks what is the thing that scared me the most. I take a minute, then reveal my deepest darkest scariest heart-shattering fear. In that moment, all I'd thought was that if I died, Ilaria would not have a mother.

The therapist nods as if I just said, "I enjoy croutons," and says, "Let's explore that."

I say I don't want to.

She urges me to really look at this terrible fear.

So even though I don't like this path we're on, I decide to trust since I don't know the arena of therapy. I tell her again my fear was that I would be killed on the front lawn and Ilaria would not have a mother. And the therapist makes me describe this. Uh-huh. Really, she does. She wants me to describe the manner in which I might be murdered. When I say I truly don't want to, she sighs and sits back with that disapproving pursed mouth.

Hoping it will help . . . I do it. And it is really frightening to talk about. I describe how he would have killed me. If that's not cringe-worthy enough, oh, there's more. Now she makes me tell her what my funeral looks like and I do that even though it's so morose, so elegiacal I can't stand it. It's the worst thing I have ever envisioned and described. The therapist is nodding as if I'm reciting my musical theater credits and then asks, "Can you see Ilaria at your funeral? Is she all right?" I say, "No, I see her very sad—"

Abruptly, she concludes the session. Just like that—time's up, so she says she'll see me in a few days.

I'm stunned. Slowly, I pick up my purse and leave the room. My skin hurts.

I drive home cursing in my car. What the hell was that? It didn't help at all. In fact, I'm shaking again. Now I'm even more scared. In the next few days I tell a few friends who've been in therapy about this method, and their outrage fuels my own exasperation. They say this is not healthy. I mean, I knew instinctively at the time it was verging on cuckoo, but it feels validating to hear this from friends who have had good therapy experiences.

I go to the next appointment and do something that's not the norm for me: I confront the therapist. I gingerly yet firmly tell her I found her method to be perhaps irresponsible and not a formula or path I can see ever working. She pauses and says . . . are you ready, oh gentle reader? She says, "Yes, I had heard about this new method and I was trying it—"

I stammer, "What are you telling me? You didn't know what you were doing?"

She admits that my assessment is correct.

Then she quickly adds, "There is a new drug you can take that may help you forget the incident. There are many methods. Can you trust me to guide you?"

I say "Nope" and walk out.

Cue the end credits temple-pounding music of a gritty tough-girl-detective show as I strut down that hall.

But I'm not feeling any stronger, so I keep looking for help.

Over the next few months, I try a few more therapists. I tell the story over and over, but this is just not working for me.

One therapist asks, "Why do you think he picked you to attack?," and I deadpan, "Maybe he was a film critic."

She tells me I should be angrier, that I should rage that I was "victimized." Look, maybe I felt that in the moment, but afterward and now I feel I was just "randomized." I was in the wrong mall parking lot at the wrong time with a lot of stuff that would attract a thief. I think this is what is my problem with these therapy sessions. It's the same thing with the fertility situation or whatever happens or doesn't in my career. I've just never looked at myself in a poor-me way. Sure, I'm bummed when dismal events occur, but I'd rather just move on than sink into the quicksand of a why-me scenario. I've gotten to do so many fun things in my life from finding my daughter to chatting with Barbra Streisand and Bette Midler to singing in a Broadway charity benefit with people like Audra McDonald and Paul McCartney. I have a fun life. It just makes sense some execrable things will happen too. I get it. Maybe I have this balanced outlook because I'm a Libra. I actually don't believe in astrology at all, so I think it's my mom's optimism. Like her, I just don't dwell on negative events.

But I try to get better, I really do. I stay in therapy for six months and then one day I see things very clearly. The parking lot attendant of this one therapist's office is pleasantly greeting me as usual. As she gives me my car ticket and I start toward the therapist's door, she gives me an encouraging upbeat nod, as in "Go get cured, lady." I can tell she is used to seeing melancholy patients all day long. When I come out of the office today, she raises her eyebrows to me in the universal sign of "Better?" I shake my head, "Nah." And she shrugs acceptingly . . . and I realize no one is ever better! This parking lot attendant hasn't seen *anyone* ever get better. What's better, anyway? I want to be able to stand in my front yard without shaking. I want to be able to be out after dark without being on edge. I want this behind me. I know what will make it pass. I need to stop hiding this from my parents and family. I need to tell my mom so she will hold me and stroke my hair and tell me I'm okay. But I can't. I won't burden her with this while it's still freaking me out because she will never sleep again if she sees me this distraught.

Politically correct disclaimer: I know there are some fine therapists. We have therapists in our family, and many of our friends have great experiences. Family therapists helped us settle Ilaria into our home. But on this victim-of-a-crime issue, I never quite connect with one. If there's anything I learned from the years of trying to be a parent, it's this: if something isn't working, try something else.

I decide to leave therapy. So how do I get better? At their suggestion and urging, I tell my friends the story over and over. It's like when you've been dumped and your friends listen. They tell me to just talk it out. And I do, until I am bored with the sound of my own voice. That works. I actually don't want to hear myself tell the story again.

After a while, I can stand in my front yard and not shake. I hear a noise on the street and I don't scream. I now carry pepper spray in my purse, and I give it out like party favors to any women leaving my house. I have decided the best thing I can do with the experience is remind people to look behind them on a dark street.

Once again, it all comes back to control—being pinned to the ground by a stranger is the same as my weight gain and equal to putting myself through all those fertility treatments. In all these situations, of course I just wanted the control of my body back. Who doesn't?

This also ties into the same methodology I use with parenting—even though I have rules and guidelines, I give Ilaria the control to make her own decisions. I think problem solving is the best tool I can give her.

Now, I feel like the incident is behind me. Writing it out was not easy and if I am impetuous enough to keep it in this book, I will have to sit my mom down first and tell her. This will be terrible because she will be scared. No mother wants to hear this story about their daughter. But I hope my mom and dad will take it better because they'll see it's behind me and I feel stronger because of it. I really do. I actually want to get a Wonder Woman T-shirt and wear it outside with nothing but lipstick and a smile. If you come within ten paces of my front yard, I will pepper-spray your eyeballs out of your face.

Also, my friend Dan tells me something that makes me see the incident in a different way: so many people wonder what they would do in that situation and he points out that now I *know* that I didn't go silent and I didn't freeze up. I punched and kicked and screamed. Like my daughter kicking that eight-year-old boy off her on that slide, I kicked that guy off me.

Other than looking over my shoulder on a dark street, I don't give it much thought anymore. I have other things to think about.

Since it's time to baptize Ilaria . . .

19

Greek Baptism

Ilaria enjoys hearing about heaven. Maybe because I describe it as a place where everyone rides a soft little white pony and has popcorn for breakfast. As hokey as this sounds, I tell Ilaria I felt her presence the day she was born. I tell her I saw her blond-streaked hair in my dreams. I tell her she sent me signs she was coming. I tell her about the girl in Spain who held my hand as if she was conveying Ilaria was coming to me soon. I tell her all this because it helps her know how much she was wanted. She likes to discuss these stories before bed . . . probably because for most kids the deep thoughts are revealed when they're trying to stall. This is when the good stuff comes out.

Ilaria likes to tell me what's going on in her world. Which is good. A nice mom in the line at Kmart once gave me the advice to just listen and not make everything a life lesson. We're lying in bed and Ilaria tells me in detail that she has what would amount to a blood feud with a girl at preschool. Yes, I want to rush over there in the morning and fix it, but I just cover my mouth in the dark and let her spill it out. A few days later, I see her playing with the mortal enemy again, so of course it's actually fine without my meddling. As evidenced by the experience in my front yard, I need to talk things out, as do my sisters, sister-in-law, and cousins. Maybe it's a girl thing, maybe it's a Vardalos trait. Either way, Ilaria likes to talk things out too.

Ilaria asks me why God didn't give me a baby. This isn't an uncomfortable question for me anymore. I tell her there was another plan for me; I was supposed to wait for her. I tell her it was hard to wait but she is worth it. I say, "I used to look up at heaven and say, 'When, when will I be a mother?' And you were on a cloud looking down at me, saying, 'Wait for me, I'm coming.'" She likes this story and asks for it a lot.

There is a new mountain of presents in the front hall. Our friends and family have been overly generous up to now, so we come up with the idea that instead of presents for her baptism, if they wish to, they can donate money to any foster family agency. So our friends and family donate . . . *and* still send presents.

Again and again, Ian and I are touched by the generosity of our family and friends. Here's a celebrity name-drop story. As I've mentioned, one of my closest friends is Sean Hayes. One of the things I love about him is he is unchanged since he became a superstar. He is a lovable and smart guy and never puts on airs. I adore him. Plus he is soooooo caring that one night when I showed him the pepper spray I now carry, he pokerface-offered to attack me so I could spray him for practice.

One of the things Sean and his grounded and good-natured boyfriend, Scotty, and I often talk about is how we grew up comfortable but without wealth and we don't want our lifestyle to change us and make us out-of-touch L.A. types. Of course, we're probably more out-of-touch jerks than we think, but we're trying to retain some normalcy in our lives so we don't become full-blown windbags.

Anyway, after years of this conversation, when I became a mom, Sean and I had a big discussion about how I don't want to spoil my daughter. Sean agreed and cautioned me to be really careful because of some of the entitled L.A. kids we've encountered.

But for Ilaria's baptism today, Sean and Scotty come over this morning and give me a gift: it's a necklace of a diamond heart. Diamonds! When I look up, Sean's eyes are misty, and he tells me how happy he is to see me as a mom, finally. I protest that the gift is too extravagant and he tells me to "shut it" and that I can keep it until Ilaria is old enough to wear it or hawk it if times get tough.

So I'm keeping it hidden to see which comes first.

I add the gift to the crag of swag and think about today's baptism. From the very beginning, every time Ilaria clutched a burger as she strode across the back patio in her bikini, someone in the family would declare, "She's a little gypsy. Just like us." The first time my family saw her gnaw a lamb bone and power through a plate of olives, they squealed, "She's Greek, she's Greeeeeeeeeek." I am not sure of her ethnic background, but the truth is, like Ian getting sucked into the vortex of my giant family, Ilaria is Greek now too. It seems fitting that she get baptized.

But while we're getting ready to go to the church, and Ilaria is quiet in her room, I become apprehensive. Ilaria is opinionated and therefore not easily cajoled into doing things that don't interest her. I've explained baptizing her is a way of thanking God in heaven for her. I don't think she's buying it. Because she now insolently struts downstairs, not in the pretty silk party dress I'd bought her, but rather in the now-ripped yellow polyester princess costume she'd lifted from Ann's house a while ago. This is my first indication this is not a good day. That and the huge pout she's sporting. Her bottom lip is taking over her face.

I have described to my daughter what her baptism will be like. In the Greek church we fully immerse babies in a tub of holy water. Pieces of hair are trimmed. Of course, there's olive oil involved since every ceremony seems to tie in somehow to Greek salad.

I'm not sure Ilaria is going to go for it. She's almost four years old now and quite dogmatic. At school, they call her a "leader," which I know is just a Reggio word for "bossy." This is not going to be easy. I hear her cousins in the TV room telling her that her baptism will be fun, and Ilaria replies: "I'm not doing it." Everyone quickly switches gears and assures her it will be over quickly. I look in: the dark thunder of Ilaria's expression foreshadows the storm a-brewing. But with my parents and family in tow, we all head to church.

My family is visiting for the premiere of *My Life In Ruins*. One fun fact about my family: when I'm filming, they show up to be extras. They're all over my movies—you can spot them if you imagine my face with different wigs. I ask my parents and Ian to be in my movies because it's funny and, also, film lasts forever. Ian is usually working on a TV show or another film, but we figure out a part for him to play (actually he quickly flips though my scripts then states, "I'll play the bartender if I can carry a gun"), then he flies to whatever city I'm in for what seems to be his personal goal: to get me fired by making me laugh on camera. In *Connie and Carla* I had to change my usual not-laughing technique of thinking of that disgusting worm sandwich into now imagining myself slurping up a heaping bowl of lemon-poached eyeballs. Because when the camera is on me, Ian is off camera imitating my dancing to make me laugh. In his scene in *My Life In Ruins,* which we shot on our actual wedding anniversary, Ian plays the hotel clerk with the (added) hair in his ears who suggestively propositions my character. Ian improvised most of what he did. The more he came on to me, the more I laughed. My hot costar, Alexis Georgoulis, is a giant star in Greece so there were tons of rumors in the magazines that we were having an affair even though my parents were chaperoning me all over Greece. In truth, making a movie can be really lonely, so it's really nice to have my family around. My mom even ran lines with me as we perched against the ruins of Delphi. One of the greatest joys of my career was the day we filmed at the Acropolis. As I was standing in position at the base of the ancient Parthenon and about to say my lines, my parents walked right through the shot handing out sacks of fruit and cookies to the cast and crew. Everyone loves having my parents around. They're comical and demonstrative and so excited to be a part of it, their affection and excitement is contagious to even the most jaded crew member. So it's great that my family comes to the premieres too, along with many cousins, aunts, and uncles. Because we live all over—from Greece to Australia, the States and Canada—the premieres are mini-reunions for us.

So since the family is coming for the *My Life In Ruins* premiere, we've decided to have Ilaria's baptism in the same week. We've asked my cousin George Skoufis and Rita Wilson to be Ilaria's godfather and godmother. Traditionally, you ask your best man to baptize your child. To be a best man in our church you have to be Greek. Years ago at our wedding, Ian's friend Kerry was Ian's honorary best man, and my cousin George, whom I'm very close with, was also our best man because he's Greek Orthodox.

Rita had been such a good friend to me during the blegh years. As I said, you really find out who your friends are when you don't feel like being a shiny, happy movie star. Often Rita would take me for lunches in Beverly Hills. She never mentioned how run-down I looked or how glum I seemed. We'd shop and laugh together, and it felt good to forget that I had rented a condo in the Pit of Despair. During that time, Tom and I started writing *Larry Crowne*. They both knew what I was going through, but they never asked invasive questions. I always say Rita is like my fairy godsister, so it seems fitting she now baptize my daughter. Ian and I like this combo of

George and Rita. It seems fitting to have George, our best man, be Ilaria's godfather, but because he lives in Australia and as I've mentioned we don't have family close by, now Ilaria will have Rita as her godmother in Los Angeles. Tom will also be Ilaria's godfather since he's married to Rita and is now Greek Orthodox. My cousin George is married to a man named Jim. Yes, my cousin is cool and out (snap fingers, bob head here) but gay marriage is not recognized by my church. Yet.

Congenial Father John welcomes us all, and I see Ilaria is calm as she watches the ceremony begin. She became quite serene when I reminded her in the car we're having a party at home afterward to celebrate her baptism. Cousin Nike and Core have stayed behind to decorate. To give Ilaria a goal to work toward, I whisper the party details, and on my phone, show her the picture of the giant mermaid cake. (The mermaid theme is her joke on the dunking that's coming her way.) She's excited about the cake—to keep her attention, I describe the creamy and abundant frosting. Before you judge me on bribing my kid with sugar, just can it; sometimes food *is* a reward.

The priest begins to chant, and Rita and George carry Ilaria out of the church to denounce the devil. Yes, really. We Greeks are serious about this good and evil stuff.

They come back in and now I see it on Ilaria's face: this is *not* happening. Because she has just spotted the baptismal font of water, which to a kid looks like a warlock's cauldron of boiling brew. Her expression says *No, no, people let's cut to the cake*. She is not into this at all. She'd rather stay pagan than go into that giant swirling toilet.

Now I have to carry her toward that basin, and she starts screaming. I mean, yelling like we're sacrificing her to cannibals. I look up at my mom, dad, siblings, Rita, Tom, George, relatives, and think . . . *Hmm, why am I doing this exactly? Do I care if she's Greek Orthodox? Is this so important to me?*

As the priest trims three locks of Ilaria's hair, for the Father, Son, and Holy Spirit, she is shouting as loud as she can to summon them all to help her. I look upward so I won't cry. The icons all around look back at me: Why are you doing this to your kid?

I want her to think of the church as a peaceful refuge. For Greeks, our church is also our community center. Growing up, we socialized with other kids, and it brought a sentiment of solidarity to all make fun of our parents' accents and primal yearning to cook lamb on a spit in the front yard. We all learned Greek, and some of us found spouses. Being a part of a Greek church gave me roots, traditions, and a feeling of community. Never mind that it's a never-ending fountain of comedic material.

I want Ilaria to think of church as a place she can always come to, at the very least to gather her thoughts. When I was in preproduction for *My Big Fat Greek Wedding*, we lost three friends. Three. As my career dream was coming true, three friends were dealing with the reality of disease and lost their lives. They were in their thirties and died of illnesses they were too young to get. I had come to this church, sat in a back pew, and asked God if there was some reason at all that would make sense to take three people before they'd really lived. There isn't an answer that will ever satisfy me or anyone, but I did find tranquillity at that church. I had always been welcomed, the parishioners had made my stage show a success, and we'd been members for a long time. It made sense that I would baptize my daughter here.

But Ilaria has another plan. Ian and I cannot console her. She is screaming that this must stop. Rita is soothing her, softly whispering that the baptismal font is just like a warm bath. I watch my friend Rita. Our shared background is what immediately bonded us the night we met in that small theater. We *knew* each other right away. And because of our same culture, we moved so easily into a friendship. I want Ilaria to know this sense of community. Being Greek is so much more than the tzatziki-sauce-garlic-breath jokes I make. I am immensely proud of my heritage and therefore want to pass it on to my daughter. I now look up at Tom. He looks back at me with a nod, as in, it'll be okay. In that moment, I see him not as Tom the movie star, not as Tom my friend, but as a parent. I see he knows that sometimes as the parent, you just have to do what you think is right for your child.

I glance at my own parents, my siblings, my nieces and nephews. They're all waiting to see what I will do.

Now, as I said, I am not a grown-up. I would rather take Ilaria now and run off to join a circus than cause her pain. Ilaria is shrieking and pointing at the cauldron of water as if we're about to make a broth out of her. I look at Ian and think . . . *This isn't a wrong choice we're doing here, is it?*

I just want her to have some traditions and community in her life. This is a symbol that I am trusting God with her life. So I make a decision and, just like that, I dunk her in the basin. And Ilaria goes apeshit.

She is completely furious at all of us.

Ian helps, Rita and George pitch in, the priest dunks her some more, and she never stops screaming.

Suddenly it's over, so Rita and I quickly take her away to change her into a new outfit. Rita's experience as a mother shows as she is tender and gentle with Ilaria and eventually even gets her to laugh. In her pretty white dress, my small daughter looks as disheveled and vulnerable as if she's just been through a prom-night parking-lot rumble. But she smiles back at Rita and even gives her a small kiss on the cheek.

As we're driving home Ilaria says to Ian and me, "I'm really mad at you."

I say, "I know."

Sitting beside her in the backseat, I take her hand and squeeze it. I am not sure I did the right thing. I wonder if this is what being a grown-up is supposed to feel like? Are we supposed to do things like this to our kid?

Ilaria declares, "I don't like it there."

Now I should spout off about how great church is, how it will always be a place she belongs. But I don't. I just touch her face and say, "You don't have to go back there again until you get married." So I guess I'm not really a grown-up.

For the record, she goes back a lot. Because a few months later, she starts Greek school at the community center. Okay fine . . . some parts of *My Big Fat Greek Wedding* are a documentary after all.

So besides chomping on a lamb shank, Ilaria is fully Greek. She speaks the language and is learning to write it. But I see today at church as we head to get Communion from Father John, we have to pass by that big baptismal font. Ilaria walks a wiiiiiide circle around and away from it.

She has not gone near it since.

20

Where's the Off Switch?

You work. I work. Whether your job is full-time mom or corporate CEO, raise your hand if you've accidentally napped in the sweater department at Walmart.

As I try to parallel park with one hand, while cursing that unnecessarily tight shrink-wrap I can't peel off the juice box three-pack, I wonder how my mom did it all. I am so sleep deprived my chin skin hangs into my neck like I'm perpetually texting. But I'm not.

I check myself in the rearview mirror. . . . Well, I do look happy. Like a happy, gaunt hag.

It's been well over a year of motherhood in which I have spent every waking moment with Ilaria in between fulfilling those work commitments I'd made before I became a mom. I directed and acted in a film I wrote, turned in a new script, and premiered two films. I don't feel superhuman. I've seen the same bedraggled expression on the faces of many women, from Gap cashiers to hairstylists to moms who work full-time being moms—if you're a mom, you just get it all done.

Without a smidgen of contrition, I'm going to say this out loud: barring a few exceptions, the planning, and by this I mean, the household upkeep, playdates, lunch making, school volunteering, and general socialization of a child, is still primarily considered mom territory. Sure, I've seen some dads with day planners in hand too; they're marvelous, but they're rare.

I can walk Ilaria into preschool every day for six weeks in a row, and nobody blinks. But if Ian does it one day, the other moms and teachers make such a big deal of it. I'll hear them all dreamily coo about it for weeks: "Saw Ian last week. He's so good with kids." I want to say to the moms, "Um, you mean like you and I are every day?" Plus isn't it a little demeaning to men to applaud them for simple human behavior? Most of the dads I know, even if they're not doing the planning, are present and hands-on. Then again, one dad at preschool said his wife had attended a parenting class the night before so he'd "stayed home and babysat." I didn't say, "You mean parented?"

Luckily, my own husband is not a slacker. And I'm not just saying that because he'll read this book. He won't. He's still working on *Seabiscuit.* The truth is, Ian has risen to the tasks of parenthood. Another truth is, all babies love Ian—probably because he looks like one. Subsequently, he and Ilaria got along right away and Ian jumped into the dad thing.

Ian changed diapers too, dutifully sleeps on that cot, and hauls kid stuff to the park. By the way, no one told us there'd be so much stuff. Just to get out the door with a kid means extra underwear, a change of clothes, a cooler of milk and snacks and juice, plus a blanket to sit on in the park and some activity like a coloring book and crayons. An archetypal guy, Ian used to walk out the door with only his wallet, phone, and keys. And in the classic guy move, he would come right back because he'd forgotten one of these items. Now he has a huge knapsack that is just Ilaria's stuff. We made sure to purchase a very au courant Kenneth Cole shoulder bag for our kid stuff because for years we'd felt sorry for those sad-sack parents carrying a urine-yellow diaper bag with duckies on it. The haunted look in their eyes, as if their sexuality was dripping out of them with every plodding step, made us shudder with fear.

We were so determined to remain young and virile when we became parents. But now we mutter "I gotta get to the gym" as we doze off, only to wake up with our necks cricked at those algebraic angles. Our zombie exoskeletons are gray and flaky from surely the sleep-deprived malnutrition of rickets. We need counseling for our Goldfish cracker addiction. Breakfast has been replaced with apple juice from foil bags we've switched to even though it always geysers up through that teeny straw hole, so in the car our legs stick to our forearms. I know the cereal dust at the bottom of a box is not a real dinner for me. We're lucky we have Anna to babysit . . . but we can't go out because we're so tired we'd face-plant into the entrée.

But really (tight smile masking trauma), it's going so much better!!! (I insert many exclamation points to keep myself awake as I write.) We tell ourselves Ilaria's sparkling self-assured personality is the reward for the loss of our vim and vigor.

Today, I'm driving her to preschool and have to blink several times to stay awake. Not good. I acknowledge I'm in a state of unremitting brain fog.

The sleeping a few hours at a time has completely thrown my own rhythms off. Sure, Ilaria is sleeping through the night—the cot is completely down the hall, which means when I walk out of the bathroom I get to trip and hydroplane across it. But now it's me who is hyper-diligent at night, watching over Ilaria, not wanting to leave her alone. Any sound in the house makes me bolt awake or instinctively reach for the bottles she's long given up.

I'm waking up more tired than I went to bed. I'm sure all parents would agree with this feeling: I haven't been in REM since I became a mom.

Even if I could, I don't want to sleep in. I like to take her to preschool. I put my convertible top down, blare a song on Sirius Kids Place Live, and Ilaria throws her hands in the air and squeals "Rock and Roll!" as we peel out the driveway.

I could nap when Ilaria is at preschool, but I learn so much when I stay there. Plus, we'd ascertained from the sleep therapist that napping doesn't add up to a good night's sleep. If I make some lifestyle changes so that I get more rest, does this mean I won't be able to be with Ilaria as much? The guilt of this realization is really hard for me. Ian and I consider ourselves fortunate that we're both employed. But we don't have any family living in Los Angeles to help out. . . .

By the time we pull up to preschool, I accept I can't be here all day anymore. I have new work commitments that are gnawing at my psyche, and I'm exhausted. I've got to be disciplined and get some sleep, plus find time to exercise and get my energy back. My mom and siblings tell me: you can't take care of your kid unless you take care of yourself.

So tonight I go to bed at nine P.M. . . . but I can't turn off my brain. I lie here until three A.M., thinking of all the things I have to get done. I wake up at six A.M. feeling crummy again.

Therefore, I do what my mom always did: I make a list. I itemize all the things that are plaguing my subconscious and scribble across the top—

How to Sleep

Exercise Sucks: But I have to do it. I set the TiVo in front of the treadmill to record programs other than *Scooby-Doo* so I can watch adult content like *Mad Men* (and, yes, I do pretend

I'm walking toward John Slattery as he's handing me a martini). For other days, I find a morning dance class that begins right after my daughter's school drop-off time, so eighty minutes later I can be showered and at my desk writing.

Kid Kryptonite: A recipe in the *Sneaky Chef* cookbook is an ingenious mélange of pureed spinach, broccoli, peas, and a bit of lemon juice to remove that tinny spinach-sweater off your tongue. One cup can be mixed with a bit of ketchup or tomato sauce—it goes brown, thus hiding the gross green, then added to ground turkey burgers for more than the daily recommended serving of vegetables. To save time, I make a silo of it to be frozen in one-cup portioned Ziploc bags for quick mixing into pasta sauces or meatballs. (As I type this, I'm imagining myself making it with Rachel Ray—we're wearing matching outfits.) In a trembling voice, I tell Ian he must hide the Goldfish crackers from me. I slice some chicken and eat the concoction as soup. Within days, my eyes look bright, I'm standing taller . . . forgive my forthcoming admission, but that potion is truly nature's broom.

Pain In The Neck: An osteopath assesses the damage to my shoulder and neck muscles from the constant rocking plus cot-sleeping. In a few sessions it feels like she oiled the sockets in my neck and I think I am seeing my own aura until I remember I actually do have peripheral vision.

Modern Gift Horse: Nobody told me there'd be so many birthday parties and that at least once a weekend I'd have to yell, "Drop the cupcake, Cupcake, we've got to get home and walk Manny!" Just taking Ilaria to a toy store to get a birthday gift takes hours with parking, plus walking through multiple aisles of choices, and like every kid she has to touch every single toy in there. On Amazon.com, I order twenty-five age-appropriate gifts. (With Prime, it's free delivery! You're welcome for the free ad, Amazon. Please send me a purse.) A gi-normous box of gifts arrives and I shove it deep into a closet. Before a party, Ilaria goes "shopping" in there and it only takes five minutes.

The Complexities of Complexion: I throw out all my dried-up face creams and go back to my previous much easier regimen of inexpensive Dove soap, plus La Mer cream that costs more than a Prius. But I tell myself to spend the money on the moisturizer because it works, and within a few days I feel my skin slough and soften. The beauty of European skin is that even our grandmothers don't have wrinkles. The downside is I still get pimples. Plus, I sometimes need to see a dermatologist for blocked oil glands that look like speed bumps. I never know when they're going to erupt and appointments are two months away. So I schedule twelve dermatologist appointments to have one on standby every month, and if my skin isn't acting up, I can cancel twenty-four hours before and not be charged. Derm appointments are such a commodity in Los Angeles, I could sell mine on eBay.

Stubborn Stubble: For many of us ladies, daily grooming takes a lot of time. The days of my luxuriously long showers are over, and there's no time to run a razor over any part of me. Therefore, I resume the laser treatments I'd started on my legs years ago and slowly achieve my goal of becoming a hairless cat.

The "No" Word: I begin to limit my fundraising events to topics like adoption, poverty, and the elderly. I duck and ask my agent to explain to the angry groups who don't understand why I've declined hosting the opening of their artifacts museum in a country nineteen hours away, that there are only fifty-two weekends a year. And that I'm a mom now.

Tote That Purse: Nothing, except my daughter and dog, makes me more chipper than a new purse. So for my new organizing project, of course I need a special purse. I purposefully stride into the department store, avoid the sparkly evening clutches that seemingly call my name, and instead steer myself toward the satchels and totes. I find a big one with a zippered-off section just for Ilaria's stuff—the antibacterial wipes, Band-Aids, toys, activity books, crayons, and snacks go in one crumb-filled sector. So in a big-shot meeting, I can pull out my script notes and know there won't be Tinkerbell stickers all over the pages (unless I stuck them on there myself . . . because they really are pretty).

Clutter Is A Dirty Word: I grab every form of cleaning supply (insert Windex joke here) and attack the gummy surfaces of my home. Opening doors and airing out the musty rugs, curtains, and pillows, I now attack the viscous floors. After I clean my house, sure, like leaving the dental hygienist's chair, it feels great and I vow to keep it that way. Our new and wonderful housekeeper, Carmen, comes over, tames the laundry, and helps keep the grunge sponged. But a few days later, that layer of chaos is back. I see why now: every room is a kid room; there's child paraphernalia everywhere. I go a step farther: in the living room, I take apart the entire Playmobil safari and hospital structures plus gather all the diminutive occupants. I put *all* the toys in *one* play-room. It's as if I'm reclaiming the house as adult territory. Or at least shared space. When I finally get all the toys, books, CDs, and DVDs put away and actually see my couch upholstery again, it is a moment of sweet grown-up victory.

I will myself to make the time to exercise, cook, write, plus still be with my daughter a few days at her preschool. As I cross items off my list, I am now sleeping about five hours at a time. My goal is a solid eight.

Sometimes my agent calls to tell me there's an acting job . . . for tax and budgetary reasons many productions shoot outside of Los Angeles. But when I read the scripts, they're not life-changing roles. I hear myself turning the acting jobs down. I'm also asked to go into new businesses and endorse My Big Fat Greek product spin-offs, from wine to cookbooks to restaurants. For the record, no matter what that diner owner tells you about me being a silent partner, I am not in any way affiliated or involved in any of these My Big Fat Greek products. The brand has never been licensed out. Anyway, I keep saying no to everything. As much as I hate writing because it is such a solitary pursuit, at least I can do it on my own time. If something truly cool happens, like I get offered a bad-ass cop role in an es-teemed director's film, I wonder if I'd bring Ilaria with me for that film shoot. Would she adapt to New York's lifestyle if I fulfill a life-long goal of doing a Broadway musical for a year or two? I wonder if it is prudent or reckless to bring my young daughter along on my adventures.

Do I miss being on camera? Yes. But more than I'd miss seeing my daughter clear another hurdle, reach another milestone? No. Ilaria is really responding to routine, truly flourishing from the schedule we've now established. So I decide unless the job is in Los Angeles, it's best to stay near her for the time being. But before you applaud me for being altruistic supermom . . . again it's not like Scorsese called.

I know I need to stick to a sleep schedule to truly change my body's rhythms. If I was organized before out of an unbridled enjoyment of efficiency, I am methodic encroaching on psychotic now as I diligently and proudly cross items off my list. The more clearheaded and focused I feel, the more I get done. I wish I could say I pulverize Ilaria's fruit smoothies from my own organic garden, in between scrubbing down my husband's feet with a homemade almond and quinoa paste . . . but I'm not that mom.

Three months later, as I cross all the items off my list, I achieve my goal and sleep eight full hours . . . and I wake up so rested, I check to see if there are bluebirds chirping around my head.

I'll admit, I am quite pleased with myself as I yawn and stretch in bed this morning. I mentally resolve to stick to this regimen and not add one more thing to my day . . . when Ilaria walks in to ask me to become her preschool's room mom.

As my mouth says, "Yes," my brain screams, "Nooooooooooo."

21

More Than Our Bodies

My four-year-old daughter is growing long legs and straight, long rock-'n'-roll hair. I'm not equipped to raise a cool girl. A nerd with bangs hiding a pimple-terrained forehead and glasses covering half her face, yes, I'm that girl's mentor. But if there's one thing I will not squelch in my daughter, it's her natural body confidence. That, I also have. But I had it when I was heavier too. I'm not saying I'll shop for groceries in a thong, I'm just saying I never abhorred or reveled in my physicality.

Here's one thing I used to eye-roll—slim actresses on a red carpet answering the workout-regimen question with a lying shrug "I just have a fast metabolism" or "I run after my kids." But now I know why some actresses say it, and even I once said it too to make my publicist laugh. Because if I answer thirty questions about screenwriting or adoption but just one about weight, just *one* . . . the *entire* article will only be about weight loss with a title: "I Broke Up With Cheese."

My weight loss is lauded and applauded, which is just asinine. Let's be frank, I don't look that good, yet there have been rumors of plastic surgery and a face-lift. The only thing I can say in my defense is (1) you know I'd tell you and (2) would I keep this nose?

Many reporters constantly feel the need to ask me for my "diet secret." Aren't we all sick of this innocuous topic? Aren't we all tired of headlines "Thin Is Out." Or "Thin Is In," "She's a Full-Figured Beauty," "Actresses Who Have Real Woman Bodies." Puh-leeze. Is it quixotic of me to request we stop letting our psyches be trampled by the media's desire to cajole us that no woman's accomplishment is as lofty and exalted as fitting again into our high school jeans?

But it's not just the press. Strangers comment on my weight loss. A woman in my new workout class screamed, "What have you done? You look amaaaaaaaaahhhhzing," as if I was Jabba the Hut before. A reminder: I was never Guinness-record-book fat. Admittedly, I'll never be model skinny. Oh yes, I would love to be model skinny for a day or two. It'd be terrific to sulkily slink into a retro lounge and have every brooding male model wish he was hot enough to be with me. But this is never going to happen. I will never look like those women. Which is why I write romantic comedies in which I, Every-Woman, trip into some bar and kiss the guys way out of my league. This is my job, ladies, and I do it for all of us. But mostly for me. Here's probably the only career tip in this whole book: if you're going to write and act in your own movies, always write a line where the guy calls you pretty.

I'm not super disciplined and so harmoniously balanced that I churn my own vegan butter, but I have to keep it together or I blow up, resulting in the complete loss of energy I've described.

So to be in control, I weigh myself every morning. But my daughter never knew what I was doing. Once, as soon as I got off the scale, Ilaria got on it and declared, "Yup, three years old." I never weighed myself in front of her again.

I never talk about weight or calories in my daughter's presence. I tell her I walk on our treadmill to get energy. It's true: that treadmill keeps my weight down or I feel sluggish. And by sluggish, I mean I'll look like a gray slimy slug.

I want my daughter to know she's in control of her own body, but I try to not make her entire existence be about her appearance—I don't constantly comment on how "cute" she is. I try to empower her by asking, "Who do you like to play with?" or "What's your favorite book?" Yes, sometimes I do blurt out how cute she is, because most of the outlandish outfits kids put together are reminiscent of a *Grey Gardens* character, so I can't help it.

But here's the thing about Ilaria and how she thinks—on that day she first tasted strawberry ice cream, I noticed she did something I've never seen before. She ate a bit of the ice cream, truly enjoyed it . . . and handed it back to me.

This is not how a Vardalos eats. We push past the point of full. When I was growing up, at family gatherings, we'd overload a plate at the buffet, then after dinner, lie down on various couches and make each other laugh until we could eat some more. We're happy and emotional eaters. I'm not familiar with a person who has a natural shutoff valve.

If I could, I would eat cake every ten minutes, but I have to be cautious or I'll turn my veins into crème brûlée. If there's anything I do know how to do now, it's shut my pie hole. So I take advantage of my daughter's natural leaning away from the Vardalos "if your stretch pants haven't ripped, you're not fat" mantra. I grit my teeth and pinkie-swear myself that I will help her stay healthy but not have food issues. I want my daughter to grow up in a world where women are more than their bodies. That self-confidence that's already in her has to be reinforced by Ian and me so she is impervious to media images, peer pressure, and stupid human comments.

So I never use the word *treat* for a sweet food. "Treat" means a toy or trip. I've established a lingo: Growing Food and Sometime Food. I tell her a sandwich and apple are foods we need to eat to "grow" and a cookie or ice cream is something we have "sometimes." I say "sometimes" and do a huge shrug as if, hey, it's no big deal. Inwardly, I wonder if she knows I could eat a bag of Oreos in the time it takes me to explain this to her. I do my best to help her choose "growing" foods for meals. I don't congratulate her for finishing an entire meal or admonish her for calorically high food requests like chocolate chip pancakes for dinner. Twice we've gone out to a local café and ordered those and it takes all the pressure off it as an out-of-reach dream food. It's only eight semisweet chocolate chips, and she never finishes the pancakes anyway. I'm trying to not make "sometime" foods so desirable they become binge-worthy. I myself eat chocolate every day. Yes, every day. A little bit every day makes me never eat a lot of it. Why do I eat it? (1) It's delicious. And (2) because if this is the day I get hit by a bus, I don't want my last thought to be, *Shoulda had the chocolate*.

With Ilaria, I am trying everything I know to bolster her natural inclination toward not overeating. But at the same time, if she ends up gaining weight, so what? As I said, I was a fat and happy kid. I have a natural self-confidence that is frustrating to the many directors who have made comments about my weight. When I hear a director make a comment about my weight, I do my best work as I "act" like I can't hear them.

I once had a female costumer who seemed to need to exert power over me by being nasty about my weight. I had never encountered this before from a woman. On *Connie and Carla,* when I was struggling with my fluctuating weight because of fertility treatments, our costumer Ruth Myers was kind and understanding and went out of her way to make me feel attractive in my costumes. My stylist Jessica Paster is always nurturing and kind. But this woman on this project had a peculiar attitude about weight. I was slim at the time, but she kept trying to put me in cavernous clothes that looked suspiciously reminiscent of Golden Girls muumuus. I pored through the clothing racks, wondering if maybe I wasn't comprehending my role. She now showed me Polaroids of what the other actresses were wearing. They were all slim, but according to this costumer, every one of these actresses was "too fat for film." Clearly this woman's perception was skewed and could not be changed. She was a Fat-ist. As I turned to reach for a smaller shirt on the costume rack, she actually pushed it away from me, grabbed my stomach, and said, "I'm just trying to help you hide this."

Even though my stomach was flat thanks to months of Pilates and Cardio Barre classes. I have an almost irresponsible lack of concern about my body. This came from growing up in my family where you were noticed for how funny you were, not how you looked. This was further reinforced by my years of working at Second City. In Joyce's world, you weren't promoted and applauded for being hot; you were esteemed for being smart and funny. By the way, acting is about honesty in your eyes, not hiding your stomach in a boxy housedress. Small secret: most film scenes are shot from the waist up anyway.

But in that moment, with my stomach in that costumer's hands, I stared down with horror. No matter how impervious one is to criticism, nobody enjoys their flab kneaded like bread dough and declared a hideous flaw. Now . . . we Canadians are nice but we're not pushovers. We get you back and you don't even know. I made it my personal goal to drive this woman nuts.

As I've mentioned, although I'm not fanatical about it every day, I do have to eat very healthfully. When filming, my energy level stays so high because I consume six small meals a day and avoid sugar and white starch completely. But for this entire shoot, when I saw that costumer anywhere on the set, I would head for the Craft Services cart, grab the gooiest, plumpest fried donut . . . and walk by her while pretending to eat it. She'd gasp at the visual of an actress eating a carbohydrate and loudly bray, "Your costume won't fit if you eat that," and I'd shrug and say, "Oh well, it'll have to be let out then, huh?" I'd then turn the corner and dump the donut into a garbage can so I wouldn't faint from the glucose. I'll admit it brought me immense satisfaction to see her flummoxed.

It also brings me great joy to see my girlfriends laugh when I tell them the story. Sure, we are at the gym when I tell them. Which is why I tell them now . . . because we are out of my daughter's earshot.

22

Mother Nurture

Please excuse the "quips and tales" coming now. The truth is, most people think their own kids are charming in the same way everyone secretly loves their own feet no matter how Jurassic their toes are. I am only including these stories for this discussion of nature versus nurture.

A bonus in raising a child you don't have a biological tie to is you will never saddle them with watching their every move and declaring their musical talent as "that's from your dad's side; his old Auntie Beulah played pianola." Or their bad penmanship as "well, there's Grandpa Frank's meat paws once again."

Also, when someone says, "Your daughter is beautiful," you don't have to murmur modestly. You can just boomingly and boisterously concur at the gorgeousness that is your kid and even point out her perfect bow mouth and tiny fairy ears, 'til that person backs away slowly.

The benefit in raising the child you got to adopt is you just get to watch them unfold and become who they are. Ilaria is unfolding with ease and grace. She is doing really well, and, interestingly, she is still continuing to adapt to her environment.

In that first year we became a family, I got to have my first Mother's Day and it was a disaster of course. Because for years I didn't want to even venture out of the house on that day, Ian had made a celebratory brunch reservation at a fancy-pants place. But we were seated way too close to an older persnickety couple who gave us the stink-eye when Ilaria banged on the table with her spoon. I couldn't even look at them when she spilled an entire glass of milk and it cascaded like a flowing albino river across our table and theirs. When Ian reached for the milk glass, he spilled all our beverages, and I tried to help but instead flung their basket of bread on their laps and the floor. Ian and I locked eyes. Ah, perfect. Our mouths twitch. Because the more awkward the situation, the more we want to laugh. Here's the thing we then noticed: Ilaria saw us smiling at the maladroit mishap, and she was grinning too.

Father's Day wasn't much better—a trip to the beach involved Manny peeing right onto a stranger's blanket. Again, Ilaria saw Ian and me laughing. I wondered if we should be admonishing Manny and steering him away, but c'mon, he's a dog. Plus it's funny. It was extra awkward because the person whose blanket he'd peed on had been uptight since we'd all arrived like the loudest and clumsiest band of street musician grifters complete with a Tupperware of aromatic feta cheese. We couldn't help laughing. But we worry more grown-up parents would hide subversive reactions from their daughter. Should we be doing that?

In these first eighteen months, I am still trying to fully grasp that I'm the one in charge here. Today after the park, I'm making lunch when I notice a dark spot inside my daughter's ear. I peer in . . . and come face-to-face with a disgusting, wiggling tick. Without hesitating, I grab tweezers and as I pull it out, think, *Yuck, this is what a mom should do. Oh riiiight,* I'm *a mom.*

I'm just not completely comfortable yet. Maybe nerds never feel like they belong anywhere.

Conversely, I am in awe of how confident my daughter is.

She now takes the tweezers and holds my face steady so she can get the "crazy hair" out of my eyebrow. This is her new pursuit—she delicately uses the tweezers to do everything from pulling crabgrass from the yard to removing those teeny Playmobil pieces that stealthily work their way back into the living room to get wedged in the fat part of adult soles. Ian and I marvel at her manual dexterity mostly because we fantasize about retiring and having our daughter the brain surgeon take care of us. She is fascinated with friends' cuts and older relatives' surgical stitches and isn't squeamish at all. One time as I seasoned pieces of short ribs spread out on the kitchen counter, Ilaria picked up each one and inspected the marbling and bones. Then she asked, "Is this from a human?" Blegh. I feel like if I'd stated, "Yes, I bludgeoned Auntie Renee and now we'll eat her," Ilaria would only tell me it's wrong to hit.

Our friend Brian had meniscus surgery and the stitches are due out today. Because his doctor is across the city, Brian asked if he could just remove the five stitches himself and the doctor agreed it would be all right. But because Brian knows Ilaria so well, he comes over and asks me if he can get her to do it. I'm videotaping her now as she wears surgical gloves and is sterilizing the entire bathroom area with rubbing alcohol. She admonishes Brian to stay still, leans into his wound, then gently snips and pulls out the stitches. She is so methodical and unfazed by the gash, I'm fast-forwarding in my mind to when I'll play this tape at her medical school graduation party. Or parole board hearing. When she is finished, she pats Brian, tells him he is a good patient and to go to the front lobby and choose a toy.

For a crafts project, we make a dog costume using brown leggings and cut-out white felt polka dots. Ilaria wears it every day.

I mean every day. We're walking to the drugstore when a brash boy gets right in her face on the sidewalk and goads, "Why are you wearing that?," and she looks him dead in the eye and laughs. "I don't know." She stares him down . . . until he sheepishly admits, "It's cool." My daughter has more confidence than that lady we've all heard moan in exercise class. You know her. My own dance class is big, chock-full with people, and after all these years I still can't spot who The Moaner is. But I admire that she can just release that guttural, ecstatic moan in front of us all and clearly not care what we think. I wonder if all kids are just naturally confident until we tell them they're wrong or too loud or in the way.

Last year, I had to travel for work and Ilaria was so well behaved on a plane, the flight attendants even commented on it (inner back pat). Maybe it was the DVD player and six kid movies, coloring books, nine dolls plus other junk I lugged around. By the way, I am bemused by how people watch me parent, and in close quarters like on a plane, there's no escaping prying eyes. From a restaurant to the park, I hear them whisper "big fat Greek girl" then watch me admonish my daughter for winging a bun at my eardrum. I wish I had the nerve to say to these people, "Um, I'm not watching you scarfing that hoagie or leaving pee on the toilet seat; how about ya turn around while I do human stuff too?"

One time I happened to meet a man who told me he'd once sat behind us on a plane trip from Los Angeles to New York. I am not being coy, as disingenuous as this may sound: I am still surprised to be recognized. I remember that flight—the airline reservation agent did not recognize me at all and I recall her tongue almost caught on fire trying to pronounce my last name. She started with "Valdro . . . Veros . . . Vart-vart" then defaulted to "Have a good flight, Nina." I don't take being recognized for granted, so it's unexpected to discover I'm sometimes being watched, spied on, as I parent. Even though this man was being complimentary on how I speak to my daughter respectfully, empowering her with choices, he was revealing he had eavesdropped on us for the entire plane trip.

So I just keep trying to do the best I can with an audience because, really, they don't realize they're staring. I'll admit if I was sitting behind Steven Tyler and his kids, I'd absolutely lean an ear against that seat and listen in too. Curiosity is just human. By the way, years ago my mom gave me some of her always-astute advice (in our family, we've named these nuggets "Doreenies"). Way before people even had phones with cameras my mom once told me: "Always conduct yourself as if a video camera is on you at all times." Judicious advice. Other Doreenies include: "Just put some lipstick on and you'll feel better." And "There's no better feeling of confidence than the one that comes with having a black tie dress in your closet and a moussaka in your freezer."

Anyway, it's good advice to always conduct yourself with dignity, but Ian and I forget this all too often. Another time Ian, Ilaria, and I were flying together for work and were seated in first class. As we all took our seats, a couple saw Ilaria and grumbled about how a four-year-old wouldn't behave well enough for the front cabin. The woman boozily told us, in her opinion anyone under twenty-one years of age shouldn't be in first class. I just nodded and smiled courteously as my brain gave her the finger. On the flight, Ilaria barely spoke and fell asleep, yet this woman and her husband got so drunk they got into a fight with another passenger. It was a case of air rage, and the flight attendants had to intervene and calm them all down. As Boozilla burped and hunched back into her seat, Ian and I were goading each other to tap the couple on a shoulder and say, "Would you mind keeping your voices down, you're disturbing our sleeping daughter," but we didn't want to get coldcocked. Of course, because we're not grown-ups, we couldn't just let it go. Later, the couple was passed out and snoring and I got up to remove my purse from the overhead bin. Ian pushed me and I fell against their seats, jolting them awake. I threw my purse at Ian and we were both cracking up . . . until I saw Ilaria watching. She laughed too . . . but were we setting a good example? I don't think so.

But then again, she has always seemed remarkably solid and self-assured. On a trip to Toronto, Ilaria meets Kathy Greenwood, John, and their two girls. I'm not just saying this next part because Kathy will read this book (she will—twice), but their children are remarkably benevolent and considerate. In preparation for our arrival, they have sweetly pulled out all their toys to share. Almost immediately Ilaria is playing with the girls as Kathy and I grip each other's forearms with glee. The girls all jump up and down on the couch cushions, I feel like I'm seeing it in the dream Kathy and I shared of this day when we'd be mothers. The girls' hair flies up, as if in slow motion. It all feels thoroughly surreal, and Kathy and I cannot even look at each other or we will lose it and scare our daughters with our "ugly cry" faces.

Suddenly, Ilaria slips, and my blood pressure drops. But before I can even move, she quickly rights herself, looks at Kathy and me, and declares "I'm okay!" in that worldly way she has.

Kathy exclaims, "Okay, I *love* her."

Ilaria is adept and competent. She could have milked that little slip with maximum tears for attention and Kathy's homemade cookies but she doesn't bother. She lets us know it's all good and to carry on. By the way, I knew my best friend would love my daughter, but to hear her say it out loud is wonderful. I see the moment as a testament to what good things can come your way when you have a best friend who is honest with you. And you listen.

Ilaria has become extremely sociable as well. Now that we've managed to get some rest (because I sleep eight hours and she sleeps ten!), we have reinstated the fun loud adult dinners at our place.

I suspect this need to have people over is in my heritage. I just enjoy it, and I'd really missed it. But as a parent, I would prefer not going out as often so I can be home for bedtime. With Core around for dinner parties, it's loud and fun at our house again.

We also invite people over we don't know that well. This was inspired years ago by a dinner invitation to Mary Steenburgen and Ted Danson's. We didn't know them that well, but we accepted the invitation. It was so much fun, very comfortable, and we found out most of the guests didn't know each other either. Mary announced that's what people used to do—she and Malcolm McDowell would invite colleagues they admired over to dinner—so she was keeping the tradition alive. Mary advised they all got to know one another better in a more intimate setting than they ever could at a professional event. So Ian and I started doing it too. It's not like I just go up to Sean Penn and ask him over for a chimichanga in our backyard. It's much more organic than that—if Ian or I find ourselves chatting with a colleague we like—famous or not—and they suggest we keep in touch, we exchange info. Then we invite them over for a holiday party, loud dinner, or casual barbecue with a few members of the ever-sociable Core to buffer and start conversations so it's not awkward. These new friends come back often, maybe because we never hit anyone up for fundraising or hand out a religious pamphlet. We don't take pictures, so guests feel comfortable undoing their pants after dinner knowing they won't end up on my Twitter page. Hanging out is a much better way to get to know people than standing around an event with your stomach sucked in because press cameras are around. (Maybe just I do that.) Also, I don't panic if more people show up at my home than I anticipated . . . because I take my mom's advice and always have an extra moussaka in the freezer.

Ilaria now helps me cook the meal and set the dining room table, then gets to stay up for an extra thirty minutes to welcome everyone. We request her to do "eyes-to-eyes" when greeting adults but no need—she is not shy. She holds court, loudly telling everyone about the boy she's chosen to marry or explaining exactly how she finger-painted a mustache on Manny. She's not precocious or performative, so I see adults are drawn to her. Like many a Vardalos girl before her, she enjoys hostessing. I learned from my mom to set out Post-it-note-labeled serving dishes and utensils beforehand, then tape a "running order" of the entire dinner so I won't forget the rolls in the oven. If I happen to make fewer potatoes than I estimated for, I just whisper to Core my own family's signal to lay back on that dish: "FHB" (stands for "Family Hold Back"). My mom also taught me nothing that occurs during a party is so egregious that you can't scramble and cover. This covers all aspects of life—from my wedding day when I slipped on a hailstone and fell into the limo, to when I was nominated for a Golden Globe Award and turned on the red carpet to wave madly to the cheering stands, thus ripping the entire armpit out of my gown. Thanks to my mom's entertaining advice, if my dog sat on the dessert, I'd microwave Popsicles and call it sorbet (I won't admit in print I'd serve the dessert anyway). So to me Ilaria's jovial attitude is pitch-perfect as she asks arriving adult guests if they would like a juice box. I'm not telling you this to brag (okay, a little); I'm telling you this to point out that less than two years after her arrival, there aren't any traces left of the angry behavior of the withdrawn, pale toddler who kicked and punched her way into our hearts. Fortunately, her personality is the same as the day we met her.

Ilaria is inquisitive bordering on nosy, and this has evolved into her being thoughtful and remembering characteristics about each person, from who enjoys grapes to who plays hockey. To make friends feel appreciated, she brings out gifts they once gave her, like a heart-shaped beach rock from Mark and Yeni. She asks adults questions about their day and work life as if she cares. She has so much charisma, we ponder if she'll either be president or running her cell block. Hey, I figure either way she's a leader.

She has those ideas I wonder if we all once had before adult common sense squashed our imaginations. Once she said: "Mom, I'm gonna make a purse for you that's a robot and it'll pay for anything." The simplicity kids see things with is eye-opening. Once during a sleepover, I hear a female cousin she adores whisper to her, "Don't tell anyone, but when I grow up, I'm going to be a wizard." There is a pause in the dark, and I hear Ilaria innocently ask, "You're gonna grow a beard?"

She has those existentially puzzling thoughts four-year-olds have. One time before bed, she asks me, "Is God dead?" I say, "No." And she says, "Well, you said he's in heaven and when we die we go to heaven, so how did God get there?" Hm. This is not something you can boot up your search engine on.

She is already reading. Yes, sure, so is your four-year-old. But my kid didn't speak for a while so that's why I'm boring you with these updates. Ilaria tested as being ready a year earlier than usual for public kindergarten. We didn't start her in school early because kids' development can progress in fits and starts and also stall. She could have mastered some skills today and yet struggle tomorrow. Because we've had the benefit of my siblings being parents long before us, we get good advice that kids' maturation during the heaviest years of acquiring knowledge is not a steady road without bumps and potholes. Also, we've promised ourselves we'll give our daughter a normal life. As much as we can. Maybe she just thinks everyone's mom teaches their daughter to do a spit take. With milk. Maybe she thinks everyone's parents get asked for autographs and pictures. She still doesn't know or care what we do for a living. She hasn't asked.

When I have had to travel alone for work, Ilaria acknowledges it's part of my job. Even though we have Anna to babysit, Ian and I have never been away from our daughter together overnight. If there's out-of-town travel involved for work, we all go along, or one of us always stays in Los Angeles with her. She's okay with one of her parents traveling . . . probably because she looks forward to the treasure hunts. My mom did this when she and my dad went on a vacation, and I remembered how the time passed effortlessly, as everything does with the promise of hidden candy. So I make small postcards like my mom did, put them in envelopes, and give them to her when I travel—one for each day. Inside are clues she has to solve around the house and yard to find the hidden treasure—usually candy or a plastic ring or a Scooby-Doo toy. She loves to discover the treasure. Except one time I hid a pencil. In my defense, it was a shimmering red pencil. When I got home, Ian described her expression when she found that dud gift. Her face was on par to Charlie Brown getting the rock in his stocking. She'd dropped the pencil, looked at Ian, and deadpanned, "Get some chocolate."

Like most kids, sometimes she embarrasses her parents out of total innocence: we are meeting a new pediatrician and she announces, "My daddy has a big, big penis."

Sometimes, her humor is observational: I had a lot of cheese at a Christmas party so the next day my face is literally swollen from the salt consumption. Ilaria wakes up and exclaims, "Mom, are you wearing a different nose?!"

When Ian heads out the front door to take her to preschool, she now asks, "Wallet, phone, keys, daughter?"

Once on a Friday night, I asked her to please try to sleep in the next morning so we could all get some rest and she slyly smiles, then at dawn whispers into my eyeball, "Let's get this party started."

Because we don't make her eat everything off her plate—we just ask her to eat until her body is full—and I say "listen to your body," now at the end of a meal, she cocks a hand beside her ear to listen and out of the side of her mouth ventriloquist style, says, "I'm full."

The days of her Jackie Chan drop-kicks to my thorax are gone. She is gentle and amenable. And so droll that I can now wake her up in the morning by putting a cold water bottle against her upper arm.

She jolts awake, squeals with laughter, and spends the rest of the day plotting to get me back. Later in the day, I take her to a studio lot with me because I'm just dropping off a casting list. As I'm speaking with the producer, she gets me back by lifting up my skirt and screaming "Ew!" at my black satin panties. (I'm only telling you this story because I had good underwear on.)

Tonight, she asks me to tell her the story again about when she was up in heaven looking down on me. I start it as usual: "I was looking up asking, when, *when* will I be a mother? And you were on a cloud, looking down at me saying 'wait for me I'm'"—and she interrupts me with a wry smile and says, "No, I said, 'Why is that lady crying? I'm trying to take a nap.'"

It's a huge moment. Sure, I laugh so hard I can barely breathe, but because I see something so interesting in Ilaria's expression. Deep satisfaction at making her mom laugh. I have the same feeling when I make my mom laugh until she can't catch her breath. I love to make my mom laugh with my stories. And now I have a funny girl too.

The extra cot is long gone from the hallway—it's now stored in the garage. But at night before she sleeps, because this is when the good stuff comes out, Ian and I lie in bed with her to talk. One night, Ilaria and I are looking up at the neon stars her godfather, my cousin George, sent from Australia. They're pasted on her ceiling and when the lights first go out, they glow in the dark. Ilaria tells me all about Australian animals and how one day she'll be an animal rescue worker. As Ilaria drifts off, I think about George, my ironic cousin, who as a teen upon seeing one of our aunt's vast fleshy arms in a summer dress, drily declared to me, "Always remember darling, sleeveless is a privilege not a right." He was always funny. Yes, of course he was always gay. In the same way I was always going to be an actress. We are who we are. So when people compliment us on our daughter, Ian and I thank them. But we know we did not make her funny and smart—Ilaria arrived this way.

Then, did she adapt to her environment because it's a match made in heaven, or because she is biologically wired like us?

For example, in terms of how I feel about gay and lesbian equal rights, there isn't any teaching to do. Ilaria has seen our own group has many same-sex couples and she is part of a generation of kids who started preschool with the kids of same-sex parents. To her it's as common and accepted as I hope it can be soon to the generations older than her. I know she's blasé about it because one day, we were in a diner and two cute guys in their twenties were holding hands at another table. I saw Ilaria watching them for a while. Then she turned to me and straightforwardly asked, "Do you think *he* asked him for the date, or *he* asked him?"

Is her reaction biological logic or environmental education?

Again, I'm not telling you all this to brag (okay, I am). I am now fascinated by any discussion of nature versus nurture. Maybe our human growth is a combination of both facets.

In truth, I'm telling you all these stories to dispel the myth that adopted kids are damaged. There is nothing done that a lot of love can't undo. Someone once asked me if I think adopted children have abandonment issues. My answer is yes. We all do. That's why so many love songs are written and we play Adele's CDs over and over and wail to our cats about the one who left us.

But for now, Ilaria is comfortable. I always say she just walked in and turned our house into a home.

By the way, we have a new dog too.

I don't know what it is about us, but Ian and I find a lot of dogs on the street. We'll see one running without a collar and just groan because we know what's coming: months of trying to find the owner. Years ago, we'd found a stray, dirty dog running along a street. No one in the neighborhood knew her or claimed her. We took her in and called her Trudy Trouble because after weeks and weeks of trying to find her a home, she'd chewed through all our screens and eaten a doorknob. She didn't have a microchip, and no one responded to our many signs and calls to shelters. Finally someone did call and said she was theirs for a while but they didn't want her anymore because she was "untrainable."

We were advised if we dropped her at a shelter, she'd be put down in ten days. Trudy was very sweet, very affectionate, and very odd. She'd eat anything from shoes to hardware. I'm not talking chew. I mean eat. As in digest. No one could figure out what breed she was—she was unique looking. Sort of like a white husky and a terrier with tempestuous eyes. But she was sweet, she loved petting—she would arch her back as you stroked her fur—something I'd never seen a dog do before.

Then she displayed erratic behavior more often and almost bit Ilaria, so we hired a professional trainer. But Trudy Trouble was loving and still acted wild. She'd run around the house banging into furniture and our kneecaps. One day before I got on the plane back to Los Angeles from a New York trip, Ian informed me we had to do something about Trudy Trouble because she'd tried to bite Ilaria again. She'd wrapped her jaws around Ilaria's leg as if, when given the chance, she was testing to see how fast she could swallow it.

I got on the plane, worried about the situation. Like many travelers, I absentmindedly flipped through that in-flight magazine. It had an article on animals. I sort of glanced at each picture—from dogs to raccoons. Then I saw a picture of Trudy Trouble. I looked closer to learn what breed she was. And under her picture I saw the word—coyote.

I paced until that plane landed then called Ian and screeched out that Trudy was a coyote. I'm sure Ian picked up Ilaria and ran out of the house. That evening we found a place for Trudy—a ranch where she could run wild. I know this sounds like the fake story you heard from your parents when the dog you were allergic to oddly disappeared, but the woman trying to train Trudy agreed with our assessment that she was part coyote and actually helped us place her. The owners of the ranch did not have kids and have since called to tell us Trudy is doing well and is especially happy at night when they let her out and she howls at the hill. Of coyotes.

So it's understandable that since then we groan when we see stray dogs on the street, but we can't help ourselves when we see their sad eyes. We pull over, go door-to-door to find the owner, and if we can't, we put up signs in the neighborhood and take them home until we can find them a home. After we found another little white-spotted puppy who peed on every surface we owned until we got him placed, we vowed we had to stop picking up strays.

Then one evening on a neighborhood walk, Ian spotted a brown lump of mangled fur running toward us. This little dog's pink tongue hung out, a chewed rope was around his throat, and he had a bite clean through one ear. No one in the neighborhood claimed him. So we brought him home—the bottom of his paws were so soft, it seemed as if he'd never been outdoors. Of course he didn't have a microchip, so we put the standard signs up everywhere from the vet's office to around the neighborhood.

But we really didn't want anyone to come forward. He was as soft as a plush-toy animal. He didn't bark or shed, and he even pooped outside the house. We all loved him. It was important to Ilaria that we didn't give this dog away. She wanted to adopt him.

So after a month, the vet said no one had come forward so we could adopt him. Ever the ombudsman, Ilaria incorporated Core suggestions and named him Louie Salvatore Dominick Bagel Vardalos Gomez. The minute we got him home, Louie shed all over the furniture and pooped on my white carpet. It is once again a test. I can see it in Louie's eyes—do you really want me? The answer is, yes. I can get a new carpet. But there's only one Louie.

Manny is at first annoyed with his new little brother/shadow. We try to give Manny extra attention and assure him he's still top dog.

But Manny gives us a look as if he's saying, "That's what you said about the little girl and then she got her own room."

Plus, Louie has a habit of physically leaning against Manny. And Manny is like Ian, in that he's hot when he eats, he's hot when he sleeps, he's hot when he swims. So Manny is annoyed and tries to ditch Louie, who dutifully follows him from room to room, then leans and snores. But after a while, Manny realizes Louie has his own food bowl, doesn't take up much space, and hates squirrels too. So he decides Louie is okay. I try to house-train Louie and get him to stop tasting the piquancy of the carpets and my shoes and it is extremely time-consuming and hard for him to break these habits. Plus he has a pornographic habit of waking us all up by putting his tongue into our mouths.

But one evening Ilaria cries about not wanting to take a bath . . . and Louie sidles up to her and licks her tears from her cheeks until she laughs. Her mood is completely changed, and as she gets into the bath, I decide this little dog can poop on my pillow and I'll love him forever.

I realize adopting a dog makes Ilaria feel even safer in the family unit. Slowly, slowly Ilaria let go of the anxieties she was feeling and settled in. Is it her nature that helped her fit in so well? Or is it the nurturing? Ilaria calls Manny and Louie and herself our "kids" and I can see for her that Louie is a completion of our family.

By the way, even though like most kids, Ilaria occasionally said she wanted a sibling, that has passed. Yes, we are still on the waiting lists for various countries and know the phone could ring with a sibling. But I am living in the moment and don't think about it. By the way, it's a nosy question often posed to me and for the record: asking a woman if she's going to have more kids is like asking a man if he plans to do something about that bald spot.

Ah well, perhaps curiosity is in our nature. Maybe some nurturing might breed better manners.

23

The Real Stuff

Uh-oh . . . there is a theme emerging here. Telling all these stories even if for context or explanation feels braggy. As a card-carrying dork, this is uncomfortable for me.

I'm slightly chagrined I told you stuff I'm proud of, even small things like my nickname being Mixie. Plus, all the subsequent specifics about the process of settling my daughter in, while meant to be in the tone of discovery rather than advisory, might be construed as boasting about my parenting skills. I don't think I'm good at it; I'm just telling you what happened. So lest you think *I* think I'm cool, please allow me to assure you, oh, I do not think this about myself. I am not cool.

Therefore, I feel the need to merely pause for a moment and tell you some real facts to even out the perception of me:

1. When I was ten years old and playing in my garage, I tried to change the appearance of a wood board and accidentally spray-painted my face completely black.

2. As a kid on a July trip to Greece, I put a message in a bottle into the sea of Loutraki Beach. Months later, I received a letter from Egypt. This girl and I had a lot in common and she became my pen pal for four years. When I was in high school, in one of my letters I remarked how incredible it was that we would know each other all these years simply because my message in a bottle had traveled all the way to Egypt. In her letter back, she wondered why I thought that and assumed I knew she'd actually found my bottle on her family's July vacation at Loutraki Beach.

3. Sure, it gets cold in Winnipeg but Greek parents are overly cautious, so we had to wear snowsuits under our Halloween costumes. Even the year I went as a ballerina.

4. When I was seventeen (and my full sideburns had come in), I loved this cool guy, Steve. At the local summer fair, I got up the nerve to ask him to go on the Zipper with me. He said, sure, if I waited in line. I did. For an hour. As I was getting closer to the front of the line, I worried Steve wasn't coming back. Then I saw it—someone had puked in the red compartment car. The Zipper ride spun so the puke was all over the car. The toothless carnies stopped the ride, perfunctorily hosed down the red car without soap or alcohol, then simply ran the entire ride around once so the excess water could run out. Everyone in the line was disgusted and ducked so the water wouldn't get on them. The carnies restarted the ride and as I inched up the line, I kept worrying Steve wasn't coming back. I peered around—no sign of him anywhere around the fair. Suddenly, I was up next and as I turned forward I

saw the carny motioning me to get in . . . to the red car. Everyone watched to see if I would do it. I started to turn away when suddenly Steve appeared beside me. Ready to go, he asked? Yep, I said and got into the red car with him.

5. I cannot eat at an outdoor café if it is beside an establishment that does manicures and pedicures. Just the idea of an errant toenail clipping careening into my salad makes my insides curdle.

6. I am similarly repulsed by antique furniture. I have to walk quickly by antique stores because the thought of all the dead-skin-skull-flakes ground into a headboard makes me throw up in my mouth.

7. That daily '80s outfit I wore—the harem pants and a headband . . . I was too embarrassed to tell you I also wore leg warmers.

8. Using my headset in my car, I pretend to be on my phone but am actually singing all the parts of *Rent*.

9. I do not like smooth jazz music at all and once even offered a street saxophonist playing outside my hotel window a crisp fifty-dollar bill if he would move down the block.

10. When we were in preproduction for *My Big Fat Greek Wedding*, four days before shooting, we still had not cast the male lead of the groom, "Ian." We were all staying at the Sutton Place Hotel in Toronto and I met with one of

the producers, Gary, in the bar to discuss the situation. He assured me that he, Rita, and Tom would never cast an actor I didn't feel possessed the warmth of the real Ian. But we were all worried because for six months, we'd been through many lists of actors and didn't feel we'd found the right guy. With the beginning of filming approaching, we needed to make a decision. Then John Corbett walked into the bar. I turned to Gary and whispered, "That's John Corbett! He was first on our list. What happened?" Gary recalled we'd heard John was not available for our shoot dates—he was already committed to another project. A film (ironically) called *Serendipity*. But our shoot dates had recently been moved back two weeks. Well, Gary and I sidled over to the bar to see if we could chat with John . . . and we overheard this conversation. The bartender said, "So you wrap production soon. What's up next for you?" John replied, "I don't know but I just read this script in my room called *My Big Fat Greek Wedding* and I want to be in it." Gary and I looked at each other—whaaaaat? Gary strode around the bar, introduced himself and John said more nice things about the script. Gary offered him the role. John was incredulous. In an industry known for exaggeration and hearsay, he seemed dumbfounded to have found an honest producer. He said to Gary, "Are you telling me if I shake your hand right now, I have this role?" Gary said yes. They shook. Then Gary turned John around to meet me . . . and in this incredible moment, I cursed my earlier-in-the-evening choice to eat Greek Town's delights for dinner. I had garlic breath that could knock a buzzard off an outhouse. Handsome John Corbett leaned in to me and said, "Hi . . ." and I leaned back.

Way back. I then took two steps back, stretched a hand out, and muttered "nice to meet you" into my other hand. Weeks later, John told me he smelled my stink-breath but took the part anyway.

11. Sometimes in my workout class, if we're all facing the mirror and moving together, I pretend we're in rehearsal for a Broadway musical called *Work It*.

12. I have a crush on Robert De Niro even though I once met him and he seemed unimpressed.

13. Sometimes I Google myself.

14. In photo shoots, when the stylist dresses me in sexy clothes that require a sultry attitude and pout, I pose by pretending I'm standing on the streets of Rome, shooting a Fellini film. Actually, I recommend this mental exercise for a daily feeling of pure sex appeal: look over your shoulder at your pet and whisper sultrily: "Ciao."

15. I get self-conscious and blush when people misuse the words *nonplussed* and *bemused*.

16. I get self-conscious and blush when I misuse the word *regimen* for *regime*.

17. I have an unnatural devotion, bordering on hoarding, addiction to Tupperware.

18. I was too mortified to tell you that the second time I was on Oprah's show, I got injured. For some reason, the

show was a mash-up of actors who had movies coming out in the same month, so Noah Wyle and the Olsen twins, Mary-Kate and Ashley, were the other guests. At the end of the show, as I sat on a couch with Mary-Kate and Ashley, the producers and stagehands began to change the set over to the After the Show segment for the Oxygen network. Oprah did a friendly wave and invited us to scooch closer to her. We did. And one of those tiny Olsen twins accidentally sat on my thumb. To not make a scene, I didn't react, but as I yanked my thumb from her teeny bum cheeks, the pain ripped up into my forearm. Back in Los Angeles, an orthopedic doctor treated my torn ligaments for over twelve months with six different casts and weekly hand therapy. Years later, it's healed but I coddle my thumb so the ligaments won't snap again. Consequently, a fresh bottle of water is first handed to a friend with the phrase, "Olsen twin," and they wordlessly twist off the cap for me.

19. One day when Ilaria was away with Ian, I spent forty-eight hours in bed watching two entire seasons of *Downton Abbey,* then spoke to Manny and Louie with an English accent.

20. I love love love Beyoncé, and Ian points out I smile at her on the TV as if she can see me and we're friends.

21. Rue McClanahan was the first celebrity to attend when I was doing my one-woman stage show in that small Los Angeles theater. Afterward her assistant approached me and said, "Rue loved the show and would be honored to have you over for dinner." I was thrilled. The assistant,

oddly named "Shepherd" (really), called that week and explained Rue was so inspired by my show she wanted to throw a Greek dinner and wondered what groceries should she buy? So I gave the assistant a detailed list of ingredients for the weekend dinner. As Ian and I were driving to Rue's house, I was excited and Ian the New Yorker was suspicious. He asked if I'd actually spoken to Rue and I realized, no, I had not. We got to the door and God bless her, Rue swung open the door, quite hammered, wig askew, looked at me as if she'd never seen me before, and peered at Ian like she wasn't buying what he was selling. The assistant, Shepherd, appeared behind her and said, "Come in, come in!" Rue drifted back out to the patio. There were several people there imbibing in summer drinks, including another of my comedy idols, Estelle Getty. I started out to the patio, but the assistant stopped me and said, "I'll bring them in so you can show them." I said, "Show them what?" And she said, "How to make a Greek dinner." Ian and I looked at each other—no, no. I said, "I'm cooking?" And she said, "Yes, of course, we don't know how to cook Greek food." I stood in the kitchen, unable to make eye contact with Ian as Shepherd herded the guests into the kitchen. Rue and her male companion began to argue like a scene right out of *Who's Afraid of Virginia Woolf*? He stormed off to another room and in the awkward pause, everyone looked at me . . . so I began to cook. A few guests stayed and watched for a while, then everyone slowly trickled back out to the patio, leaving us alone in the kitchen again. Ian resolutely went into the dining room to count the place settings. At least, including the people on the patio, there were enough place settings for all of us, so we reasoned we were invited to the dinner. Ian and I were too embarrassed to join them on the patio and actually were not invited to do so. Eventually, the dinner was ready and Shepherd shepherded us all into the dining room. We ate in silence. It was so odd and awkward. Finally, Ian motioned to me that we should go. The situation was just wholly perplexing so we got up, thanked everyone, and said we would now be going. Everyone looked up as if they'd just noticed we were at the end of the table. It was quiet as we headed to the door. Suddenly Rue said, "Wait!," and we turned back thinking, well, finally, she is going to say something about this being some sort of misunderstanding. But no. She said, "Can you give Estelle Getty a ride home?"

Okay, back to our story. . . .

24

The Wonder Years

We're on a family trip to Hawaii and people are asking me for photos around the pool. (General note: poolside photos are excruciating for anyone who isn't wearing control-top panty hose under a bikini.)

Ilaria's sitting with her cousins around the wading pool and I see another kid point to me and tell her something. Ilaria turns and takes a long look at me. She's five.

Later she says, "Mom, you're famous, you know."

Ugh. This is not a word I wanted to come out of her mouth. As I said, it's not that I've hidden it, but I've made sure she's never seen us act. In helping her with her identity, we feel it's important for her to just know her parents as who we are, without having to reconcile our public personas as well. So we haven't shown her our movies and when she has visited us on our film and TV sets, we made sure she does not see us act. If the camera was rolling, we'd just walk her off the set, usually to the food area called Craft Services, which is beloved for its abundance of snacks. Every kid enjoys visiting the

Craft Services truck, even though on the first time Ilaria complained, "Where are the crafts?"

We don't take her to industry events. There are many fundraising kid-friendly events that are supposed to be photographer free. The one time we'd taken Ilaria to one of those events, there were photographers—luckily she had the kitty makeup on—so we just don't go at all now. Also, Ilaria will never come to a premiere. We don't think it's natural for any kid to see a throng of red carpet photographers calling out "Parent Name, Parent Name" and taking pictures. It's a heady experience, and I didn't even allow my nephews or nieces to see it when they were young. In my opinion, no kid should ever see it. Kids' worlds should be all about them and have nothing to do with celebrity. Daily, kids of actor-parents see strangers lavish praise on their parents. Yes, it's wonderful. But I don't want Ilaria to think I'm special because of my job. I want her to think I'm special because I'm her mom. My own self-esteem has never been in direct correlation to how well or not my career is going, so neither should her opinion of me.

I thought Ilaria didn't even know Ian and I are actors. We weren't hiding it; it's just never come up, and kids don't really care what their parents do for a living. But she has often seen kind people say nice things about our work. One time at a farmers' market Ian spotted paparazzi (or as Ilaria calls them, "rude boys"), we left, and I'd asked her if she knew why strangers want to take our picture. She replied with a shrug: "Because we're cute."

But on several work and family trips, my movies had been playing on cable or on the hotel in-room service. Guests had seen them and would sweetly tell me their favorite parts while we were all in line at the breakfast buffet. Ilaria heard it but had no expression of it really registering or mattering to her.

One time, we were in a video store on the hunt for *Hello Kitty* movies and as we turned a corner we came face-to-face with an entire wall of *My Life In Ruins* DVDs. I waited, watching her expression. She took it in for a few moments, said, "Hey, Mom, that's you," and turned away in search of her beloved *Hello Kitty*. Maybe she was silently staring at first because the DVD cover picture is so retouched she wasn't even sure who it was.

Now the incident in Hawaii seems to have given her a word for this thing she's been putting together in her mind. I reply, "What does famous mean?" She says, "It's a word that means you're good at doing dances. And shows. Daddy's a singer."

In the next few moments I figure out Ilaria hasn't asked questions because she gets it all. Since now she says, "Mom, do you write all the movies you act in?"

Okay, so she knows. I'm relieved to observe she's not that impressed with The Showbiz. So I tell her about my job and how much I love it and I describe Ian's shows, and say that I hope one day she can enjoy what she does for a living as much.

She tells me many of her friends have seen my movies and told her about them and she knows that Ian is on a show called *Cougar Town*. I'm surveying her face to see if she's okay with all this. Is she old enough? Is she really absorbing it all in the very matter-of-fact way I think she is? Is it too much for her to handle? Well, she seems totally at ease with it. She smiles nonchalantly at me. She gets it and it's not overly important to her. It's just my job.

So I ask, "Hey, do you want to see one of my movies?" And she yawns, "No, they're probably boring."

To this day, I'm immensely proud that she still has not seen us act. We're going to try to keep this going for as long as possible. Again, no secrets. If she asks, yes, she can see our movies or TV shows. But I figure the longer I can keep her perception of us unfettered, the better. We want her to grow up like we did—movies are magic. I don't want to give her a peek backstage to see the actors putting on makeup. It'd be like going behind the scenery at Disneyland and seeing the middle-aged biker playing Mickey standing around smoking while holding his giant head.

It's Ilaria's last year of preschool and I have really gone back to work now except I still won't leave town for acting jobs unless I can bring her. I keep taking writing jobs that hopefully will get made and I'll get to act in them. I like working with men and especially enjoy developing with female executives and producers because we have the tacit understanding among many women in my industry—there's enough success to go around. We don't take each other down, ninja style. Being surrounded by woman-friends—jaunty girlfriends who don't try to puncture my career-aorta—keeps me sane in this cesspool known as Hollywood. Correspondingly in my movies, the women are kind to one another. Also, I write several female roles since the average script I read seems to have merely two—the Wife who gets killed in the first scene and the Hottie the guy takes up with two scenes later. The men I write are good-hearted, mirroring the men I know. Years ago, I remember wincing when a development executive advised me, "Ian needs to cheat on Toula and win her back before the wedding." I'm not implying my scripts are marvelous, no no, not at all. But I try to avoid the formulaic pitfalls that send messages to men and women that we're at war. We're not. We can have a lot of fun when we play nice together. My entire film career exists because another woman—Rita—read my first screenplay, and, along with Tom and Gary, produced it.

It never fails to alarm and depress me that there are some women who do not support other women. But this is another reason I currently stay close by—what I teach Ilaria in these formative years will stay with her forever. Not that she needs much coaxing, but I'll urge her to stand up to discourteous girl behavior and, as a young woman, to surround herself with woman-friends. I remember a dad in preschool describing his daughters being so awful to each other. He shrugged, "Well, you know how girls can be." I blurted, "No. Some girls, sure. But not all. Help them be each other's friend." And he gave me a look like I was canvassing for a cult. I am similarly annoyed by magazine covers blaring, "Don't We Just Hate *(Actress Name)* For Having It All?" No, actually, we don't. The majority of us don't. Yes, some women do. I used to be afraid of them. But I don't run from the Coven since I discovered pepper spray.

Today, I get to see the ultimate woman-friend—Oprah—to be on her new OWN show. I talk about how therapeutic I think it is to embrace grief and just go through it to get through it. I tell her I am actually grateful for every disappointment because it led me to my real daughter. After the show, I get to thank Oprah for her thoughtfulness all those years ago in not pushing me to reveal my obvious unhappiness during the fertility treatments. I know this woman has had a lifetime of people thanking her. But as I am telling her this now, I watch her be gracious and patient in accepting my gratitude to let me experience my "full circle moment." (I don't know how she lets us all gush on her without stifling a yawn.)

What stepping back did is give me a new perspective for my line of work; I'm not enamored with this industry of rejection and criticism. But I've missed acting, and have the same ambition to become a better actor, so am slowly finding on-camera jobs that work in with parenting. I get a request to do a cameo in a Los Angeles film called *For A Good Time, Call,* written by Lauren Miller and Katie Anne Naylon. My agent tells me these two women were frustrated by their attempts to break into the industry, so they'd written their own movie. I can't say yes fast enough. They turn out to be enormously gifted and lovely women who support each other.

Also, I am giddy to play the mom in the new American Girl movie about McKenna the gymnast doll. I like the script and brand because it's about girl empowerment without being anti-boy. Also . . .

it's my first mom role. Coincidentally, it films in Winnipeg. This is my first time working in my hometown since my musical theater days. It's restorative to fulfill that moment I'd craved when Ilaria runs into my parents' home, shouting "Yiayia and Pappou!" Also, I hope being the mom in this movie might make me cool to my daughter for two or three seconds. Again, my job doesn't impress her, and if she does want to finally see this movie, I'm not sure if she'll enjoy seeing me as someone else's mom, so I'm definitely not going to encourage it. The kind people at Mattel sent a doll for her, but I hid it until a birthday. I just don't want her to know my job has benefits for her. I do want her to know we have unique and fortunate lives.

Therefore, we do a lot of community service throughout the year, plus get a Christmas list from a Foster Family Agency. We buy food and as many toys as we can fit into the cart. Then we go home and she plays elf. As Ian and I read names and ages from the list, Ilaria decides what they might like and stuffs the gift bags. There's no need to drive the point home with kids—they get it. We take the rest of the toys to a local box drop-off, and as we put them in, Ilaria whispers, "Merry Christmas, kids."

She still lives a life outside of the public eye. We'd announced her adoption by of course giving the exclusive to the reporter who'd kept it a secret—Marc Malkin at *E!* (still without releasing her name or picture)—only because I became the spokesperson for National Adoption Day. By the way, it's odd to hear myself speaking publicly about adoption and explaining how to do it. I realize how far behind me those disconsolate years are.

Like many little girls, Ilaria enjoys playing dress-up with my clothes. When I'm wearing a long gown for an event, she sighs that I'm a "real-life princess." I see things from her perspective: the glamour, getting a good table at the latest Top Chef's restaurant, and event parties *are* fun. I find myself enjoying it all again (though a couture garment fitting is like squeezing a tuba into a guitar case). I tend to choose comfort over style so I can have fun at the parties—even if that means my untethered back-fat flips over the sushi bar because I wouldn't wear the corset that goes under the dress. Undergarments and panty hose tend to take my nether regions hostage and I like to be able to sit without giving myself a urinary tract infection. So I usually don't wear them (unless that corset boosts my rack to the sky, then I'm totally in). But because I'm in awe of my daughter's unself-conscious fashion sense, I've resolved to take more risks and have more fun with my clothing. One day, I may even hit the red carpet in her dog costume.

I show Ilaria my jewelry, which will one day be hers (along with her own swanky diamond heart). For every job I've ever gotten, once the contract is signed, I donate to a charity, plus I buy a piece of jewelry to commemorate the project. Maybe I see it as a guarantee of always having something to hock or maybe I see it as taking a moment to celebrate how damn hard it is to sell a script or book an acting job. Either way, a bauble (best pronounced "baaaawwwbul") is both frivolous and pragmatic insurance for the future. A friend once told me I like jewelry so much because I have a leftover merchant gene in my DNA. When I wear a piece, it reminds me of the accomplishment of each project. And inwardly I squeal, "Ooh, sparkly!"

Her eyes are wide as I explain to Ilaria that these jewels are rewards . . . because we are strict about new toys and big treats like theme park excursions. The impetus for what I call our Pilgrim Parenting is the unwarranted pout we've seen on some L.A. kids' (and adults') faces. I do feel like Cinderella's evil stepmother when I get Ilaria to help out around the house (relax, tabloids, I don't make her sweep out the chimney). I make myself enforce rules even though I snort into my hand when I watch her try to maneuver her tiny body, gallantly trying to make her own bed. I try to be the parent. Of course I want to spoil her with her own jet. Sure, I want to dance around all day in our pajamas eating bonbons in Paris, but then I might as well just hand her a crack pipe right now.

It's just better if she learns to appreciate luxuries, plus ways to be frugal. When Ian and I were not making a lot of money, I would re-cycle our clothing with a six-dollar bottle of Rit dye and some laundry quarters. It started with a white denim jacket I'd worn for years. Then one spring, I ran it through the coin-operated washer with fuchsia Rit dye in hot water, turned the rinse cycle to cold, tossed in a cup of salt to set it . . . then posed and preened in my hot pink jacket, basking in the warm rays of girlfriend-kudos. I still do this with my clothes and have even worn the same dress on camera dyed a different color because it saves time on shopping. I'll often rinse a washer-full of faded T-shirts and jeans in black Rit Dye to show Ilaria they come out like new and it'd be wasteful to thrown them out and buy more. The only time my craft-y hobby went horribly awry was when I impudently dumped the silk Badgley Mischka gown I'd worn to a Golden Globes party into my washer. For some reason I tried to bleach the dark blue color out first and the fine ma-terial came out as a shredded chartreuse mess. I was so mortified at the waste that I wore it as a Halloween costume. Sure, I was the best-dressed witch on our street, but I was annoyed at myself because any ethnic girl with a mustache knows the power of bleach.

Ilaria also sees how much time I have to do things with her is the direct result of being organized, even though I'm leaning over the perimeter of obsessiveness when I find myself making lists of lists I have to make. She sees how many jobs I have—from acting to writ-ing, there is a multitude of fittings, script meetings, charity work, and interviews—and I never pant and panic in a whirl of chaos. As I've mentioned, my own ability to multitask with composure came from my mom. So I know Ilaria seeing how calmly I approach things, treating everyone with a smile and respect, will be the best example

I can teach her on manners. Especially when I want to scream "shut-up-shut-up-shut-up" at the checkout guy who's taking forever with our groceries while telling us about his band.

Also, Ian and I have Ilaria take responsibility for filling her own little backpack with the things she'll need for the preschool day—the snack we made her, the book she likes, a show-and-tell item. (She tries to cram Louie in there too.) It helps her think through her day and be accountable. However, lately in the mornings, I can't take my eyes off her—it's only been a little over two years and already she seems so grown up as she dresses herself. Sometimes I just want to baby her, so I put on her little socks and shoes. I can't help it. I remember when we adopted her, friends would ask, "How is the baby?" and Ian and I would be quick to point out she was a toddler. Now we look back at pictures and see she was a baby. And like every mom, I see she's growing so quickly I want to put a heavy brick on her head.

So we are very careful to raise her in an environment outside all that is Hollywood . . . but we truly pamper her on one day: In our house, we don't just have Mother's Day and Father's Day—once a year, we also celebrate Daughter Day. This is our way of acknowledging the day we met as the day Ilaria became our daughter. Daughter Day is spent celebrating with presents and cake and even a drive down to Disneyland. All day we do the things Ilaria wants to do and we celebrate meeting her. We talk about her memories from before she became our daughter, and the evening ends with her requesting if we can "do the thing"—she loves the story and it's comforting to her to reenact how we all met. So she crouches in bed to pretend she's in a social worker's arms, and Ian and I walk toward her. She does the same thing she did that day—she turns and smiles. Now I say out loud: "Oh, I found you." And we all celebrate how we became a family the instant we met.

25

Navigating Mom World

"Where is Ilaria going to school next year?"

I mumble "I'm not sure" as the inquiring mom lists her top choices and explains which curriculum is best for her child. The truth is, I don't know how to interpret the ambiguous Los Angeles school system. I buy a book and try to figure out how to get into a charter school, which public school is in our neighborhood, and what is the difference between a progressive private school and a traditional magnet school. Caught, I stare at the mom asking the question and mutter, "In Canada, we just went to the igloo up the street," while pretending to look for something in my purse. But I'm taking this seriously.

Am I doing my daughter a disservice if I don't get her into "the right school"?

Other moms seem to know what they're doing—so much more than I do.

Although Ilaria is now absolutely comfortable in her home, I'm still not completely at ease being a mom. I thought it would come with a wisdom, an all-knowing seer-like confidence. But no. I'm not like that naturally. I mean, I'm so naive, I had a coyote in my house. So I ask a lot of questions. I've had the benefit of watching my mom, siblings, and friends parent long before I became a mom, so I gleaned good information off them. The women (yes, and men!) of Core have also been very helpful and loving throughout this entire experience. But the best thing I've noticed about parenting is you get to talk to people you may not have ever met. I get to have tremendously informative and valuable conversations at a play structure or waiting in the ballet class lobby. The moms are great.

Los Angeles is laidback in that many parents are in the industry, so most moms don't care what I do for a living. They either don't recognize me, don't care that I'm an actress, or don't like my movies. I'm simply another mom, and I appreciate that I'm in this club. The conversations are so interesting and on a vast array of subjects from finding time to work to weaning kids off a sippy cup. I appreciate it when a mom at a birthday party will offer a website: "Hey, there's a new collapsible water bottle that's made out of the good plastic" or "Instead of astringent soap I just pour a cup of baking soda in my kid's bath" (which I immediately switched to and it even pH balances our lady-parts).

I love the moms I'm meeting—I love them in a gushy way. I have encountered wonderfully warm women with excellent stories and tips from a good sunscreen to the best app to identify convicted predators in your neighborhood.

I do shush anyone who says, "Oh I'm just a stay-at-home mom." Now that I know what it takes, I vociferously declare, until everyone at the yogurt shop stares, that "There's no such thing as *just* a mom."

I don't know how my own mom did it—four kids in eight years? How did she do it so humbly, never needing her own parade to fete her? I want to make her and every mom a shiny neon-glitter-festooned badge: "Chauffeur. Private Chef. Hypnotherapist." It's the most challenging job I've ever done. Because the Me years are over. When you become a mom, you come second from now on. My brain is all about my daughter now. I keep a running tally in my head of her schedule, what she's eaten from dawn to dusk, the email addresses of the moms of which friends she's asked me to plan playdates with, plus a detailed diagram of the fastest route from school to soccer to home in time to defrost a chicken and pull off that conference call while she's washing her hands. So I value any advice from the exceptional moms I'm meeting.

I don't even dodge the moms with Beautiful Woman Syndrome who wear Lululemon workout wear all day and stand too close as they "You should" the rest of us. If one of these moms overhears me asking about anything from a healthy bread to a school's curriculum, hastily they point a finger and proclaim, "You should sign up for elementary school orientation tours by now or she won't get in." Or "You should have her in gymnastics or she won't make a junior volleyball team." Or "You should only give her almond milk or she'll grow breasts on her back." Even though their perfectly groomed Children Of The Corn spawn look at me as if I could use a shower and some microdermabrasion, I now feel great affection for these women even as I try to outrun their teeny yoga butts. I like them because they know a lot. And, I'll take someone with BWS over a member of the Coven any day.

I'll admit, some advice makes me nervous when I hear if I don't have Ilaria in certain developmental programs by now or if she doesn't go to the right elementary school, she won't get into an Ivy League college. Maybe I'm just lazy, but she just turned five. . . . I don't mind if Ilaria is a bit unruly and unfocused or goes to the wrong kindergarten. I don't care if her pigtails are like a cat's yarn by the time she gets to ballet. It's fine if she steps through a puddle to get into the car. If giving her cow's milk means she doesn't go to college, that's okay.

My favorite thing to see is her getting into the bath at the end of a day. The dirtier her hands, ankles, and knees are, the more fun I know she's had. I am hoping I don't get caught up in the zeal of achieving through my child's life. I see it in some parents' eyes— they want their children to have the great, pain-free, and amazing lives they didn't have. Essentially, we all want our kid to have a better life than we did. But adversity and conflict build character. If Ilaria's destiny is living on a foreign country's beach selling woven-grass necklaces, that's her choice. If she achieves greatness (as that tweezers-wielding brain surgeon), so be it.

I think it's my parental obligation to let her be who she is. I must clench my fists at my sides, grit my teeth until they shatter, and let her form her own opinions . . . even if she disagrees with me. (Gasp, even if she doesn't like purses.) As someone who's fond of being in charge, I must find a way to stand back and let her make her mistakes. Oh, I'm not saying I've found my "bliss" and am so groovy I'd give grass-weaving the thumbs-up after twelve years of private school tuition.

But, I simply want my daughter to have a good life. More so, I want her to be happy and make her own life choices. So if I ask you to write her a recommendation letter to Harvard . . . please tell me no.

26

Run Like a Girl

I can tell this nice woman is only being polite. I know I should stop talking. Instead, I grin broadly at her and continue:

" . . . and Ilaria said a kid at the park called someone fat and the mom said it's a bad word. Now, I don't think 'fat' is a bad word at all. We attach a lot of value to certain words and therefore cause them to become painful. So I tell her, 'fat' is a *powerful* word and while some people don't like it, in our family, we don't mind it. I remind her of all the people she loves who have fat tummies, from Santa to some of our relatives, heh, heh."

Oh no, my awkward crazy laugh is back. Because I know I should stop pontificating. The cordial woman stares back at me. Her expression, while still polite, is saying, *Is there a point to your nattering?*

I should stop blabbing at this very lovely woman whose eyes I have bored shut. She'd merely stepped forward to welcome us to the

New Parents reception of Ilaria's elementary school. Now she's trapped by my child-rearing oration.

I don't know where Ian went, and I can't close my yapper. Why on earth did he leave me alone?

On the car ride over to this adult event, we'd had another warning talk with each other about making a good impression at the new school—no wife-swap jokes was again first of the no-no's. But talking too much was the next and biggest item on our list. Our conundrum is that being parents is still so new for us. You know the pure glee on a dog's face as he hangs out the car window panting with joy? That's what we look like all the time. We're so happy, we beam odious perma-grins. When anyone asks us about Ilaria, we blab their ears off.

If we met us, we'd *hate* us. Subsequently, before parties Ian and I remind and warn each other to be cool.

But he'd left me alone, I locked down some eye contact, and I immediately waxed rhapsodic on my harebrained theories of parenting.

I look around: where, where, where is Ian? I need him to hold my lips shut. I cannot stop talking about my daughter. I now blurt out:

"To develop her ability to reason, I allow her to argue, to prove her point to me. Today, she wanted to go to the park, and I asked, 'Why do you think you should get to go to the park?' She said she read a book and fed the dogs, so she deserves a treat. I said, 'Okay, you win.' I know when she's a teen, this will bite me on the butt! Heh, heh, heh."

Oh. God.

I make myself turn away from this kind woman who has surely resisted the urge to plug my gullet with a cocktail weenie. But I can't help myself, and now turn back to add just one more thing:

"I limit adult topics but don't believe in editing words. It's not like our friends are filthy drunken sailors but adults do swear. I don't make a big deal of it; I say those are words adults use when they can't think of a better way to describe something. And that she can say those words when she's as tall as me, heh, hehhhhhhh."

Oh, I truly wish I could choke on something to suppress my bogus chortle. Still no sign of Ian. I now decide he is playing a joke on me by leaving me alone here. Yes, of course, he's done it on purpose! He's probably behind a potted plant tittering into his giant hand. In my head, I plot ways to get him back and decide I will tell his costar Courteney Cox he has a secret but debilitating crush on her. Out of the corner of my eye, I see the woman I've been irking is backing away from me. It's all right. I'm done. Because I have actually put my hand over my mouth. But now I can't stop nodding vigorously, eye buggedly, with voracious eagerness at her. I think she's scared.

Swiftly, she passes me a tray of appetizers. I fervently cram a cheese puff in my gob so I can't blab anymore. Finally and suddenly, Ian is there. He feels the tension in the air, shoots me an "oh no, you've been yammering" look, and takes me aside so I can chew and calm down. I slowly do.

I look around at the parents who will become our friends for the next several years. They're all friendly, they seem as excited as us to begin school—

Suddenly, I tear up. Oh no, I'm bawling. Dammit, I'm That Mom. I don't want to be *that* blubbery mom with running mascara who everybody talks about on their car ride home. This gathering was organized so we can meet each other since our kids will be going through school together. I want to make a good impression. But I am suddenly overwhelmed with memories of the last few years flashing around my cranium like a laser light show of Ilaria's many expressions. I can't look at Ian or I will burst into gelatinous tears.

Like the ousted contestant's see-ya-later clip on *American Idol*, I see the images zip by of everything we've been through in less than three years with Ilaria. I see myself rocking her at a kids' concert, cradling her on the Toon Town roller-coaster ride, lifting her up high to see her first fireworks. I'd held her from behind and experienced everything anew while leaning softly into her. These moments were lived with my tears in her hair.

Now she starts school. Are we actually here? This soon? Is this toddler who bravely walked into her new home now ready for elementary school?

I fear the answer is a resounding yes. But I'm not ready to let her go. How did this happen so soon? Around me, I hear moms lamenting they only had five or six years with their children. Inside I think: *I barely had three. It's not fair. I want her home with me forever.* I look around . . . and I see the same fleeting thoughts on many parents' faces. I become aware that everyone has the same expression.

This makes me realize something. Nothing prepared me for the love I would feel for my child. Nothing prepared me for how quickly it happened for me. And here's what I just figure out now: no one is ever prepared. In a way, we're all instant moms. I look around at all the parents, all the moms, all the dads—the emotions crossing their faces are the same ones Ian and I are feeling. Nothing prepared us for the daunting responsibility and love we feel for our children. All of us are instant parents trying to rise to the challenge of raising our children well. It is so daunting. And unfathomably wonderful.

When it comes to control, parents don't get a safety bar to grip on this ride. I just have to grin through my chattering teeth and lean into every gut-churning dip. I see it all around me right now—I'm in a room of adults who know that sharp pang of nostalgia when we look at a picture of our child taken just yesterday.

• • •

Over the next several days, there are orientation events to accli-
mate the kids to their new school. We all get to know one another.
The parents and teachers are witty and kind, compassionate and
warm.

A few days later, as we walk Ilaria in for the first day of school,
she seems a little shy, but seeing her name on her new cubby brings
a smile of belonging. This is a relief. I want her to enjoy this day.
Once again, all the instances of turning down out-of-town work
make sense. Being completely available to her so she could begin
this experience with confidence and ease was the goal. And it
worked. Minutes later, Ilaria is walking around her new classroom
with her usual curiosity and comfort.

My concerns are mitigated about choosing the right educational
institution for my daughter. It is a good fit. The fact that Ilaria is a
student at this school in particular is yet another coincidence. This
school is special to me because I had visited it a long time ago.

So I now take a few minutes and walk over to an area beside the
gym. I have to see that railing. I need to do a ritual.

There it is. Slowly, I walk toward it.

I'd once stood at this exact railing years ago, so sad, yet so determined. This is the school I had been at four years ago, when I'd
watched my friend's daughter play volleyball.

I now take a step forward to stand on the specific area where I
had decided to find out about foster care. This was the precise moment that led me to motherhood.

And I stand here again, years later, and take a deep breath.
Huh.

I expected this moment to be bigger. Monumental actually.

I at least thought I'd cry.

Nah. Not a drop. Time can turn a scab into a beauty mark.

Well, that's done.

I go back to the school playground to find Ilaria playing with her new classmates. They shriek and scamper with abandon like puppies on caffeine.

Watching my daughter run, arms flailing, legs akimbo, just careening around—I think this is the most desirable state of happiness any of us could achieve. I never understood why it's a pejorative announcement to accuse anyone of throwing or running like a girl.

Heedless of danger or fear or self-doubt, pitching your body headlong and forward is irrefutably a transcendent and preferred state of existence. I want to run like a girl. I want to be as unfettered and carefree as a young girl crisscrossing a field. I know now I never felt like a sophisticated adult because it just doesn't come naturally to me. Maybe it never will. Maybe I just never ripened. Maybe that's okay.

I suppose it'd be prudent to now abandon my pursuit of being a grown-up. Adults most certainly are supposed to be in charge, but I still do not feel like a grown-up. Sure, I talk a good game and carry a good purse, but I'm still obscenely immature. Except for enforcing chores and baptizing my daughter, I don't feel like the adult in our relationship.

Motherhood has not brought the insight and evolvement I anticipated. What life lessons can I possibly pass on to my astute girl who seems to have more insight than I do? All I know is when I fiercely pursued my career goal, my determination was rewarded. But when I went zen and accepted there was a different motherhood path for me, I found happiness. Are we supposed to have a combination of both forces in us? Is this the overall goal? I'm not sure.

Because perhaps my childishness, my unrealistic optimism works for me. Maybe if I had grown up, I would have stopped dreaming, accepted reality, not have written my first movie . . . and never have found my daughter.

I now turn around and look at Ilaria again.

She is laughing and running.

I want to stay here and just watch her all day. I want to be a part of every moment of her life. I want to experience it all with her.

I wait and wait at the edge of the playground . . . until Ilaria looks over at me. She sees me . . . and smiles.

My heart lurches a bit.

She's happy, she's secure. She's ready.

And I know it's time for me to go now.

THIS IS THE HOW-TO-ADOPT APPENDIX

Hi again!

Oh yes, there's more.

Then again, you probably know by now that I can't stop talking. So I had to add a few more things. All right, now that you've patiently waded through twenty-six chapters of Kid Kwips, here's some information on how to become a parent. If you're interested in adoption and have questions, hopefully this appendix has some answers.

I wish you the best of luck on your adventure.

Q. What is the first step in adoption?

A. To begin the process, decide which type of adoption you would like to pursue. There are three types: domestic, fos-adopt, and international.

Q. What is domestic adoption?

A. Adoption terms vary by country, but in the United States and Canada, domestic adoption means adoption of an infant or young child by parents who are U.S. or Canadian citizens. Typically, this means a birth mother or family is placing an infant for adoption. Prospective parents are matched with that birth mother during gestation or shortly after the birth. After the birth of the infant, the time it takes to complete or finalize a domestic adoption varies by state or province from three days to six months.

Q. What is fos-adopt?

A. This is a term used to describe a child adopted from the foster care system. The child is considered a foster child (a dependent of the court) until adoption occurs. The children are in the foster care system with a plan for adoption because reunification with a parent is not probable. In most states there is a supervision period of about six months before adoption occurs, though in some states it could be up to two years.

Q. What is international adoption?

A. This type of adoption is when a child is adopted from a different country than where the adoptive parents reside. In most international adoptions, the children are legal orphans. The time frame varies from country to country, but in most countries the adoption is finalized prior to the parents leaving the country with the child.

Q. What needs to be done to begin any form of adoption?

A. Once you have chosen the type of adoption, you will need an adoption Home Study. It is best to choose an agency, attorney, or county office that specializes in the type of adoption you would like to follow. All persons who are adopting, whether by domestic, international, or fos-adopt, must have an approved Home Study.

Q. What is a Home Study?

A. It is a written assessment completed by a social worker who comes to your home. Generally it includes two to five home visits, individual interviews, a couple interview, fingerprint results, background information, and a home inspection. A complete Home Study can range from six pages to more than forty. Questions your social worker may ask range from opinions on bedtimes to religious upbringing.

Q. How long is the process from Home Study to placement of a child in your home?

A. The Home Study, including fingerprinting, physicals, plus first aid and CPR classes, can be done as quickly as a few weeks or it can take up to a year, depending on how motivated the prospective parents are.

In cases of domestic adoption, the wait for an infant is between one week and two years, depending on your attorney or agency's outreach programs.

In the fos-adopt system, there is a tremendous need for parents willing to adopt a child older than five since there are many children with terminated parental rights. This means these children are available immediately for adoption, once your Home Study is approved. The wait for a child who is newborn through five years old in the fos-adopt system is typically up to two years or more. If you are open to special-needs children or to adopting siblings, the wait can be much shorter.

In international adoptions the time it takes to place a child varies by country, but placement can occur within a few months or up to five years. See below for more information.

Q. Who may adopt via domestic, international, and fos-adopt?

A. Criteria vary from state to state and country to country. In all types of adoptions, adoptive applicants must be eighteen years or older and in most cases it is mandatory they be at least ten years older than the child they are adopting. An applicant must clear or be exempt from a criminal background or child-abuse check, be in good health, and be able to provide a safe home for a child. Currently Florida, Mississippi, Michigan, and Utah do not allow same-sex couples or single people to adopt. Arkansas does not allow same-sex couples to adopt but will allow an adoption by a single person. If you would like to see criteria for your particular state, go to www.adoptuskids.org/for-families/state-adoption-and-foster-care-information and click on the state you reside in. For international requirements, go to adoption.state.gov/country_information.php and choose the country you are interested in to see a list of criteria for an adoptive parent.

Q. What are the typical costs to adopt in the United States?

A. Domestic adoption of an infant is approximately $10,000 to $50,000. Adopting via the foster care system is usually free. Any costs incurred for fos-adopt, such as fingerprinting and Home Study fees, are typically reimbursed upon finalization. This funding is provided by the federally funded Adoption Assistance Program. International adoption fees vary by country but are between $10,000 and $60,000.

Q. What background information do prospective parents adopting via domestic, international, and fos-adopt receive on a child?

A. This depends on the method of the match. For domestic adoption, usually full parental background information is provided, plus periodic ultrasounds, drug testing, and medical checkups. For fos-adopt, full disclosure is the law and all information that is known will be provided to the adoptive parents. For international adoption, it varies per country, though usually little background information is available. It is advisable to retain a translator who may make inquiries on your behalf.

Q. How many mandatory social worker home visits are there during the process if you adopt via domestic, fos-adopt, or international adoption?

A. For domestic adoption this depends on the state where you adopt. Most require a supervision period of six months. For example, in California four visits are required, whereas in Virginia they require three visits.

For fos-adopt there are usually one to three visits per month until the adoption is finalized; most states require the child to be in the home at least six months before the adoption is finalized.

For international adoption there aren't home visits after your Home Study is completed, but if you choose to re-adopt the child in the United States, you will have one supervised home visit. More information follows.

Q. What is re-adoption?

A. In most international adoptions a final adoption decree is issued prior to the child leaving the country. When this occurs, some families choose to do a re-adoption in their state of residence, which will give the child an adoption decree from the United States and a birth certificate issued from their state of residence. Re-adoption is not required.

Q. Is an attorney necessary to finalize any form of adoption?

A. Typically yes, but it depends on the state. In California, families who do an agency adoption may finalize themselves. Also, most self-help centers at the local courthouse will help with the correct documents needed to file. For fos-adopt, it depends on the counties; some will finalize the adoption for you; others will assign an attorney to you at no cost to finalize the adoption.

If you adopt via foster care and cannot afford an attorney, on National Adoption Day, several hundred attorneys and judges work for free to finalize the adoption of several hundred children nationwide.

International adoptions are usually finalized prior to leaving the country, though a family can choose to do a re-adoption, which can be done by an agency or attorney.

Q. In a domestic adoption how are prospective parents matched with an infant?

A. Prospective parents write a short biography or letter, attach a photo, then register with a licensed adoption agency, facilitator, or attorney. Ordinarily, the birth mother and/or birth father choose the family based on the bios and pictures presented. The attorney or agency will facilitate the exchange of finances between the birth mother and the prospective parents. The adopting parents typically cover the birth mother's expenses during the period of the pregnancy.

Q. What is an open adoption?

A. In a domestic, international, or fos-adopt situation, an open adoption is when birth parents and the adopting parents know of one another and mutually decide what their ongoing relationship will be. This could mean other family members as well. For instance after the adoption, a grandmother may want phone contact or physical visitation with the child. It could mean there will be a yearly phone call between the adopting mom and the birth mother. In some open adoptions, the adopting family is present for the birth, but then further communication between the birth family and the child is completely and mutually terminated. Sometimes the birth parent and the adopting family exchange addresses and phone numbers and stay in contact for the entire upbringing of the child. Open adoption is consensual by both parties. The most common open adoption is pictures and updates yearly until the child turns eighteen. No one must participate in an open adoption unless it's initially agreed upon. Each situation is unique and depends on what is best for the child.

Q. What is a closed adoption?

A. Closed adoption means there is no contact between the birth parents and adoptive parents and usually means the birth parents and adoptive parents do not know anything about one another. The intermediaries between birth and adoptive families can be social workers, a private lawyer, or a private adoption agency. More information follows.

Q. What is a private adoption?

A. Also known as independent adoption, in North America there are usually two types of domestic adoption: agency and attorney. *Private* refers to the process being private between an attorney and client. An attorney, rather than an adoption agency, may oversee and complete the process for a private adoption. The attorney matches the prospective parents with the birth mother and is the intermediary throughout the process. The term *private* doesn't refer to the adoption being "open" or "closed." The costs, approximately $10,000 to $50,000, will cover the birth mother's expenses and the fees to terminate rights and finalize the adoption. The extent of time a birth mother has to change her mind varies from state to state; it could be anywhere from twenty-four hours to thirty days. The length of time to finalize an adoption is also different per state law; it ranges from a few days to six months, or in some cases longer. The birth parents will give their consent to the adoption and in most cases the state department will complete the supervision visit(s) and final report for finalization.

Q. What is a private adoption agency?

A. This varies by country, but in the United States or Canada, a private adoption agency is a state-licensed agency that assists prospective parents and birth parents in the adoption of children via domestic or international means. These agencies are monitored to ensure they are following the state or provincial adoption regulations. They assist in matching children with adopting parents, completing the Home Study, and supervising the adoption.

Q. What are the qualifications required to work in a private adoption agency?

A. The qualifications vary by state, though most require that social workers have a master's degree as well as many hours of initial and yearly training.

Q. In the United States and Canada, if you adopt domestically, do you have to foster before your adoption is legally finalized?

A. No.

Q. Do social workers work only for the government and Foster Family Agencies (FFAs), or could they also work for licensed private agencies?

A. All state-regulated agencies (county departments, FFAs, or licensed private agencies) are required to have social workers to complete adoptions.

Q. What's the difference between an adoption agency worker and a facilitator?

A. A private adoption agency is licensed by the state and follows strict regulations including that social workers must have a master's degree in social work. A facilitator is helpful in that this person acts as a go-between for parents and agencies and acts as a matcher, but the facilitator will refer out to an agency or an attorney to complete the adoption.

Q. In the United States and Canada, if you adopt via fos-adopt, do you have to foster before your adoption if legally finalized?

A. Normally yes. A child is placed with a family for a period of six months or longer as the state is working to legally emancipate that child. Even if the child is already legally freed, this is still called fostering because there is a six-month period of waiting for a court date to finalize the adoption. This time allows the social workers to visit the home, assess the match, and address any concerns. A person working directly with state social workers or with social workers at an FFA may voice their concern to not be matched with a child who isn't legally emancipated. In addition, a person may voice their concern if they are presented with a case they feel they're not equipped to take on. This means that if you meet a child and do not feel it is a match, you may tell your social worker how you feel. The social workers want it to fit—they do not want you to feel pressured in any way.

Q. If someone is pursuing parenthood via the fos-adopt system, does that mean they are only fostering with no hope of adoption?

A. No. When you decide to do fos-adopt you will be asked what type of risk level you are open to. These levels include low to no risk that the child would return to the birth parents. In some cases there may be a high risk that they could return to the birth parents. If you do not feel this is the route for you, tell your social worker you would feel more comfortable being matched with a child already legally emancipated. Typically, the wait is two years or longer for a legally freed child to be placed in your home.

Once you decide what risk level you are open to, your agency or social worker will try to find the best match for you. Before you agree to be matched with the child, you will know the background on the case and whether or not the child is likely to go back to their original home. Fos-adopt has a high success rate of adoption. Also, many children have been placed in homes temporarily, then returned to their birth parents, yet they continued to have a friendship with the parents who fostered them.

Q. Who may adopt a child via the United States' and Canada's fos-adopt systems?

A. Anyone who meets the standards and has an approved Home Study. American and Canadian foster care does not discriminate on the basis of sexual orientation, marital status, income level, or age. For more information on what your particular state's guidelines are, go to www.adoptuskids.org/for-families/state-adoption-and-foster-care-information, or for your Canadian province's, go to www.adoption.ca/provincial-adoptions, and click on your state or province of residence.

Q. Are there orphanages in North America?

A. No. Children without parents and children of parents who have not demonstrated the ability to care for them live in foster homes or group homes.

Q. What is the difference between a North American group home and an orphanage?

A. A group home is much smaller than an orphanage, housing only six to twelve children at a time. Group homes were originally designed to offer more of a "home" environment for children rather than an institutionalized environment that is characteristic of orphanages.

Q. What is a relinquishment?

A. This is also known as an agency adoption, when a birth parent relinquishes their parental rights to a state department or a licensed agency. The agency in turn places the child with an adoptive parent(s) and supervises the adoption until it finalizes. The extent of time a birth mother has to change her mind varies from state to state; it could be anywhere from twenty-four hours to thirty days. Once a birth parent relinquishes their rights, the agency supervises the adoption until finalization occurs.

Q. What does a Foster Family Agency (FFA) social worker do?

A. An FFA social worker works closely with the prospective parents to guide them through the process of adopting via the foster care system. The service is free.

Q. How do I find the free services of a Foster Family Agency (FFA) within my state?

A. Go to www.childwelfare.gov/nfcad.

Q. What if I am adopting via foster care and I don't get along with my social worker?

A. A prospective adoptive parent may meet with many state social workers and FFA social workers to find the right person. Also, prospective parents may change adoption agencies and attorneys and social workers. It is advisable to interview a few different agencies to find the right one for your family.

Q. Are all children in the U.S. and Canadian foster care systems victims of abuse?

A. No. Some were placed in foster care because of neglect. Some were relinquished to foster care by parents unable to care for the child because of a broken marriage or a financial issue. Prospective parents can discuss what they feel they are equipped to take on in terms of abuse and neglect.

Q. What annual income should an adopting parent have?

A. Kids don't need much more than love and acceptance from a parent.

Q. Is a fos-adopt child being fostered or adopted allowed to share a room with a sibling of the opposite sex?

A. Only up to five years old.

Q. If an older person adopts a child, what occurs if something happens to that parent?

A. In the case of a substantially older single adopting parent, an assessment would be made to be sure there is an additional caregiver or someone who would legally take responsibility if something were to happen to the adoptive parent.

Q. What is the Heart Gallery?

A. The Heart Gallery is a traveling exhibit of professional photographs taken of children in foster care who are available for adoption. You can visit www.heartgalleryofamerica.org to find an exhibit close to you or to view the photos online.

Q. May a U.S. citizen adopt a child that is an illegal resident?

A. In some fos-adopt cases it does happen that children who are illegal residents are removed from their homes in the United States, and when this occurs the state will help obtain citizenship for the child. In some cases this is done before adoption while in other cases it is completed after finalization. For domestic adoption a prospective applicant wanting to adopt a child who is an illegal resident would need to follow the international adoption laws of the country where the child is a citizen.

Q. How does a state or FFA social worker make a match via U.S. and Canadian foster care?

A. They assess the home and personality of the prospective parents. Also, they take into consideration the background of a child the prospective parents are open to. If the adopted child will be a sibling to a child already in the home, usually the social worker tries to have the child be younger than the sibling who is already in the home. The social worker who matches you will want to find the right fit for the child as well as for your family.

Q. How does someone finalize an adoption via the fos-adopt system?

A. When you are ready to finalize your fos-adopt placement, the county will assist you with your finalization. Some counties will assign an attorney to you at no cost, others may give you a voucher or payment for the cost of an attorney so you may choose your own, while many complete the adoption themselves without requiring an attorney. Regardless of how it is done, someone will be there to help you through the finalization.

Q. What if someone adopting from foster care can't afford an attorney?

A. An attorney will be assigned to you at no cost to you.

Q. What types of medical, dental, and financial assistance are available for a child adopted from foster care in the United States and Canada?

A. A child adopted from foster care will receive the state insurance (for California it is Medi-Cal; for other states it is Medicaid) until the adoption finalizes, then the parents can put the child on their insurance. However, in most states a foster child will continue to get the medical and dental coverage from the state until they are eighteen (in some cases up to twenty-one if approved). Routinely, parents adopting a child choose to put the child on their insurance and use the state insurance as secondary. There are many parents who do not have insurance so they use the state insurance as primary. The child will often qualify for the Adoption Assistance Program (AAP), which is a monthly stipend until the child is eighteen. The amount varies for age and state but, for example, a child in California who is an infant through four years of age will get a minimum of $621 a month.

There are some cases in the fos-adopt system where birth parents who are about to lose parental rights will choose to sign a relinquishment rather than have their child go into foster care. In those cases, an adoption placement agreement is signed right away so the child would be able to go on the adoptive parents' insurance at placement. To find out what your state offers for postadoption medical, dental, and financial assistance, go to www.childwelfare.gov/adoption/adopt_assistance.

In Canada, each province is different; some offer financial and medical support while others are not able. Go to the following website and click on your province, which will tell you what funding is available as well as medical benefits: www.nacac.org/adoption subsidy/provincialprofiles.html.

Q. Are many of the children in foster care over the age of five?

A. There are children who are newborns to five years of age. However, as previously described, there is a need for families who will take children over the age of five, siblings, plus ethnicities other than Caucasian. These are the children getting lost in the system who age out of foster care without families. A law was recently passed that allows children to remain in foster care until they are twenty-one years old if they go to college, have a part-time job, or go to trade school. This was passed so when foster children turn eighteen, they are not simply out on the street; this also allows the foster parent to continue to get a stipend each month.

Q. What is the process for a private adoption of a child in Canada?

A. A U.S. citizen will need an approved international Home Study to adopt from Canada. Canada only allows residents of Canada to adopt, with exceptions made for relatives of children who live out of the country. In the past five years only fourteen intercountry adoptions have occurred from Canada to the United States. For more information visit adoption.state.gov/country_information/country _specific_info.php?country-select=canada.

For Canadians to adopt, they need an approved Home Study. Regulations and limitations vary by province, though most adoptions cost between $10,000 and $25,000. The time frame varies as well, though a one-year wait is common for newborns. For information on how to get started, visit the Adoption Council of Canada at www.adoption.ca.

Q. What is the process for adopting from China?

A. A U.S. or Canadian citizen will need an approved international Home Study. The wait is forty-eight months or longer, and the cost is $15,000 to $50,000. The wait time may be shortened if one of the applicants is of Chinese descent or if an applicant has previously adopted from China. You will need to find an agency that specializes in China adoptions. Only married heterosexual couples or single heterosexual females may adopt. Applicants must be at least thirty years old and no older than fifty-five. If the applicant is single, they cannot be more than forty-five years older than the child. Only one of the applicants has to travel to China to pick up the child. For more detailed qualifications, go to adoption.state.gov/country _information/country_specific_info.php?country-select=china.

A Chinese citizen is subject to the one-child policy. In China, if your firstborn child is a girl, you can apply to have another child, though many will put the female child up for adoption in the hopes of having a male child. There is very little information on families who live in China who want to adopt from China. If you are a resident in China, then you have to follow the Chinese law and practice on adoption. If you are a resident of another country and are working or temporarily living in China, then you would follow the adoption laws from your country.

Q. What is the process for adopting from Ethiopia?

A. The current wait time is twelve to twenty-four months or longer, and the cost is $20,000 to $40,000. Married couples are eligible for adoptions from Ethiopia. Single women may currently adopt by providing financial and heath capability, but this law may change in the near future. There are age, health, and background study requirements and restrictions, such as a parent may not be more than forty-five years older than the child. Visitations by both parents to Ethiopia are required before a child may be adopted. Two short trips of approximately six days are mandatory for foster home visits with the child, paperwork, and court dates. For the second trip, only one parent needs to travel to appear at the U.S. embassy. Both parents may want to travel the second time since this is when custody of the child is awarded. An escort is advised for all meetings, travel, and transportation and usually is provided by the adoption agency for a fee. All children are tested for hepatitis and HIV. All background and medical information is available to the parents.

Q. What is the process for a private adoption from Greece?

A. A U.S. or Canadian citizen will need an approved Home Study to adopt from Greece. To adopt from a government orphanage you must be a resident of Greece or have Greek origin, the only exception being for children with special needs. The wait time is up to five years. In the past five years, only three children have been adopted by U.S. or Canadian citizens. For more information go to adoption. state.gov/country_information/country_specific_info.php? country-select=greece.

A Greek citizen wishing to adopt in Greece must be between the ages of thirty and sixty and be at least eighteen years older than the child. The applicant then files an application to adopt with the court. Social workers will be assigned to complete a list of information (similar to a Home Study), then a panel of three judges will decide if they are approved to adopt. The cost varies per case, and the wait time can be up to five years to finalize an adoption.

Q. What is the process for adopting from India?

A. A U.S. or Canadian citizen will need an approved Home Study to adopt from India. The entire cost of the adoption, including legal fees, is from $10,000 to $30,000, depending on the special needs of the child. The wait time varies anywhere from one to three years. India requires that potential adoptive parents be between thirty to fifty-five years old, and a couple cannot have a combined age of more than ninety. Single applicants may adopt but cannot be older than forty-five years old. Applicants may be required to stay a minimum of seven days in India, depending on the agency. For more detailed information go to adoption.state.gov/country_information/country_specific_info.php?country-select=india.

Citizens of India who are Hindu, Jain, Sikh, or Buddhist may formally adopt a child in India. Under the Hindu adoption and Maintenance Act of 1956, a single parent or married couple can adopt but are not permitted to adopt more than one child of the same sex. All others, including Muslims, Parsis, Christians, Jewish people, or foreign citizens, are only the legal guardians of the child until they reach the age of eighteen.

*

Q. What is the process for adopting from Mexico?

A. A U.S. or Canadian adoptive applicant must have an approved Home Study. The wait time is currently six months to two years. The cost of an adoption in Mexico is $13,000 to $40,000. Applicants must be over twenty-five years old and at least seventeen years older than the child. There is a required one- to three-week pre-adoption trial period, though agencies advise you to prepare to stay in Mexico an average of three months to complete the adoption. Detailed information is available at adoption.state.gov/country_information/country_specific_info.php?country-select=mexico.

A citizen from Mexico can adopt within the country. Go to your local social services agency or orphanage to begin the process. Currently Mexico is encouraging citizens to adopt older children. There is a six-month trial period before the adoption finalizes.

Q. What is the process for adopting from Russia?*

A. A U.S. or Canadian citizen will need an approved international Home Study. The cost for an adoption from Russia is on average $50,000. The wait time varies depending on if you are open to special needs. The wait time can be from one to two years, or even longer. Married couples and single people may adopt, though if the applicant is single they have to be at least sixteen years older than the child and no more than forty-eight years old. The prospective adopting parents are required to go to Russia two times. For more information on adopting from Russia, go to adoption.state.gov/country _information/country_specific_info.php?country-select=russia.

Russian citizens living in Russia can foster, do guardianship, or adopt a child. The process is similar to that of the United States and Canada. There also is a monthly stipend for guardianship and foster care. Russia also requires a Home Study to be completed on a family who wishes to adopt. There are a large number of children adopted by Russian citizens every year.

Q. What is the process for adopting from the UK?

A. U.S. or Canadian citizens who want to adopt from the United Kingdom must have an approved Home Study. Because of the UK's long waiting list of British prospective adoptive parents, there are very few out-of-country adoptions. In fact only sixteen have occurred in the past five years. The waiting time is extreme, though the cost is low. For more information, visit adoption.state.gov/country_ information/country_specific_info.php?country-select=united_ kingdom.

---

* Just before *Instant Mom* went to press, the Russian government passed a law banning adoptions of Russian children by American citizens. We've kept this information in, in the hope that these adoptions will soon be allowed again.

A citizen of the UK must contact their local authority social services to complete a Home Study. The UK offers in-country adoptions, international adoptions, as well as adopting from foster care. For more information, go to www.adoptionuk.org.

Q. What countries are currently closed to international adoptions?

A. At the writing of this appendix, the following countries are closed to international adoptions: Bhutan, Cambodia, Guatemala, Haiti, Montenegro, Rwanda, and Vietnam. For an update on a specific country, go to adoption.state.gov/country_information.php.

Q. Where can I find information on adoption from other countries?

A. To learn about adoption requirements from other countries, visit adoption.state.gov/country_information.php.

Q. Is it common practice for social workers and adoption agencies to suggest counseling for all types of adoption?

A. Sure, and they can connect you with responsible and qualified counselors. If you adopt via foster care, there is funding available for counseling.

Q. Are there specific U.S. and Canadian organizations that provide support to parents and families after an adoption?

A. Most agencies have post-adoption services for families once their adoption is complete. There are also many adoption support groups. To find a local adoption support group, go to adoptive families.com/support_group.php.

Q. What is Helpusadopt.org?

A. Created and run by Becky Fawcett, Helpusadopt.org is a financial grant program providing monetary assistance for adoption to couples and individuals. They award grants of up to $15,000— regardless of race, religion, ethnicity, gender, marital status, or sexual orientation—to defray the costs associated with adoptions via domestic, international, or foster care. For more information, visit www.helpusadopt.org.

Q. Are there other groups who assist with costs associated with private, international, and fos-adopt adoption?

A. There are many organizations that offer grants or loans for adoption. For a listing of grants and loans available for adoption, visit www.iadopt.info/grantsloans.php.

RECOMMENDED BOOKS AND RESOURCES

Books

Tell Me Again About the Night I Was Born by Jamie Lee Curtis

I Wished for You by Marianne Richmond

I Don't Have Your Eyes by Carrie A. Kitze

Adoption Nation: How the Adoption Revolution Is Transforming Our Families—and America by Adam Pertman

The Connected Child by Karyn B. Purvis, Ph.D., David Cross, Ph.D., and Wendy Sunshine

Twenty Things Adopted Kids Wish Their Adoptive Parents Knew by Sherri Eldridge

Being Adopted by David M. Brodzinsky, Ph.D., Marshall D. Schechter, M.D., and Robin Marantz Henig

Children of Open Adoption by Kathleen Silber and Patricia Martinez Dorner

Resources

Sleepy Planet: sleepyplanet.com

National Adoption Day: www.nationaladoptionday.org

Children's Action Network: www.childrensactionnetwork.org

The Alliance for Children's Rights: www.kids-alliance.org

Adopt US Kids: www.adoptuskids.org

Congressional Coalition on Adoption Institute: www.ccainstitute.org

North American Council on Adoptable Children: www.nacac.org

Evan B. Donaldson Adoption Institute: www.adoptioninstitute.org

Helpusadopt.org (financial grant services): www.helpusadopt.org

ACKNOWLEDGMENTS

I'd like to thank social workers, facilitators, birth and foster parents, attorneys and health care professionals—all the women and men who help create families for those of us who walk a different path to parenthood.

To the team who matched us with our daughter: Thank you for making me a mom. I think of you every day and wish I could print your names in bold and giant font.

To my editor, Jeanette Perez, and all the lovely, kind, and talented people who embody the offices of HarperOne and Harper-Collins: I appreciate how you shone a light and threw a buoy as I went over the terrifying comprehensive candor waterfall. I value your expertise and compassion. Mostly, I am grateful for your desire to get a how-to-adopt book into the marketplace. You're good people.

To my agent, Laura Nolan: Thank you for waiting until I was ready to tell the true story.

Dear Family, Friends, Core, and Colleagues: Although I couldn't mention you all by name and tell every story, every one of you is a part of this book. It is my auspicious privilege to have all you sparkly, delightful people in my life. Come over. I will cook.

Manny and Louie: Thank you for keeping me company as I wrote.

Ian: Thank you for reading this book before you will ever finish *Seabiscuit*.

And Ilaria . . . thank you for understanding why I sometimes cry when I look at you.